The Lion House Cookbook

The Lion House Cookbook

MORE THAN 500 FAVORITE RECIPES

DESERET
BOOK

Salt Lake City, Utah

Photo Credits:

Robert Casey: pages 16, 21, 22, 25, 29, 32, 35, 38, 41, 42, 45, 49, 52, 55, 56, 61, 91, 126, 140, 150, 214, 226, 234, 238, 249, 253, 259, 273, 274, 286, 289, 295, 305, 313, 314, 318, 325, 331, 339, 340, 343, 346, 349, 354, 357, 387

Alan Blakely: pages 2, 9, 10, 13, 62, 65, 69, 70, 73, 77, 78, 100, 106, 119, 139, 143, 144, 153, 154, 156, 160, 168, 175, 178, 181, 184, 187, 195, 205, 220, 225, 241, 266, 279, 301, 306, 362

John Luke: pages 7, 66, 74, 81, 82, 87, 94, 105, 109, 120, 123, 124, 133, 147, 165, 188, 190, 200, 210, 246, 250, 256, 262, 269, 280, 290, 326, 334, 350, 377, 378, 384

Russell Winegar: pages 113, 116, 233, 245, 358, 361

Kimberly Hall/Shutterstock: page 321

Food styling for photos on pages 113, 116, 233, 245, 358, and 361 by Susan Massey. All other food styling by Maxine Bramwell.

Back cover and flap photos, right to left: Robert Casey, John Luke, Alan Blakely, Robert Casey, Lion House/Temple Square Hospitality, Russell Winegar, John Luke, Robert Casey

Library of Congress Cataloging-in-Publication Data

Names: Temple Square Hospitality (Firm) | Lion House (Restaurant)
Title: The Lion House cookbook : more than 500 favorite recipes / Temple Square Hospitality.
Description: Salt Lake City, Utah : Deseret Book, [2016] | ?2016 | Includes index.
Identifiers: LCCN 2015035378 | ISBN 9781629721736 (hardbound : alk. paper)
Subjects: LCSH: Cooking, American. | Lion House (Restaurant) | LCGFT: Cookbooks.
Classification: LCC TX715 .L75939 2016 | DDC 641.5973—dc23
LC record available at http://lccn.loc.gov/2015035378

Printed in China
RR Donnelley, Shenzhen, China

10 9 8 7 6 5 4 3 2 1

CONTENTS

INTRODUCTION

From 1856 to the present, the Lion House has been making a wide variety of food for the enjoyment of all those who have ever lived or visited there.

When Brigham Young's family resided in the Lion House, baking and cooking went on almost around the clock. Approximately seventy-five people needed to be fed three meals a day, and there was only one wood-burning stove on which to cook everything. Brigham Young's wives became very skilled at turning out the best food of that day.

Today the Lion House Pantry is still turning out the best food of the day. The skilled staff takes pride in providing baked goods and hot entrées for fans throughout the world, including the many new fans who happen to visit one of the Lion House Pantries located in a Deseret Book store. Of course, they don't use a wood-burning stove anymore, but just as much love goes into the baking of each roll or cookie and preparing each soup and meal as it did in Brigham's day.

Now you can create the same magic in your own home with *The Lion House Cookbook,* featuring more than 500 favorite recipes. With the assistance of Executive Chef David Bench, this cookbook encompasses the best of the best recipes that have been crafted within the walls of the Lion House and will bring savory delight to your family dinners, parties, and traditions.

Join the culinary traditions of the Lion House as you prepare, share, and enjoy in the delights of timeless family recipes. Happy cooking!

Stuffed Mushrooms

Stuffed Mushrooms

50 medium-sized fresh mushrooms
½ pound country-style sausage
1 (8-ounce) package cream cheese, softened
3 tablespoons chopped fresh parsley
¾ teaspoon garlic powder
Salt and pepper to taste

Preheat oven to 400 degrees F. Wash and remove stems from mushrooms. Combine uncooked sausage, cream cheese, parsley, garlic powder, salt, and pepper. Roll stuffing into small balls and fill mushroom caps. Place stuffed mushrooms in a 9x13-inch pan, cover with foil, and bake 30 minutes. Drain drippings and serve hot.

Broiled Mushroom Appetizers

Crab Filling
Makes about 30 appetizers

1 pound fresh button mushrooms
2 tablespoons margarine
1 (7½-ounce) can crabmeat, drained and flaked
1 cup mashed potatoes
1 cup grated cheddar cheese
2 teaspoons lemon juice
1 teaspoon seasoned salt

Clean mushrooms and air dry on paper towels. Remove stems; set caps aside. Chop stems into a small dice and sauté in 2 tablespoons margarine over medium-high heat for 2 to 3 minutes. Remove from heat and stir in remaining ingredients, except reserved mushroom caps, mixing well. Spoon enough mixture to fill each mushroom cap (amount will vary depending on size of mushroom cap). Place on baking sheet and broil until lightly browned.

Bacon-Chive Filling
Makes about 15 appetizers

½ pound fresh mushrooms
½ pound bacon, cooked and crumbled
2 to 3 tablespoons cream cheese, softened
2 tablespoons minced green onion

Clean mushrooms and remove stems. Discard stems or use for another purpose. Combine bacon, cream cheese, and green onion in a small bowl. Fill mushroom caps with mixture and place on baking sheet. Broil until lightly browned.

Onion-Cheese Filling
Makes about 15 appetizers

½ pound fresh mushrooms
1 (3-ounce) package cream cheese, softened
3 tablespoons fine dry bread crumbs
2 tablespoons finely chopped fresh parsley
2 teaspoons freshly grated onion
¼ teaspoon paprika
¼ teaspoon salt

Clean mushrooms and remove stems. Discard stems or use for another purpose. Combine remaining ingredients in a small bowl and fill each mushroom cap. Place mushroom caps on a baking sheet and broil until lightly browned.

Honey Yogurt Dip

Makes 20 servings

1 (16-ounce) carton cottage cheese
½ cup plain yogurt
¼ cup honey

½ cup grated coconut
2 teaspoons orange zest

Blend cottage cheese and yogurt in a food processor or blender until smooth. Stir in remaining ingredients; chill approximately 1 hour. Serve as a dip for fresh fruit.

Fruit Salsa

1 (15.5-ounce) can crushed pineapple, drained
2 (11-ounce) cans mandarin oranges, drained and chopped
2 bunches green onions, chopped

2 small jalapeño peppers, seeded and diced
1 bunch cilantro, chopped

In large bowl, mix pineapple, oranges, green onions, jalapeños, and cilantro. Serve with tortilla chips.

Hot Spinach Dip

1 (10-ounce) package frozen creamed spinach, thawed
1 (8-ounce) package cream cheese, softened
¼ cup mayonnaise

2 tablespoons chopped green onion
½ cup, plus 1 tablespoon grated Parmesan cheese, divided

Preheat oven to 350 degrees F. In a medium bowl, combine spinach, cream cheese, mayonnaise, green onion, and half of the Parmesan cheese. Spread in 9x9-inch pan, and sprinkle remaining Parmesan on top. Bake 25 minutes. Serve with chips or crackers.

Tangy Party Dip

Makes 1¼ cups

1 (8-ounce) package cream cheese, softened
¼ cup mayonnaise
½ teaspoon red pepper sauce
1 teaspoon Worcestershire sauce

4 green onions, finely chopped
1 teaspoon seasoned salt
½ teaspoon paprika
1 (3½-ounce) package thinly sliced beef

In a small bowl, whip cream cheese and mayonnaise with electric mixer on low speed. Stir in seasonings. Finely chop the sliced beef and blend into cream-cheese mixture. Serve as a dip for fresh vegetables or as a spread for crackers.

Festive Cheese Ball

Makes 2 small cheese balls

2 (8-ounce) packages cream cheese, softened
2 cups grated sharp cheddar cheese
2 tablespoons finely chopped green onion
2 teaspoons Worcestershire sauce

1 teaspoon lemon juice
½ teaspoon lemon pepper
1 cup finely chopped nuts
½ cup chopped parsley

Combine all ingredients, except nuts and parsley, in a medium bowl and mix until well blended. Divide the mixture in half and spoon into 2 small bowls lined with waxed paper. Refrigerate for several hours. Lift out waxed paper from each bowl and mold cheese into a ball, using waxed paper to protect hands. Roll each ball in chopped nuts and parsley. Refrigerate. Remove about 15 minutes before serving; serve with a variety of crackers.

Lion House Cheese Ball

1 (8-ounce) package cream cheese, softened
1½ cups grated cheddar cheese
1 tablespoon dried chives

2 teaspoons dry ranch dressing mix
½ cup chopped pecans

Combine cheeses, chives, and ranch dressing mix in a medium bowl. Chill until mixture can be easily formed into a ball, about 1 hour. Form into a ball and roll in chopped pecans. Refrigerate until ready to serve. Serve with assorted crackers.

Pineapple Cheese Roll

Makes 1 roll

2 (8-ounce) packages cream cheese, softened
1 (8.5-ounce) can crushed pineapple, drained well
2 tablespoons finely chopped green onion

¼ cup minced green pepper
1 tablespoon seasoned salt
1 cup chopped pecans

In a large bowl, combine cream cheese, pineapple, onions, green pepper, and seasoned salt. Mix well with a wooden spoon and refrigerate for several hours. Once firm and chilled, shape mixture into a log and roll in chopped pecans. Refrigerate until ready to serve.

Glazed Meatballs

Makes about 100 ¾-inch or 50 1-inch meatballs (25 servings)

3 slices bread (white or wheat)
⅔ cup milk
2 eggs, beaten well
1½ pounds ground beef
1 tablespoon Dijon mustard

½ teaspoon salt
½ teaspoon pepper
1 recipe Sweet-Sour Glaze or Swedish Meatball Sauce (see below)
Hot, fluffy cooked rice (optional)

Note: To save time, you can use pre-cooked meatballs, which are available at your local grocery store. You can also use your favorite gravy in place of the glaze or sauce.

Preheat oven to 450 degrees F. In a large bowl, soak bread slices in milk until soft. Add eggs, ground beef, and seasonings; mix until well blended. Shape mixture into ¾-inch or 1-inch balls; place meatballs on shallow baking sheets and bake 10 to 15 minutes. (Meatballs may be made to this point and then refrigerated until shortly before serving time.)

Pour Sweet-Sour Glaze or Swedish Meatball Sauce in a large pan; add meatballs and warm over medium heat. Serve in a chafing dish with toothpicks to spear the meatballs, or as a main course with hot, fluffy rice.

Sweet-Sour Glaze

1½ cups chicken broth
¾ cup pineapple chunks
2 green peppers, cut in chunks
4 tablespoons cornstarch

1 tablespoon soy sauce
¾ cup rice vinegar
¾ cup sugar

Heat chicken broth, pineapple chunks, and green pepper chunks in a medium saucepan over medium heat; simmer 5 minutes. Stir in remaining ingredients. Cook and stir until thickened, approximately 1 minute.

Swedish Meatball Sauce

1 (10.5-ounce) can cream of chicken soup
1 (10.5-ounce) can cream of mushroom soup
1 soup can water

Combine all ingredients in a medium saucepan and heat over medium heat until warm.

Coconut Shrimp (shown on facing page)

Makes 20 servings of 3 shrimp each

1 cup flour	2 cups coconut shreds, chopped
1 cup cornstarch	60 shrimp
2 tablespoons Old Bay® seafood seasoning	4 cups peanut oil
4 eggs	1 recipe Orange Marmalade Sauce (see below)
2 cups heavy cream	

Combine flour, cornstarch, and seafood seasoning in a bowl. Combine eggs and cream in a separate bowl; beat well. Place shredded coconut in an additional bowl. Coat shrimp, one at a time, with flour mixture and dredge in cream mixture, then roll in shredded coconut. Set the finished shrimp in the refrigerator for at least 1 hour to set. Just before you are ready to serve the shrimp, heat a large skillet with peanut oil. Fry the shrimp for 3 minutes or until golden brown. Check one shrimp to see if it is done inside. It will no longer be opaque. Serve with Orange Marmalade Sauce.

Orange Marmalade Sauce

2 tablespoons butter	2 cups mandarin oranges
1 medium onion, diced	2 tablespoons cornstarch
½ cup sugar	2 tablespoons water

Heat a large skillet over medium heat until a drop of water sizzles on the pan. Add butter and onions, cooking and stirring until caramelized, at least 15 minutes. (You want the onions to be browned to release their sweet flavor.) Add the sugar and the oranges. Cook until the oranges begin to fall apart.

In a small bowl, mix the cornstarch and water to make a paste. Add cornstarch mixture to sauce in small amounts and thicken until sauce just coats the back of a spoon.

You can hold this sauce in a double boiler set on low for 1 hour before serving.

Shrimp Crostini (shown on page 10)

Makes 20 servings

20 slices dinner roll (4 rolls cut into 5 ¼-inch slices)
¼ cup butter, melted
1 (8-ounce) package cream cheese
1 bunch cilantro, chopped

1 tablespoon lime juice
½ teaspoon salt
20 large, cooked shrimp, tails removed

Preheat oven to 350 degrees F. Brush one side of each roll slice with the melted butter, and place, buttered side up, on a baking sheet in a single layer. Bake 6 to 8 minutes, or until golden brown. Meanwhile, whip the cream cheese with an electric mixer on medium speed. Add the cilantro, lime juice, and salt. Mix until the ingredients are incorporated. The crostini may be made immediately or just before service. Spread an ⅛-inch thick layer of the cream cheese mixture over the toasted bread slices. Place a shrimp on each slice of bread and garnish with a sprig of cilantro.

Coconut Shrimp

Crab Napoleon (shown below)

Makes 20 servings

1 (16-ounce) package wonton wrappers

1 (8-ounce) package cream cheese, softened

2 tablespoons Old Bay® seafood seasoning

1 pound crabmeat, defrosted if frozen

1 cup alfalfa sprouts

Heat a deep saucepan or fryer with shortening to 350 degrees F. according to manufacturer's directions. Carefully place individual wonton wrappers into the hot oil and fry until golden brown. The wontons will continue to brown when removed from the oil so care must be taken with this step. Drain on paper towels.

In a medium bowl, mix the cream cheese and the Old Bay seasoning with a metal spoon. (For a stronger flavor, add more Old Bay.) Add the crabmeat and incorporate into the cream cheese. Organize a work area with the crab mixture, fried wontons, and the sprouts within easy reach. Take a wonton skin and spread a small amount of the sprouts onto the skin. Spoon a tablespoon of the crab mixture onto the sprouts. Place on a serving platter and serve immediately or hold for up to 2 hours.

Crab
Napoleon

Wonton Wrapped Shrimp
Shrimp Crostini

Wonton Wrapped Shrimp with Sauce Orientale

(shown on facing page)

1 (12-ounce) jar hoisin sauce
2 cups honey
30 to 40 raw shrimp, thawed if frozen
Fresh chives, cut into 2-inch pieces

2 (16-ounce) packages wonton wrappers
Bowl of water for sealing wrapper skins
1 recipe Sauce Orientale (see below)

In a large bowl, mix the hoisin sauce and the honey. Set up a workstation with separate bowls of shrimp, the hoisin mix, the cut chives, and the wrappers.

Dip one shrimp in the hoisin mixture but do not coat completely. Place the shrimp and two pieces of chive in the wrapper. Roll the wrapper around the shrimp and seal with a small amount of water.

Repeat to finish all the shrimp. Place the shrimp on a baking sheet lined with parchment paper. Store in the refrigerator until service.

About 45 minutes before serving, heat the fryer to 350 degrees F. Fry the wrapped shrimp in small batches for 3 minutes; place on paper towels to absorb grease. Serve with Sauce Orientale.

Sauce Orientale

½ yellow fresh onion, peeled and diced
½ bunch fresh thyme, chopped
½ bay leaf
4 cups heavy cream
2 tablespoons butter

2 tablespoons flour
2½ tablespoons lobster base
1 tablespoon curry powder
1 cup butter
Salt and white pepper to taste

In a 3-gallon saucepan, sauté the onion, thyme, and bay leaf until the onions become translucent. Add the cream and cook over medium heat to just boiling.

Make a roux in a small sauté pan over medium heat by melting the butter and then adding the flour. Stir to incorporate the flour. Do not overmix. Cook for one minute. Remove from heat.

When the cream mixture begins to boil, add the roux, a little at a time, to thicken the sauce.

Mix in the lobster base and the curry powder and bring to a boil. Remove from heat and strain through a fine sieve.

Cut the butter into small cubes and add it to the sauce. Finish with salt and white pepper to taste.

Open Face Sandwiches

Breads

A variety of white, wheat, rye, pumpernickel, and sourdough breads

Ham Spread

Makes 20 servings

1 (8-ounce) tub soft-style cream cheese with chives and onion
½ teaspoon Dijon mustard

1 tablespoon mayonnaise
⅓ cup cooked, finely diced ham

To make ham spread, stir together cream cheese, mustard, mayonnaise, and ham in a small mixing bowl. Cover and chill.

Almond-Bacon Cheese Spread

Makes 20 servings

¼ cup unblanched almonds, roasted and finely chopped
2 strips bacon, cooked and crumbled
8 ounces Velveeta® cheese, grated

1 tablespoon chopped green onion
½ cup mayonnaise

To make almond-bacon cheese spread, combine almonds, bacon, Velveeta, green onion, and mayonnaise. Mix lightly. Store in refrigerator until ready to serve.

Green Chili Artichoke Spread

Makes 20 servings

1 (14-ounce) can artichoke hearts, drained
1 (6-ounce) jar marinated artichoke hearts, drained
1 cup shredded cheddar cheese

1 (3-ounce) package cream cheese
1 (4-ounce) can diced green chili peppers, drained

To make green chili artichoke spread, place drained artichoke hearts and marinated artichoke hearts in a blender or food processor. Cover and process until finely chopped, stopping to scrape down sides as necessary. Put blended artichokes in medium saucepan, then stir in cheddar cheese, cream cheese, and chili peppers. Heat over low heat, stirring constantly, for 12 to 15 minutes or until the cheese is melted and the mixture is heated through.

Make sandwiches using one or all of the spreads, on one type or a variety of breads. Use bread that is sliced lengthwise, if possible. Coat each slice of bread with the spread of your choice. Cut crusts off bread. (Note: it is much easier to cut crusts off bread after you have covered it with the spread.) For bread that is sliced lengthwise, cut into one-inch slices. Cut regular sandwich bread into triangles by cutting each slice of bread diagonally into quarters.

Serve with garnishes such as a small carrot curl, half a cherry tomato, a thin slice of pickle, a slice of black olive, or a small sprig of parsley, if desired. Store in refrigerator until ready to serve.

Hot Creamed Chicken in a Puff Pastry

Makes 20 servings

20 prepared puff pastries
2 tablespoons butter
1 cup finely diced onion
2 cloves garlic, minced
8 cups diced chicken breasts

1 teaspoon chopped fresh thyme
4 cups chicken stock
2 cups heavy cream
Salt and pepper to taste

Cut the tops of each puff pastry and set aside. Melt butter in a large saucepan over medium heat. Add onions and sauté until translucent; do not let brown. Add diced chicken and thyme and cook until chicken is done. Add chicken stock and cream and bring to a boil over medium heat; let mixture simmer and reduce to a thick consistency. Add salt and pepper to taste. Spoon into puff pastries, replace tops, and serve immediately.

Note: Chicken stock can be replaced by a good quality chicken base. Do not use bouillon cubes—they contain too much salt.

Ribbon Sandwiches

Makes approximately 24 sandwiches

2 loaves bread, sliced horizontally (this can be ordered through most bakeries; ask for ribbon sandwich bread)
1 recipe Cream Cheese Filling (see below)
Mayonnaise

1 recipe Chicken Salad Filling (see below)
Paprika
Parsley flakes

Combine all ingredients and stir until well blended.

Using 3 slices of bread (loaf sliced horizontally), spread cream cheese mixture on bottom layer. Add the next layer of bread, spread with a small amount of mayonnaise, then cover layer with the chicken mixture. Add the last layer of bread, spreading top and bottom with mayonnaise. If desired, sprinkle top with paprika and dry parsley flakes. Trim crusts on all four sides. Slice each loaf into 12 sandwiches.

Cream Cheese Filling

1 (8-ounce) package cream cheese, softened
1¼ cups crushed pineapple, drained slightly
¼ cup sugar
Combine all ingredients and mix well.

Chicken Salad Filling

4 cups cooked shredded chicken
1 cup minced celery
⅓ cup minced yellow onion
½ teaspoon salt
Pepper to taste
1 cup mayonnaise

Party Roll-Ups

Makes 12 appetizers

12 thin slices white bread
8 slices bacon, cooked, drained, and crumbled
2 (3-ounce) packages cream cheese, softened

12 spears asparagus, cooked and cooled
Melted butter

Trim crusts from slices of bread; roll with rolling pin to flatten slightly. Blend bacon bits with cream cheese and spread mixture on bread slices. Lay one cooled asparagus spear on each slice of bread and roll up. Place on baking sheet, seam side down. Cover and refrigerate until serving time. Brush with melted butter and toast in a 350-degree oven until lightly browned, 15 to 18 minutes. Serve hot.

Bacon-Chestnut Tidbits

Makes 72 pieces

1 pound bacon
2 (8-ounce) cans whole water chestnuts

1 cup ketchup
½ cup sugar

Preheat oven to 375 degrees F. Cut each bacon strip into four pieces. Wrap each piece of bacon around a water chestnut and secure with a toothpick. Place skewers on a cookie sheet and bake for 10 minutes. Drain off fat and place bacon-wrapped tidbits in casserole dish. Combine ketchup and sugar and pour over top of tidbits. Cover and bake 15 minutes more.

Variation: In place of ketchup and sugar mixture, use favorite commercial or homemade barbecue sauce.

Party Deviled Eggs

Makes 12 deviled eggs

6 hard-cooked eggs
¼ cup mayonnaise
1 teaspoon vinegar
1 teaspoon prepared mustard
⅛ teaspoon salt

Dash white pepper
⅛ teaspoon Worcestershire sauce
Drop red pepper sauce (optional)
Paprika, pimientos, and parsley, for garnishing

Peel eggs and cut in half lengthwise. Slip out yolks; mash with fork in a small bowl. Add remaining ingredients, except garnishes, to yolks and mix until well blended. Spoon mixture into egg-white halves. Sprinkle with paprika and garnish with pimiento and parsley, if desired.

Figure 1

Figure 2

Figure 3

Figure 4

Beef Stock

Makes 2 to 3 quarts

5 to 6 pounds beef soup bones cut into 1-inch pieces by butcher
1 large onion, chopped but unpeeled
3 large carrots, chopped into ½-inch pieces
3 ribs celery, including some leaves, chopped into ½-inch pieces
½ cup water plus water to cover ingredients

1 (6-ounce) can tomato paste
8 peppercorns
6 sprigs fresh parsley with stems
1 bay leaf
1 tablespoon salt
4 sprigs fresh thyme
2 cloves garlic, peeled

Preheat oven to 450 degrees F. Place bones, onion, carrots, and celery in a large, shallow roasting pan (Figure 1). Bake, uncovered, about 30 minutes or until bones are well browned, turning occasionally (Figure 2). Drain off fat.

Place browned ingredients in a large soup pot or Dutch oven. Pour ½ cup water into the roasting pan and stir with a wooden spoon to loosen all the browned bits (Figure 3). Pour this liquid into the soup pot. Add tomato paste, peppercorns, parsley, bay leaf, salt, thyme, and garlic. Add enough cold water to cover ingredients. Bring mixture to a boil (Figure 4). Reduce heat to a low simmer and cook 5 to 6 hours, skimming the top several times with a spoon or fine mesh strainer. Strain stock through a fine mesh strainer into another large stockpot or heatproof container, discarding the solids.

Cool immediately in a large cooler of ice or a sink full of ice water to below 40 degrees F. Refrigerate overnight. Remove and discard solidified fat from surface of liquid. Store stock in a covered container in the refrigerator 2 to 3 days or in the freezer up to 3 months. Use as the base for any broth soup.

Chef's tip: The smaller the bones are cut, the more flavor the stock will have.

Chicken Stock

Makes 2 to 3 quarts

3 to 4 pounds chicken carcasses, including necks and backs
1 large onion, roughly chopped into large pieces
4 carrots, chopped
4 ribs celery, chopped
10 sprigs fresh thyme

10 sprigs fresh parsley with stems
2 bay leaves
8 to 10 peppercorns
2 whole cloves garlic, peeled
Water to cover all ingredients

Place chicken carcasses, vegetables, herbs, and spices in a large stockpot. Cover ingredients with cold water. Cook on high heat until bubbles break through the surface of the liquid. Turn heat down to medium-low so stock maintains a low, gentle simmer. Skim the top layer from the stock with a spoon or fine mesh strainer three or four times for the first hour of cooking and twice each hour for the next 2 hours. Add hot water as needed to keep bones covered. Simmer, uncovered, 6 to 8 hours.

Strain stock through a fine mesh strainer into another large stockpot or heatproof container, discarding the solids. Cool immediately in a large cooler of ice or a sink full of ice water to below 40 degrees F. Refrigerate overnight. Remove and discard solidified fat from surface of liquid. Store stock in a covered container in the refrigerator 2 to 3 days or in the freezer up to 3 months. Use as the base for any broth soup. Boil 2 minutes prior to use.

Brown Soup Stock

Makes about 2 quarts stock.

1 or 2 marrow bones, cracked
4 pounds beef shin, cut in small pieces
3 quarts cold water
⅓ cup each chopped celery, carrots, onion, white turnips
2 sprigs parsley, chopped

5 whole cloves
8 to 10 peppercorns
1 bay leaf
¼ teaspoon each marjoram and thyme
1 tablespoon salt

Scrape marrow from bones; melt in kettle over moderate heat. Brown about half the beef in marrow fat. Add remaining beef, bones, and water; cover and slowly bring to a boil. Remove scum. Add vegetables and seasonings; cover and simmer gently, about 4 hours, removing scum occasionally. Strain, chill, remove fat, and strain again. Use for soups and sauces.

Note: Vegetables and seasonings may be varied as desired. For added flavor, vegetables may be simmered in butter for 10 minutes before adding to soup.

White Sauce (Béchamel)

1 recipe White Roux (see page 20)
1 small onion, finely chopped
1 tablespoon butter
¾ cup heavy cream

4 cups milk
¼ teaspoon ground cloves
¼ teaspoon nutmeg, or to taste
Salt and pepper, to taste

Prepare a White Roux according to directions on page 20. Allow roux to cool completely in the refrigerator. Sauté onion in butter in a large saucepan until onion is translucent. Add cream, milk, cloves, and nutmeg. Bring to a slow, simmering boil. Add 3 tablespoons cold roux to hot liquid and allow to come to a boil, stirring gently. Continue to add roux, 2 tablespoons at a time, bringing to a boil and stirring gently after each addition, until sauce reaches desired consistency. Season to taste with salt and pepper. This recipe may be used as a base for soups and sauces, such as with the following:

- Roasted red peppers
- Roasted corn and potatoes
- Baked potato and all your favorite toppings
- Roasted tomatoes
- Roasted root vegetables
- Cauliflower, broccoli, and carrots
- Clams, diced potatoes, crumbled bacon, celery, and thyme
- Zucchini and other garden vegetables you need to use
- Pumpkin or squash pureed with a little nutmeg
- Chopped spinach
- Sautéed mushrooms
- Any cheese for a sauce or soup
- Roasted garlic
- Pesto

Chef's tip: White sauce may be made ahead and frozen. Allow the sauce to cool a bit and then place 1 to 2 cup portions in zip-top freezer bags and place in freezer. Thaw by placing unopened bag in a bowl of warm water. Place thawed sauce in a pan and heat over medium heat until warm.

Roux

1 cup flour
½ cup butter (no substitutions)

Roux is the most common thickener for soups and sauces. It is made by combining flour and butter, cooked to form a paste. The butterfat coats the starch granules, preventing them from lumping together when added to liquid. Roux can be prepared in larger batches and stored in the refrigerator for use in many recipes. Different types of roux are used in different recipes, and they vary depending on the amount of time they are cooked and how dark they are.

White roux is cooked only briefly and should be removed from heat as soon as it develops a bubbly appearance. It is used in white sauces and soups when no color is desired.

Blonde roux is cooked just long enough to take on some color as the flour caramelizes. Blonde roux is used the most and has a richer flavor than white roux.

Brown roux is cooked considerably longer than white or blonde roux. It needs to develop a dark color and a rich, nutty aroma and flavor. It is used in brown sauces and dishes where dark color is desired. Because cooking breaks down starches and prevents gelatinization, more brown roux is required to thicken a liquid than blonde roux.

Chef's tip: Never *add hot roux to hot liquid. Cold roux may be added to hot liquid or cold liquid to hot roux, but* never *hot to hot.*

Bruschetta

Bruschetta is a crostini topped with savory ingredients such as julianned, roasted red bell peppers; diced tomatoes and basil with fresh mozzarella; minced sautéed mushrooms, onions, and garlic; fresh pesto and a slice of sundried tomato; or any cheese at room temperature (return the crostini to the oven and bake the cheese in).

Crostini

Crostini are a fun, easy accompaniment or garnish for any soup. To make, slice an Italian-style baguette on a 45-degree bias about ¼-inch thick. Brush each piece with melted butter or olive oil and season with a sprinkle of salt or your favorite dry herb. Bake in a 325-degree F. oven until golden brown. Remove from the oven and let stand on the hot pan and continue to dry.

Iced Melon Soup

Makes 6 to 8 servings

2 tablespoons sugar

½ cup water

10 to 10½ pounds very ripe melon, divided (cantaloupe and honeydew both work well)

Juice of 2 limes

2 tablespoons chopped fresh mint

3 tablespoons orange juice

2 tablespoons lemon juice

Mint leaves to garnish

For the sorbet: Place sugar and water in a pan and heat gently until the sugar dissolves. Bring to a boil and simmer 4 to 5 minutes. Remove from heat and allow to cool. Using half of the melons, cut each melon in half. Scrape out and discard the seeds and then scoop out the flesh. Puree in a food processor or blender with the cooled syrup and lime juice. Stir in the mint and pour the melon mixture into an ice-cream maker. Churn, following the manufacturer's instructions, until the sorbet is smooth and firm.

For the soup: Cut the remaining melons in half, scrape out and discard the seeds, and scoop out the flesh. Puree in a food processor or blender. Pour puree into a bowl and stir in orange and lemon juices. Place soup in refrigerator for 30 to 40 minutes, but do not chill it too long, as this will dull the flavor.

Ladle soup into bowls and add a large scoop of sorbet. Garnish with mint leaves and serve at once.

Chef's tip: If you don't have an ice-cream maker, follow these instructions. Pour melon mixture into a gallon-sized zip-top bag and lay the bag flat in the freezer until it is icy around the edges. Transfer to a food processor or blender and process until smooth. Repeat the freezing and processing two or three times or until the mixture is smooth and holding its shape. Then freeze until firm. For a color contrast between sorbet and the soup, use different color melons.

Chilled Banana Bisque

Chilled Banana Bisque

Makes 6 servings

1½ cups whole milk
1½ cups heavy cream
4 bananas, sliced
¼ cup sugar
1 tablespoon vanilla extract
1 teaspoon molasses
Pinch of salt

Cinnamon Sugar Croutons

½ ciabatta loaf, cut into 1-inch cubes
6 tablespoons unsalted butter, melted
1 tablespoon sugar
1 tablespoon cinnamon

Put all soup ingredients together in a soup pot and blend with a hand immersion blender (a blender will work as well). Chill. Place 3 or 4 croutons in the bottom of each bowl. Pour ice-cold bisque over the croutons and garnish with a few more croutons on top. Serve immediately.

For croutons: Preheat oven to 400 degrees F. In a medium bowl, toss together bread cubes and melted butter. Stir sugar and cinnamon together until well mixed. Sprinkle on bread cubes and toss to coat. Arrange cubes on a baking sheet and bake until golden brown, about 8 minutes. Cool completely.

Carrot Apple Bisque

Makes 6 to 8 servings

5 to 6 large carrots, peeled
1 tablespoon butter or margarine
4 cups chicken broth, divided, plus more if needed
1 large apple, or ½ cup unsweetened applesauce

½ cup heavy cream
½ teaspoon nutmeg
⅓ cup sliced green onion, including tops, for garnish

Cut carrots into ½-inch chunks. Combine in saucepan with butter and 1 cup chicken broth. Cook, covered, until carrots are very tender, about 20 minutes. In the meantime, peel, core, and slice apple, adding it (or applesauce) to carrots during the last 5 minutes of cooking. Remove pan from heat, uncover, and allow to cool about 10 minutes.

Place mixture in blender and process until smooth. Fill blender one-third full and repeat until all mixture is pureed. Vent lid of blender so steam doesn't build up pressure. Transfer to a soup pot.

Stir in cream, nutmeg, and remaining chicken broth. Additional broth may be added to reach desired consistency.

Serve hot, or cover and refrigerate to serve cold. Garnish with sliced green onion.

Lion House Tomato Bisque

12 to 15 Roma tomatoes

4 (10.5-ounce) cans tomato soup

2 cups chicken stock

1 cup beef stock, or canned beef consommé

1 bunch fresh basil, or 2 tablespoons dry basil

1 cup sugar

2 to 3 cups heavy cream

Salt and pepper

Preheat oven to 350 degrees F. Slice tomatoes in half lengthwise. Place tomatoes, cut side up, in a single layer on a large baking sheet lined with parchment paper. Roast in oven until tops begin to blacken, about 30 minutes. In large pot, combine tomato soup, chicken stock, and beef stock. Place roasted tomatoes and basil in blender and puree until smooth. (Cover blender with the lid and a towel to avoid splashing when hot tomatoes puree.) Add puree to pot and let simmer. Add sugar until mixture is slightly sweet (don't skimp on the sugar—it may take more or less, depending on the tomatoes), then add cream. Season to taste with salt and pepper.

Note: The soup should not taste like marinara sauce, but should have a slightly sweet creamy flavor.

Savory Tomato Basil Bisque

Makes 6 servings

8 medium ripe tomatoes

3 Roma tomatoes

4 tablespoons olive oil, divided

1 medium yellow onion, diced

2 tablespoons minced garlic

1 small bunch basil, stemmed and chopped

1 (14.5-ounce) can vegetable broth

1 (12-ounce) can tomato paste

4 cups heavy cream

1 tablespoon Cholula hot sauce

Salt and pepper, to taste

2 tablespoons water (optional)

2 tablespoons cornstarch (optional)

Preheat oven to 350 degrees F. Remove stems from tomatoes and place tomatoes on a baking sheet. Coat generously with 2 tablespoons oil. Bake 10 minutes, or until peels come off easily. Set aside. Sauté onion, garlic, and basil in remaining 2 tablespoons oil in a large soup pot on medium heat. Add vegetable broth and simmer 5 minutes.

Peel baked tomatoes and add to pot. Puree with an immersion blender* until smooth. Add tomato paste, cream, and hot sauce to pot and season with salt and pepper as needed. If desired, thicken with cornstarch slurry of water and cornstarch mixed together. Boil to thicken.

Garnish with sour cream and serve with bruschetta (see page 20).

*In place of an immersion blender, a regular blender may be used, with caution. Fill the blender about one-third full so that the hot liquid does not splatter over. Vent the lid of the blender so that the steam inside does not build up pressure.

Lion House Tomato Bisque

Spiced Tomato Soup

Makes 8 to 10 servings

1 (46-ounce) can tomato juice

1 tablespoon sugar

1 tablespoon chicken soup base

3 cups water

2 tablespoons taco seasoning (or to taste)

Combine ingredients and bring to a boil. Adjust seasonings to taste. Serve hot or cold.

Western Tomato Soup

Makes about 8 servings

3 slices bacon

½ cup finely chopped celery

3 tablespoons finely chopped onion

¼ cup finely chopped green pepper

3 tablespoons flour

2 cups milk

1 (10.75-ounce) can condensed tomato soup

1 (14.5-ounce) can stewed tomatoes

1½ cups tomato juice

Salt and pepper, to taste

Fry bacon until crisp; crumble and set aside. Sauté celery, onion, and green pepper in bacon fat until tender and translucent but not browned. Add flour and cook 2 to 3 minutes. Combine milk and tomato soup in a 3-quart saucepan; heat and stir until smooth. Combine all ingredients except bacon with tomato soup mixture. Heat and stir until slightly thickened. Garnish with crumbled bacon.

Gazpacho

Makes 8 servings

2 cups tomato juice

1 cup peeled, chopped tomatoes

½ cup chopped green bell pepper

½ cup chopped celery

½ cup chopped cucumber

¼ cup chopped onion

1 clove garlic, minced

2 teaspoons snipped fresh parsley

1 teaspoon snipped fresh chives

2 to 3 tablespoons vinegar

2 tablespoons olive oil

1 teaspoon salt

1 teaspoon cumin

½ teaspoon Worcestershire sauce

¼ teaspoon pepper

Combine all ingredients in a large bowl. Cover and chill in refrigerator at least 4 hours or overnight. Serve cold.

Chef's tip: Three diced avocados may be added, if desired.

Chili

Makes 8 to 10 servings

1 pound diced lean beef

1 green bell pepper, chopped

1 red bell pepper, chopped

1 medium yellow onion, chopped

1 teaspoon crushed red pepper flakes

1½ tablespoons chili powder

1 teaspoon granulated garlic, or 2 cloves fresh garlic, minced

1 teaspoon cumin

1 teaspoon crushed black pepper

1½ teaspoons kosher salt

½ teaspoon cayenne pepper

1 tablespoon canola oil

2 (8-ounce) cans diced tomatoes

1 (4-ounce) can diced green chilies

4 cups canned kidney beans, rinsed and drained

2 cups tomato soup

1 cup tomato juice

1 cup brown sugar

Sour cream

Cheese, grated

Onion, finely chopped

Preheat large heavy skillet or Dutch oven. Brown beef, bell peppers, onion, and spices together in canola oil. When beef is browned, add remaining ingredients and simmer 45 minutes, stirring occasionally. Garnish with dollop of sour cream, grated cheese, and finely chopped onion.

Vegetarian Chili

Makes 4 servings

1 cup chopped onion

3 cloves garlic, minced

1 cup water

½ cup diced green bell pepper

2 (14.5-ounce) cans stewed tomatoes, undrained and diced

1 (15-ounce) can red kidney beans, drained

1 (15-ounce) can garbanzo beans, drained

2 tablespoons chili powder

1½ teaspoons cumin

¼ cup sour cream, for garnish

Spray a large soup pot with nonstick cooking spray and preheat it on the stove. Sauté onion and garlic in heated pot over medium heat for 5 minutes. Stir in water, green pepper, tomatoes, beans, chili powder, and cumin. Bring to a boil. Reduce heat and simmer 30 minutes, uncovered, to blend flavors and thicken chili.

Ladle into individual bowls and top each serving with a dollop of sour cream.

Slow Cooker: Place all ingredients, except sour cream, in slow cooker. Cook on high 3 to 4 hours.

Creamy Butternut Squash Soup

Makes 6 servings

1 medium butternut squash	1 rib celery, roughly chopped
2 pounds baby carrots	4 cups heavy cream
1 cup butter, divided	1 teaspoon sugar, to taste
¼ cup packed brown sugar	Pinch cayenne pepper, optional
1½ teaspoon salt, divided	Pinch ground cloves, optional
1 small white onion, roughly chopped	Pinch cinnamon, optional
2 cloves garlic, minced	Sour cream, for garnish

Peel and cube butternut squash. Discard seeds. Steam baby carrots until soft.

Preheat oven to 350 degrees F. Melt ½ cup butter. Toss squash with melted butter and sprinkle with brown sugar and 1 teaspoon salt in a medium bowl. Spread on a baking sheet. Bake squash 30 to 45 minutes or until soft and brown on top.

In a soup pot, melt remaining ½ cup butter and sauté onion, garlic, and celery until soft and translucent. Add previously steamed carrots and baked squash to the soup pot. Puree the mixture well with a hand immersion blender* and slowly add cream, sugar, ½ teaspoon salt, and spices, to taste. Simmer until it reaches desired consistency.

In place of an immersion blender, a regular blender may be used. Fill the blender about one-third full so that the hot liquid does not splatter over. Vent the lid of the blender so that the steam inside does not build up pressure.

Oatmeal Zucchini Soup

Makes 6 to 8 servings

5 tablespoons butter, divided	1 tablespoon Worcestershire sauce
1 tablespoon minced onion	2 cups heavy cream
1 pinch dried thyme	2 cups milk
1¼ pounds small zucchini, chopped, plus 1 zucchini, sliced, for garnish	2 cups water
½ cup quick-cooking oats	Salt, to taste

Melt butter in a large saucepan, add onion, and sauté 2 minutes or until onion is translucent. Add thyme and zucchini and sauté 4 minutes. Add oats and cook, stirring for 2 minutes. Add Worcestershire sauce, cream, milk, and water, stirring constantly. Cover and cook 15 minutes on low heat or until zucchini is tender. Season with salt, to taste.

Sauté sliced zucchini in 1 tablespoon butter, for garnish.

Creamy Butternut
Squash Soup

Minestrone

Makes 12 (1-cup) servings

1 cup dry navy beans
½ pound diced bacon
⅓ pound diced, cooked ham
½ cup chopped onion
2 cups beef stock
2 tablespoons Worcestershire sauce
1½ cups canned tomatoes, diced

1½ cups peeled, chopped carrots
1 cup fresh, cut green beans
2 cups coarsely chopped cabbage
1 cup chopped celery
1 cup small shell pasta or macaroni
Salt and pepper, to taste

Soak beans overnight in enough water to cover. Drain, rinse, and drain again. Boil beans in fresh water until tender, about 2 hours; add more water as needed. Cook bacon until crisp; drain, and crumble. Sauté ham and onion in bacon fat. Add beef stock, Worcestershire sauce, bacon, ham, onion, tomatoes, carrots, green beans, cabbage, celery, and pasta to the beans. Cook until fresh vegetables are tender, 10 to 15 minutes. Add salt and pepper, to taste.

Chef's tip: For quicker preparation use 2 (15-ounce) cans navy beans, drained and rinsed, in place of soaked navy beans.

Lentil Stew

Makes 8 servings

1 cup dried lentils
4 cups beef broth
2 (14.5-ounce) cans stewed tomatoes, undrained and diced
1 medium onion, chopped
2 ribs celery, diced
2 cloves garlic, minced
1 teaspoon rosemary

¼ teaspoon pepper
4 carrots, peeled and cubed, divided
2 tablespoons butter or margarine
8 small white boiling onions (pearl onions), peeled
¼ pound small fresh mushrooms, halved
4 potatoes (about 1 pound), peeled and cubed

Rinse and sort lentils and combine in a large soup pot with beef broth, tomatoes, onion, celery, garlic, rosemary, pepper, and half of the carrots. Bring mixture to simmer over medium heat. Cover and cook gently 30 to 35 minutes.

While mixture is simmering, melt butter in a large, heavy skillet. Sauté the remaining carrots along with white onions until lightly browned, about 5 to 7 minutes. Stir in mushrooms and cook an additional 2 to 3 minutes, stirring constantly. Add potatoes and sautéed vegetables to soup in soup pot. Cover and simmer an additional 20 to 25 minutes or until potatoes and lentils are tender.

Peasant Soup

Makes 8 servings

1 cup dry great northern beans

7 cups water, divided, plus additional for soaking benas

1 teaspoon salt

1 ham hock (or ½ pound bacon or diced ham)

3 carrots, peeled and diced

1 onion, chopped

1 cup chopped celery

2 cups chopped cabbage, plus cabbage wedges for garnish

½ teaspoon garlic powder

½ teaspoon pepper

1 tablespoon taco seasoning

Cover beans with water and soak overnight (or bring to a boil for 2 minutes, remove from heat, and let stand, covered, 1 hour). Drain beans and combine with 3 cups water, salt, and ham hock in a large soup pot. Cover and simmer until beans are tender, about 2 hours. Add carrots, onion, celery, chopped cabbage, garlic powder, pepper, taco seasoning, and remaining 4 cups water. Simmer, covered, until vegetables are tender. Remove ham hock and strip meat from bone. Dice meat and return to soup.

To serve, cut a cabbage wedge in half and slice thin wedges (½-inch wide on the long end), leaving a piece of the core attached. After ladling soup into bowls, place wedges on piping hot soup to soften them.

Chef's tip: For easier preparation, substitute 2 (15-ounce) cans great northern beans, undrained, and omit the first three cups of water.

Slow Cooker: Prepare beans as above. Place all ingredients in slow cooker. Cook on high 3 to 3½ hours.

Bean and Bacon Soup

Makes 2½ quarts, or 10 (1-cup) servings

¼ pound bacon

¼ cup chopped onion

4 cups water

1 (11.5-ounce) can condensed bean with bacon soup

1½ cups cooked navy beans

Roux, optional (see page 20)

Salt and pepper to taste

Sauté bacon; remove from pan and pour off fat. Measure 2 tablespoons bacon fat into large, heavy kettle. Cook onion in bacon fat until soft but not brown, about 5 minutes. Add water, soup, and beans. Bring to a boil; thicken with a little roux, if desired. Add salt and pepper to taste. Add cooked bacon and serve.

Cream of Broccoli Soup
with Cheddar Cheese

Cream of Broccoli Soup with Cheddar Cheese

Makes 6 servings

4 tablespoons unsalted butter
½ cup chopped onion
½ cup peeled, chopped carrots
½ cup chopped celery
2 cloves garlic, minced
4 cups chopped broccoli
¼ cup all-purpose flour

4 cups heavy cream
1 cup chicken broth
1½ cups shredded cheddar cheese, divided
2 teaspoons Worcestershire sauce
Salt and pepper, to taste
Broccoli florets, steamed, for garnish

Melt butter in a large soup pot over medium heat. Add onion, carrots, celery, garlic, and broccoli and sauté until the vegetables are very soft. Add flour to the vegetables, making a roux. Pour in cream and chicken broth, mixing well. Simmer until mixture has thickened, about 4 minutes. Add 1 cup cheddar cheese and stir until cheese has melted into the soup. Season with Worcestershire sauce, salt, and pepper.

To serve, ladle into individual bowls and garnish with remaining ½ cup cheddar cheese and steamed broccoli florets.

Broccoli-Cheese Soup

Makes 6 servings

1½ pounds fresh broccoli, chopped, or 2 (10-ounce) packages frozen chopped broccoli
3 tablespoons margarine
¼ cup chopped onion
3 tablespoons flour

2 cups chicken broth (or 2 cups water and 2 tablespoons chicken soup base)
2 cups light cream
1 teaspoon salt
¼ teaspoon nutmeg
1 cup grated cheddar cheese

Cook broccoli in small amount of salted water until tender; drain and set aside. Make a roux by melting margarine in a heavy soup pot over medium heat until margarine is foamy. Add onion and cook until translucent. Stir in flour. Slowly add broth and cream, cooking and stirring until thickened. Add salt, nutmeg, and cooked broccoli. Warm through. Just before serving, stir in cheese.

Cream of Asparagus Soup

Makes 6 servings

¾ pound fresh or frozen asparagus, reserving 6 spears for garnish

1 cup salted water

3 tablespoons butter or margarine

¼ cup minced onion

3 tablespoons flour

1 (14.5-ounce) can chicken broth

1 cup milk

¼ teaspoon paprika

½ teaspoon salt

Simmer asparagus in water, covered, until tender. Cool slightly, reserve 6 spears for garnish, and puree remaining asparagus and water in blender; set aside.

In a heavy soup pot, melt butter or margarine over medium-high heat; add onion and sauté until soft. Stir in flour, making a roux. Add pureed asparagus, chicken broth, milk, paprika, and salt. Cook and stir until slightly thickened.

To garnish, slice reserved asparagus spears diagonally into ½-inch pieces and place on individual servings of soup.

Chef's tip: One (15-ounce) can asparagus, undrained, may be substituted for fresh asparagus. Puree and follow rest of directions.

Cream of Spinach and Mushroom Soup

Makes 8 servings

2 tablespoons butter

¼ cup diced yellow onion

2 cloves garlic, minced

3 cups sliced mushrooms

4 cups heavy cream

6 cups milk

½ cup water

5 tablespoons cornstarch

1 teaspoon salt

1 teaspoon white pepper

2 cups chopped fresh spinach

Garlic Croutons

6 to 8 slices bread

4 tablespoons melted butter or salad oil

2 teaspoons minced garlic

2 teaspoons Italian seasoning

Melt butter in a soup pot and sauté onion and garlic for 3 minutes. Add mushrooms and continue cooking while stirring with a whisk until mushrooms look soft, about 4 minutes. Add cream and milk. Stir over low heat until surface bubbles.

Mix water with cornstarch to make cornstarch slurry to thicken the soup. Add slurry, salt, pepper, and spinach to soup. To serve, ladle soup into bowls and top with homemade or purchased croutons.

For croutons: Cut bread into small cubes and put into a bowl. Add butter or salad oil, garlic, and Italian seasoning. Mix well and transfer to baking pan. Bake 8 to 12 minutes at 350 degrees F. or until golden brown.

Cream of Asparagus Soup

Golden Squash Soup

Makes 6 servings

1 small onion, sliced	1½ teaspoons salt
2 tablespoons butter or margarine	¼ teaspoon celery salt
¼ cup flour	⅛ teaspoon curry powder
5 cups milk	Pepper, to taste
1½ cups peeled, cooked, and pureed winter squash (hubbard, banana, etc.)	2 tablespoons chopped parsley, for garnish

Cook onion in butter in large saucepan until onion is translucent. Blend flour into butter and onion; add milk. Cook over low heat, stirring constantly, until thickened. Remove from heat; gently blend in squash, salt, celery salt, curry powder, and pepper. Heat to serving temperature but do not boil. Sprinkle each serving with parsley.

Chef's tip: One (12-ounce) package of frozen pureed squash may be used in this recipe. After adding frozen squash, continue to heat soup only until squash is defrosted.

Corn Chowder

Makes 4 servings

2 slices bacon, for garnish	½ teaspoon salt
1 small onion, chopped	Dash pepper
1½ cups boiling water	1 (12-ounce) can evaporated milk
1 (16-ounce) package frozen corn, or 1 (15.25-ounce) whole kernel can corn, undrained	1 tablespoon butter, melted
	1 tablespoon flour

Cook bacon slowly in large saucepan until crisp; remove and drain on paper towels; crumble and set aside. Add onion to pan and cook until translucent but not brown, about 5 to 10 minutes. Add boiling water, corn, salt, pepper, and evaporated milk. Blend butter and flour to make a roux. Stir into soup mixture; mix until smooth. Cook until thickened.

Garnish with crumbled bacon.

California Chowder

Makes 12 servings

½ cup butter

1 cup flour

1 tablespoon chicken soup base

2 cups heavy cream

4 cups milk

4 cups water

2 cups peeled, diced carrots

4 cups peeled, diced potatoes

2 cups diced celery

1 teaspoon granulated garlic, or 2 cloves fresh minced garlic

1 tablespoon salt

1 tablespoon Worcestershire sauce

1 cup finely chopped onion

1 tablespoon vegetable oil

2 cups fresh, chopped broccoli

2 cups fresh, chopped cauliflower

Fresh parsley or thyme, for garnish

Melt butter in a large soup pot. Add flour and mix well. Add chicken base, cream, milk, and water. Bring to a low boil and then add carrots, potatoes, celery, garlic, salt, and Worcestershire sauce. Cook 45 minutes. In a separate saucepan, sauté onion in oil for 3 minutes and add to soup with broccoli and cauliflower. Cook another 15 minutes or until vegetables are tender. Garnish with fresh parsley or thyme.

Chef's tip: Two (12-ounce) bags frozen California-blend vegetables, thawed and slightly chopped, may be substituted for carrots, cauliflower, and broccoli.

Vegetable Soup

Makes 3 quarts, about 12 servings

1 cup diced tomatoes

1½ cups diced carrots

1 cup diced celery

1½ quarts water

¼ cup chopped onion

1 tablespoon beef soup base, or beef consommé

½ cup green beans

1 cup diced potatoes

½ pound cooked beef, cut in pieces

1 cup peas

Cook together tomatoes, carrots, celery, water, onion, and beef soup base until carrots and celery are tender. Add green beans, potatoes, beef, and an additional cup of water. Simmer until vegetables are tender. Add peas about 5 minutes before serving. Adjust seasonings to taste.

Canadian Cheese Soup

Canadian Cheese Soup

Makes 10 servings

½ cup chopped onion
½ cup butter or margarine
1 cup flour
⅓ cup cornstarch
½ teaspoon paprika
½ teaspoon salt
¼ teaspoon white pepper

4 cups half and half or milk, heated
4 cups chicken stock, heated
¾ cup peeled, diced carrots, cooked
¾ cup diced celery, cooked
1 cup shredded sharp cheddar cheese
⅓ cup chopped parsley

Sauté onion in melted butter until translucent but not brown, 5 to 10 minutes. Add flour, cornstarch, paprika, salt, and pepper. Cook about 10 minutes on low heat. Add half and half or milk and chicken stock; cook, stirring constantly, until thickened. With a fork, slightly mash cooked vegetables and add to milk mixture. Adjust seasonings to taste. Just before serving, stir in shredded cheese and chopped parsley.

Chef's tip: Amounts of vegetables may be increased if thicker soup is desired.

Potato Soup

Makes 8 servings

1½ cups sliced leeks or green onions, plus more for garnish
2¼ cups water, divided
5 cups peeled, cubed potatoes
¾ cup chopped celery
1⅓ cups peeled, cubed carrots
2 teaspoons salt, divided

¼ cup butter or margarine
¼ cup flour
¼ teaspoon pepper
4 cups milk
2 cubes chicken bouillon

Place leeks in a sinkful of cold water. Vigorously stir leeks to remove grit. Place leeks in a colander and run cold water over them until there is no more grit in the water.

Sauté leeks or green onions in ¼ cup water in a large soup pot until tender. Add potatoes, celery, carrots, 1 teaspoon salt, and remaining 2 cups water. Cover and simmer 20 to 25 minutes or until vegetables are tender.

Meanwhile, melt butter or margarine in a medium saucepan. Add flour, pepper, and 1 teaspoon salt. Cook until smooth and bubbly. Gradually add milk and bouillon. Cook and stir until mixture thickens. Stir into vegetables. Simmer, stirring occasionally, until heated through. Garnish with sliced green onions.

Clam Chowder

Makes 6 to 8 servings

½ cup butter
½ cup finely chopped onion
½ cup flour
⅓ cup cornstarch
6 cups half and half or milk
3 (6½-ounce) cans chopped clams in clam juice, drained, reserving clam juice
1 cup peeled, diced potatoes, cooked

1 cup diced celery, cooked
1 teaspoon garlic salt
1 tablespoon Worcestershire sauce, optional
½ pound bacon, cooked and crumbled, optional
½ teaspoon dried thyme
1 teaspoon salt
½ teaspoon pepper
2 to 3 sprigs chopped parsley, for garnish

Melt butter in a large soup pot over medium heat; add onion, and sauté. Add flour and cornstarch; cook 10 minutes, stirring often. Add milk and reserved clam juice; cook until slightly thickened, stirring constantly. Add clams, potatoes, celery, garlic salt, Worcestershire sauce, bacon, and thyme. Season with salt and pepper, to taste.

Serve in bread bowls and garnish with chopped parsley.

Lion House Oyster Stew

Makes 6 servings

4½ tablespoons butter or margarine, divided
2½ tablespoons flour
2 cups milk
2 cups light cream

2 (8-ounce) cans oysters, undrained
½ teaspoon salt
¼ teaspoon black pepper

Make a roux by melting 2½ tablespoons butter in a heavy soup pot over medium-high heat until foamy. Stir in flour and cook until fragrant and golden brown. Reduce heat to medium. Gradually stir in milk and light cream, cooking and stirring until thickened. Add oysters, salt, and pepper. Heat slowly to simmer; do not boil.

When ready to serve, garnish with 1 teaspoon butter placed in the middle of each soup bowl and serve with crackers on the side.

Clam Chowder

Shrimp Bisque

Shrimp Bisque

Makes 6 to 8 servings

2 tablespoons butter

1 teaspoon chopped garlic

½ cup diced yellow onion

1½ cups tomato puree

1 tablespoon Old Bay Seasoning

2 cups clam juice

4 cups heavy cream

1 teaspoon salt

2 cups cooked bay shrimp

Salt and pepper, to taste

3 chopped green onions, for garnish

Melt butter in a soup pot; add garlic and onion and sauté 3 minutes. Add tomato puree and Old Bay Seasoning; stir and cook 3 more minutes. When mixture starts to bubble, add clam juice, cream, and salt and return to a low boil to heat through. Add cooked shrimp at the last minute. Season with salt and pepper.

To serve, place in soup bowls and garnish with chopped green onions.

Crab Bisque

Makes 12 servings

1 (10.5-ounce) can each condensed cream of tomato, celery,
    mushroom, and green pea soups

5 cups milk (part cream, if desired)

1 or 2 cans crab meat

Salt

Pepper

Parsley

Combine and blend soups. Heat milk; gradually add to soups, then add crab meat. Heat slowly, stirring constantly to prevent scorching. Season to taste; add chopped parsley.

Salmon Chowder

Makes 6 to 8 servings

2 (8-ounce) salmon fillets, reserving ½ cup cut-up pieces, for garnish
1 teaspoon kosher salt, divided
¼ teaspoon ground black pepper
¼ cup butter
1 cup chopped onion
½ cup chopped celery
½ cup peeled, chopped carrots
3 tablespoons flour

3 cups milk
1 teaspoon thyme
½ teaspoon paprika
½ teaspoon Cholula hot sauce
1 teaspoon Worcestershire sauce
1 pound red potatoes, cut into ½-inch pieces
2 cups half and half
Lemon wedges, for garnish

Preheat oven to 400 degrees F. Sprinkle salmon with ½ teaspoon kosher salt and pepper; place on a foil-lined baking sheet. Bake 15 minutes or until desired degree of doneness. Break fish into ½-inch pieces; set aside. Melt butter in a heavy soup pot over medium heat. Add onion, celery, and carrots and sauté 5 minutes or until tender. Add flour; stir until mixture is smooth. Gradually add milk, using a whisk. Cook over medium heat, stirring constantly, until thickened and bubbly. Stir in ½ teaspoon salt, thyme, paprika, Cholula sauce, and Worcestershire sauce. Add potatoes; reduce heat and simmer 20 minutes or until potatoes are tender. Add half and half. Cook 6 minutes or until heated. Add cooked salmon. Garnish with reserved salmon and lemon wedge.

Gumbo Soup

Makes 12 to 16 servings

¼ cup butter
3 large yellow onions, diced
2 large red bell peppers, diced
1 stalk celery, diced
1 (14.5-ounce) can diced tomatoes, undrained
1 (7-ounce) can diced green chilies, undrained
2 cups clam juice
1 cup tomato juice
4 cups water
1 (15-ounce) can black beans, rinsed

½ pound salad shrimp
¼ cup uncooked rice
½ pound pork sausage
½ teaspoon minced garlic
1 teaspoon cayenne pepper
2 tablespoons paprika
½ cup brown sugar
1½ teaspoons salt
3 cups frozen sliced okra

Melt butter in a large soup pot over medium-high heat. Add onions, peppers, and celery and sauté until tender. Stir in tomatoes and chilies. Add clam juice, tomato juice, and water; bring to a boil. Stir in beans, shrimp, and rice. Reduce to medium heat and simmer. While soup simmers, brown sausage in a medium skillet; drain off fat. Add sausage, garlic, cayenne pepper, paprika, brown sugar, salt, and okra to soup. Cook until rice is tender.

Slow Cooker: Place all ingredients in slow cooker and cook on high 3 to 4 hours or on low 6 to 8 hours.

Salmon Chowder

Cancun Tortilla Soup

Makes 8 to 10 servings

2 tablespoons paste-style chicken base or 1 tablespoon granulated soup base

4 cups diced canned tomatoes

½ cup butter

1 (7-ounce) can diced green chiles, undrained

3 cups diced onion

10 cups water

5 cups dried (dehydrated instant) refried beans

2 cups crushed corn tortilla chips

1 tablespoon cumin

1 teaspoon garlic powder

⅔ cup diced green onions

⅔ cup fresh chopped cilantro

Tortilla chips, for garnish

Sour cream, for garnish

Combine chicken base, tomatoes, butter, chiles, and onion in a large soup pot. Cook until onion is translucent. Add water, beans, chips, cumin, and garlic powder. Heat until thickened and beans are soft, about 5 minutes. Add green onions and cilantro about 5 minutes before serving. Garnish with crisp tortilla chips and sour cream.

Taco Soup

Makes 8 servings

1 pound ground beef

1 cup chopped onion

1 package mild taco seasoning mix

2 cups frozen corn

1 (15-ounce) can kidney beans, drained and rinsed

1 (28-ounce) can stewed tomatoes, undrained

1 (8-ounce) can tomato sauce

2 cups water

Tortilla chips, for garnish

Shredded cheddar or pepper Jack cheese, for garnish

Brown ground beef and onion in a large soup pot; drain off fat. Stir in taco seasoning, corn, kidney beans, stewed tomatoes, tomato sauce, and water. Bring to a simmer over medium heat and simmer 20 to 30 minutes.

Serve topped with tortilla chips and shredded cheese.

Slow Cooker: Brown ground beef and onion in a frying pan. Place all ingredients, except for garnishes, in slow cooker. Cook on high 3 to 4 hours.

Creamy Southwestern Chicken Soup

Makes 6 servings

2 tablespoons butter
2 tablespoons flour
2 cups heavy cream
3 cups milk
2 teaspoons taco seasoning
2 teaspoons paprika
1 chicken bouillon cube

2 chicken breasts, cooked and diced
1 (4-ounce) can diced green chiles
½ cup cooked rice
1 cup frozen corn
1 cup canned black beans, drained and rinsed
Chopped cilantro, for garnish

Make a roux by melting butter in a heavy soup pot over medium heat until butter is foamy. Mix in flour, stir, and cook 1½ to 2 minutes. Slowly add cream and milk. Mix in taco seasoning, paprika, and bouillon cube. Cook and stir until thickened. Add chicken, chiles, rice, corn, and beans. Warm through. Garnish with chopped cilantro.

Chicken and Rice Soup

Makes 8 servings

1 (2.5- to 3-pound) fryer chicken
4 cups water
1 peeled carrot, cut in chunks
2 onions, divided (1 cut in chunks for broth, 1 chopped for soup)
1 celery rib, cut in chunks
1 teaspoon salt

1 clove garlic, crushed
1 cup cooked rice
2 fresh tomatoes, cut in wedges
½ cup chopped green pepper
1 cup frozen peas
¼ cup sliced pimiento-stuffed olives

Place chicken, water, carrot, onion chunks, celery, salt, and garlic in a large soup pot. Bring to a slow boil and then reduce heat to simmer. Cover and simmer 1 hour. Remove chicken from broth and set aside to cool slightly. Strain vegetables from broth and discard; set broth aside to cool. Once chicken is cool enough to handle, remove and discard bones and skin. Cut chicken into bite-sized pieces.

Skim fat off the broth and return broth to stove top. Stir in cut-up chicken, rice, tomatoes, green pepper, chopped onion, peas, and olives. Heat, uncovered, until hot and peppers and onion are tender, about 10 minutes.

Southwest Chicken Tortilla Soup

Makes 6 to 8 servings

2 tablespoons butter

2 cups diced boneless, skinless chicken breasts

2 teaspoons minced garlic

2 tablespoons diced yellow onion

2 (4-ounce) cans diced green chiles

2 cups tomato puree

1 cup frozen whole kernel corn, thawed

2 cups diced yellow corn tortillas

4 cups water

2 cups heavy cream

½ teaspoon cumin

2 teaspoons salt

½ teaspoon Cajun seasoning

1 diced tomato, for garnish

1 cup sour cream, for garnish

10 to 16 tortilla chips or 3 cups tortilla strips, for garnish

Melt butter in a soup pot and sauté raw chicken until almost cooked. Add garlic and onion, cooking 4 minutes. Add chiles, tomato puree, corn, tortillas, water, and cream; simmer. Blend with an immersion blender* until smooth. Season with cumin, salt, and Cajun seasoning.

To serve, ladle into serving bowls and garnish with diced tomato, sour cream, and tortilla chips or strips.

In place of an immersion blender, a regular blender may be used, with caution. Fill the blender about one-third full so that the hot liquid does not splatter over. Vent the lid of the blender so that the steam inside does not build up pressure.

Chicken Dumpling Soup

Makes 12 servings

Dumplings

1 cup milk

½ cup butter

½ teaspoon salt

½ teaspoon nutmeg

1 cup flour

3 eggs

Soup

1 large yellow onion, diced

½ stalk celery, diced

2 carrots, diced

2 tablespoons vegetable oil

Meat from 1 whole chicken, cooked and shredded (about 3 cups)

4 to 6 cups chicken broth

1 cup frozen French-cut or fresh cut green beans

1 cup pearl barley, optional

1 teaspoon celery salt

1 tablespoon fresh chopped parsley

2 bay leaves

1 teaspoon thyme

Salt and pepper, to taste

For dumplings: Bring milk and butter to a boil; add salt and nutmeg. Remove from heat and immediately add flour, stirring until dough leaves sides of pan. Add eggs one at a time, forming a sticky dough.

For soup: Sauté onion, celery, and carrots in oil. Add remaining ingredients and simmer until barley is tender and vegetables are softened. Season to taste with salt and pepper. Add spoon-sized balls of dumpling dough (they will sink to the bottom) and simmer until dumplings rise.

Southwest Chicken Tortilla Soup

Country-Style Chicken Noodle Soup

Makes 6 servings

½ cup diced yellow onion
1 cup diced celery
1 cup diced carrots
2 tablespoons vegetable oil
1 pound boneless, skinless chicken breast, diced

8 cups chicken broth or stock,* canned or homemade
4 ounces egg noodles, uncooked
Salt and pepper, to taste
1 small bunch parsley, finely chopped, for garnish

Sauté onion, celery, and carrots in oil in a heavy soup pot until onion is translucent; do not let them brown. Add diced chicken and cook until done. Add chicken broth and bring to a boil. Add uncooked noodles. Return to a boil and cook until noodles are done. Add salt and pepper, to taste, and garnish with fresh parsley.

This soup is best when made with chicken broth. If broth is not available, you may substitute 8 cups water and 8 chicken bouillon cubes. Adjust the flavor with salt. Alternately, you may use the breast meat of a rotisserie chicken and the juice from its container as part of the stock. Add cut-up chicken after noodles are cooked.

Hearty Chicken Noodle Soup

Makes about 2½ quarts, or 10 servings

2 teaspoons paste-style chicken soup base, or 2 bouillon
  cubes, or 1 teaspoon granulated base
3 cups canned or homemade chicken stock
2 cups peeled and chopped carrots
2 cups chopped celery
¾ cup chopped onion
2 (10.75-ounce) cans condensed cream of chicken soup

¼ cup evaporated milk, or ½ cup milk
Roux (see page 20), optional
2 cups cooked diced chicken
4 cups cooked noodles (see Homemade Herb Noodles
  below)
Salt and pepper, to taste

Heat chicken soup base and stock together. Add carrots, celery, and onion and simmer until vegetables are crisp-tender. Add cream of chicken soup, milk, cooked chicken, and noodles. Thicken with roux, if needed. Add salt and pepper, to taste.

Homemade Herb Noodles

1 cup flour
1 teaspoon herb of choice (such as parsley, thyme, basil,
  oregano, or chives)

1 egg
Water to bind

Combine flour and herb on work surface. Form a cone in flour and work egg into flour. Add water a spoonful at a time to make a firm yet workable dough. Allow dough to rest 15 to 20 minutes. Roll out paper-thin; cut into strips. Allow noodles to dry to store for later use or cook 12 to 16 minutes in 2 quarts boiling, salted water until tender, stirring gently. Drain and add noodles to desired soup.

Lamb Stew

Makes 6 to 8 servings

2 pounds lean lamb meat, cut in chunks
2 tablespoons flour
1½ teaspoons salt
¼ teaspoon pepper
2 tablespoons cooking oil
1 clove garlic, minced or pressed
1 onion, finely chopped

½ cup thinly sliced celery
½ teaspoon dill weed
2 cups water
1½ teaspoons sugar
1 cup sliced carrots
1 cup green beans
1 cup pearl onions, peeled

In a large bowl, combine flour, salt, and pepper. Dredge lamb chunks in mixture. Heat oil in a Dutch oven over medium heat; add lamb chunks and brown slightly. Add garlic, onion, and celery to meat as it browns. Add dill weed and water; cover and simmer until meat is tender, about 2 hours. Add sugar and remaining vegetables, and simmer until vegetables are tender, 10 to 15 minutes. Thicken liquid with a little additional flour mixed with cold water, if desired. Good served with dumplings.

Hearty Turkey Vegetable Soup

Makes 8 servings

Turkey Broth

1 roasted turkey
1 small carrot, sliced
1 small onion, chopped
Celery leaves
2 teaspoons salt
1 bay leaf

Soup

8 cups canned or homemade turkey broth (see directions below)
1 cup cubed potatoes
1 cup sliced carrots
1 cup sliced celery
¼ cup chopped onion
1 teaspoon salt
Pepper, to taste
1 cup uncooked egg noodles
2 cups chopped cooked turkey meat
1 cup frozen peas

For broth: Strip as much meat as possible from bones of roasted turkey; refrigerate meat for later use in soup. Place bones and skin into a large stockpot and barely cover with water. Add carrot, onion, a few celery leaves, salt, and bay leaf. Bring to a simmer over medium heat. Reduce heat, cover, and simmer 2 to 3 hours. Strain broth, discarding carcass and other solids. Use broth immediately or refrigerate and use within 2 days. You may also freeze broth for 3 to 6 months.

For soup: Combine turkey broth, potatoes, carrots, celery, onion, salt, and pepper in a large soup pot. Bring to a boil over medium-high heat. Add noodles, reduce heat, and simmer 30 minutes. Stir in turkey and frozen peas; heat thoroughly and serve.

Turkey Dutch Oven Stew

Turkey Dutch Oven Stew

Makes 6 to 8 servings

2 tablespoons vegetable oil

1½ pounds raw turkey (breast or thigh), cut into 1-inch cubes

1 large onion, chopped

4 medium potatoes, peeled and each cut into 12 to 16 pieces

4 carrots, peeled and sliced in ½-inch slices

4 ribs celery, sliced in ½-inch slices

1 teaspoon granulated garlic or 2 cloves minced garlic

1 tablespoon Italian seasoning

Water to cover the vegetables and meat in pan

2 (10.75-ounce) cans condensed golden mushroom soup

Salt, to taste

1 teaspoon coarse cracked black pepper

Heat oil in a large Dutch oven or soup pot until it is almost smoking. Add turkey and onion and cook until well browned. Add potatoes, carrots, celery, garlic, and Italian seasoning and enough water to cover them. Bring to a boil and then turn heat down to simmer and cook until the carrots are tender. Add mushroom soup, salt, and pepper and simmer 10 minutes.

Serve with a Lion House dinner roll (see page 83).

Chef's tip: Any cream soup can be used: cream of celery, cream of chicken, cream of mushroom. A favorite is golden mushroom.

Slow Cooker: Brown turkey in 2 or 3 batches in a very hot frying pan. Add the onions about halfway through the cooking process of the third batch. Browning meat in small batches allows the pan to stay hot enough to brown well. You will need 2 additional tablespoons oil for browning batches. Put all ingredients in slow cooker and cook on low 6 to 8 hours.

Country Bacon Soup

Makes 6 servings

1 tablespoon butter or margarine

½ cup chopped onion

7 slices bacon, fried, drained, and crumbled, reserving 2 slices for garnish

1 (10.75-ounce) can condensed cream of mushroom soup

1 (10.5-ounce) can condensed vegetarian vegetable soup

1 (11.5-ounce) can condensed bean with bacon soup

1 cup whole kernel corn (canned or frozen), drained

1¼ cups milk

¾ cup water

2 medium potatoes, peeled, diced, and cooked

Salt and pepper, to taste

Melt butter or margarine in a large, heavy saucepan over medium heat; add onion and sauté until translucent. Stir in bacon, soups, corn, milk, water, and potatoes. Cook over medium heat, stirring frequently, until heated through. Season with salt and pepper, to taste.

To serve, ladle into bowls and garnish with crumbled bacon in the middle.

Pozole (Mexican Stew)

Makes 10 servings

2 pounds boneless pork loin, cut in 1x2-inch pieces

1 pound boneless pork butt, cut in 1x2-inch pieces

14 cups water

4 teaspoons salt

¾ cup diced onion

1 tablespoon dried oregano

1 sprig cilantro

3 cloves garlic, minced

2 (14.5- to 16-ounce) cans hominy

Red sauce (see below)

1 tablespoon Cholula hot sauce, optional

Shredded cabbage, for garnish

Chopped onion, optional, for garnish

Lime or lemon wedges, optional, for garnish

Tostadas, for garnish

Red Sauce

10 chiles guerillas (dried chiles)

½ cup water

¼ cup onion, chopped

4 cloves garlic

Place pork in a large soup pot and cover with water. Add salt, onion, oregano, cilantro, and garlic and bring to a boil. As it boils, skim top layer of foam off surface of soup. Cook over medium heat until pork is tender, about 30 to 40 minutes. Do not cover with a lid while cooking. Add hominy, Red Sauce, and Cholula hot sauce, if desired, and cook another 15 minutes.

For the sauce: Boil chiles in water for 5 to 10 minutes. Transfer to a blender and puree with onion and garlic. Add to the Pozole. Garnish with shredded cabbage, chopped onion, a wedge of lemon or lime, and tostadas.

Brunswick Stew

Makes 10 to 12 servings

2 sweet onions, chopped

2 tablespoons butter

2 (14.5-ounce) cans chicken broth

2½ to 3 cups water

2 (28-ounce) cans petite-cut tomatoes, undrained

⅔ cup ketchup

⅔ cup Worcestershire sauce

1½ teaspoons salt

½ teaspoon pepper

2 tablespoons Cholula hot sauce

1 pound pulled pork

3 to 4 medium potatoes, peeled and diced in ½-inch or smaller cubes

½ (22-ounce) bottle barbecue sauce (your favorite brand)

3 tablespoons white vinegar

1 (15-ounce) can peas

1 (15-ounce) can great northern beans, drained and rinsed

1 (15-ounce) can navy beans, drained and rinsed

2 (14.75-ounce) cans cream-style corn

Sauté onion in butter in a 6-quart saucepan until onions are translucent. Add chicken broth, water, tomatoes, ketchup, Worcestershire sauce, salt, pepper, and hot sauce and bring to a boil. Simmer, uncovered, 1 hour, stirring occasionally. Stir in pork, potatoes, barbecue sauce, and vinegar. Cook 30 minutes on medium heat until potatoes are tender. Add peas and beans and simmer 20 minutes on low. Add corn and simmer until heated through.

Pozole (Mexican Stew)

French Onion Soup

French Onion Soup

Makes 4 servings

3 cups sliced onion
¼ cup butter
2 cups beef stock (or 2 cups water and 2 teaspoons beef soup base)
2 cups chicken stock (or 2 cups water and 2 teaspoons chicken soup base)
½ teaspoon thyme
1 teaspoon salt
¼ teaspoon pepper

Parmesan Toast Slices

1 loaf French bread
Butter, room temperature
Parmesan, Swiss, or favorite cheese, shredded

Sauté onion in melted butter in a medium saucepan over medium heat until dark golden brown (caramelized), but not burned, about 30 minutes. Add beef stock, chicken stock, thyme, salt, and pepper. Simmer 30 minutes. Ladle into bowls and top with Parmesan Toast Slices just before serving.

For toast slices: Slice French bread into thin slices and place on a large baking sheet. Spread each slice with softened butter. Sprinkle liberally with Parmesan cheese. Place slices under broiler and toast until light brown. Serve whole or sliced.

French Soup Pot

Makes 12 servings

3 pounds lean beef brisket
¼ pound salt pork
1 whole onion, pierced with 2 whole cloves
3 leeks, cut in chunks, or 1 bunch green onions, sliced in 1-inch lengths
8 ribs celery, cut in chunks
9 carrots, peeled and halved lengthwise, divided
1 turnip, peeled and cut in chunks
1 teaspoon thyme
Parsley, to taste
Water to cover ingredients
1 tablespoon salt
1 (3½- to 4-pound) whole chicken, legs and wings bound to body
6 potatoes, peeled
1 small head cabbage, cut in 6 pieces

Place brisket, pork, onion, leeks or green onions, celery, 6 carrot halves, turnip, thyme, and parsley in a large, heavy soup pot. Cover with water and bring to a boil. Add salt. Reduce heat and simmer, covered, for 1½ hours. Add chicken, cover, and cook 30 minutes more. Add potatoes, remaining carrots, and cabbage; cover and cook 30 minutes or until vegetables are tender.

Serve strained broth in soup dishes with meat and vegetables on plates on the side.

Hearty Beef Stew

Makes 8 servings

1½ pounds lean boneless round steak	1 bay leaf
1 (14.5-ounce) can stewed tomatoes, undrained and diced	1 tablespoon lemon juice
3½ cups water, divided	1 teaspoon Worcestershire sauce
1 medium onion, sliced thin	6 carrots, peeled and cubed
1 clove garlic, minced	4 potatoes, peeled and cubed
1 teaspoon salt	1 cup sliced celery
¼ teaspoon pepper	¼ cup flour

Prepare steak by trimming visible fat and cutting meat into 1-inch cubes. Coat a large soup pot with nonstick cooking spray and brown meat in pot over high heat. Add tomatoes, 3 cups water, onion, garlic, salt, pepper, bay leaf, lemon juice, and Worcestershire sauce. Heat to boil; reduce heat, cover, and simmer 2 hours, stirring occasionally to prevent meat from sticking to bottom. Add carrots, potatoes, and celery and cook, covered, an additional 30 to 35 minutes until meat and vegetables are tender. Blend ½ cup water with flour until smooth; pour gradually into stew and cook, stirring, until thickened, about 5 minutes. Remove and discard bay leaf.

Serve with toasted Italian-style bread or breadsticks.

Slow Cooker: Brown meat. Add all ingredients to cooker, but omit flour. Cook on high 3½ to 4 hours or until vegetables are tender.

Steak Soup

Makes 4 servings

1 large onion, thinly sliced	1 or 2 cloves garlic, minced
1 tablespoon vegetable oil	¼ teaspoon cumin
12 ounces top sirloin steak, cooked and cut into thin strips (leftover steak is fine)	¼ teaspoon paprika
	2 large potatoes, peeled and cut in strips
3 cups beef broth	2 eggs, separated
½ to 1 teaspoon salt	½ cup heavy cream
¼ teaspoon pepper	2 sprigs parsley, chopped, for garnish

Sauté onion in oil in a large saucepan. Add steak strips, beef broth, salt, pepper, garlic, cumin, and paprika. Simmer 5 minutes. Add potatoes and simmer until potatoes are tender. Remove from heat. Beat egg whites slightly and add slowly to hot broth, stirring constantly. Blend egg yolks with cream and stir into soup, stirring slightly just to blend.

Garnish with parsley and serve immediately.

Beef Minestrone

Makes 6 to 8 servings

1 pound ground beef

1 cup diced onion

1 teaspoon minced garlic

1 tablespoon olive oil

1 (29-ounce) can tomato puree

3 cups water

1 teaspoon salt

1 teaspoon Italian seasoning

1 (10- to 12-ounce) package frozen mixed vegetables (or fresh carrots, peas, zucchini)

½ (12-ounce) package spiral noodles, uncooked

Pepper, to taste

½ cup grated Asiago cheese, for garnish

Brown ground beef, onion, and garlic in oil in a large soup pot. Add tomato puree, water, salt, and Italian seasoning. Add vegetables and noodles and continue to cook until vegetables are tender and noodles are cooked. Add pepper, to taste.

To serve, garnish with Asiago cheese.

Slow Cooker: Prepare ground beef, onion, and garlic as above. Place all ingredients, except garnish, in slow cooker and cook on high 2 to 3 hours.

Cowboy Stew

Makes 6 servings

1½ pounds ground beef

¾ cup chopped onion

1 teaspoon salt

¼ teaspoon pepper

1 (10.75-ounce) can condensed tomato soup

1 (10.75-ounce) can condensed cream of mushroom soup

1 (10.75-ounce) soup can of water

4 potatoes, peeled and cut into ½-inch cubes

4 carrots, peeled and sliced into ⅛-inch slices

3 ribs celery, diced

Preheat oven to 350 degrees F. Brown ground beef and onion in a large frying pan. Add salt and pepper while meat is browning. When meat is done and onion is soft and translucent, transfer into a colander to drain excess fat. Return mixture to frying pan and add soups and water. Simmer 5 minutes. Arrange potatoes, carrots, and celery in a 9x13-inch baking pan. Pour meat and soup mixture over vegetables and stir. Cover with aluminum foil. Bake 1½ to 2 hours or until vegetables are tender.

Serve with Angel Biscuits (see page 86).

Chef's tip: Serving yield can easily be increased by adding more vegetables, 1 can tomato soup, and ½ can water.

Slow Cooker: Brown ground beef and onion and drain off excess fat. Add remaining ingredients and cook on low 4 to 5 hours.

Beef and Barley Soup

Makes 10 servings

½ pound lean boneless round steak

9 cups water

1 (14.5-ounce) can stewed tomatoes, undrained and diced

1 (10.5-ounce) can beef broth

½ cup chopped onion

1 clove garlic, minced

½ teaspoon basil

¼ teaspoon salt

2 bay leaves

½ cup pearl barley

1 (10- to 12-ounce) package frozen mixed vegetables

Prepare steak by trimming fat and cutting steak into 1-inch cubes. In a large soup pot (at least 4-quart capacity), stir together 8 cups water, steak cubes, tomatoes, broth, onion, garlic, basil, salt, and bay leaves. Bring to a boil. Reduce heat; cover and simmer 1 hour. Place barley in a strainer and rinse with cold water. Gradually add barley, along with 1 cup water, to soup in pot; cover and simmer again 1 hour. Skim fat from top of soup. Add frozen vegetables to soup pot; cover and simmer a third time until meat and vegetables are tender, about 30 to 40 minutes. Remove and discard bay leaves.

Serve with a crostini (see below).

Slow Cooker: Prepare meat and rinse the barley. Place all ingredients, minus 1 cup of water, in the slow cooker. Cook on high 3 to 4 hours.

Crostini

Crostini are a fun, easy accompaniment or garnish for any soup. To make, slice an Italian-style baguette on a 45-degree bias about ¼-inch thick. Brush each piece with melted butter or olive oil and season with a sprinkle of salt or your favorite dry herb. Bake in a 325-degree F. oven until golden brown. Remove from the oven and let stand on the hot pan and continue to dry.

Cantaloupe Salad

Cantaloupe Salad

Makes 8 servings

2 small cantaloupes
6 peaches, peeled and sliced
2 cups honeydew melon, cubed

3 cups grapes, halved
French Fruit Dressing (below)

Cut each cantaloupe lengthwise into 8 wedges; peel and chill. Coat peaches, honeydew melon, and grapes with dressing. (Keep remaining dressing for another use.) Chill 1 hour. For each serving, arrange 2 cantaloupe wedges to form oval or circle and fill centers with fruit mixture.

French Fruit Dressing

⅓ cup sugar
1 teaspoon salt
1 teaspoon paprika
¼ cup orange juice

1 tablespoon lemon juice
1 tablespoon vinegar
1 cup salad oil
1 teaspoon grated onion

Combine all ingredients in bottle or jar and cover. Shake thoroughly. Store any leftover dressing in refrigerator for later use. Shake well before each use.

Fruit Salad for a Crowd

Makes 20 to 25 servings

2 (3.5-ounce) packages instant pudding (coconut cream or pistachio)
1 (20-ounce) can crushed pineapple, undrained
1 (20-ounce) can pineapple tidbits, undrained
2 (8-ounce) cans mandarin oranges, drained

½ cup flaked coconut
2 cups red or green seedless grapes
2 cups miniature marshmallows
1 (20-ounce) carton frozen whipped topping, thawed

In a large bowl, mix instant pudding with crushed pineapple and pineapple tidbits, including their juices. Stir in remaining ingredients until well blended. Cover and refrigerate until ready to serve. Chill 2 to 3 hours.

Honey Lime Dressing for Fresh Fruit

½ pound honey
2½ tablespoons limeade concentrate

Beat together with hand mixer for about 2 to 3 minutes. Store at room temperature. Serve over fresh fruit.

Pear Blush Salad

Makes 4 servings

1 (3-ounce) package cream cheese, softened
¼ cup nuts, finely chopped
2 tablespoons maraschino cherries, chopped (include
cherry juice)

1 (30-ounce) can pear halves, drained
(reserve juice)
Red food coloring
Mint leaves

Combine cream cheese, nuts, cherries, and enough juice from pears to soften cheese. Put rounded teaspoon of cream cheese mixture in hollow of half the pear halves. Put 3 or 4 drops of red food coloring into reserved pear juice. Soak rest of pear halves in this liquid to tint pears pink, 5 to 10 minutes. Cover first halves with tinted halves. Stand pear on bed of lettuce and garnish with mint leaves.

Angel Salad

Makes 4 to 6 servings

1 cup miniature marshmallows
3 bananas, chopped
1 cup pineapple chunks, drained and chopped
½ cup peanuts, crushed
2 tablespoons cornstarch

2 tablespoons sugar
1 cup pineapple juice
1 egg, beaten lightly
½ cup cream, whipped

Mix marshmallows and fruit; add peanuts. Make a cooked dressing of cornstarch, sugar, juice, and egg, blended together in that order. Heat, stirring constantly, until thickened. Cool and fold in whipped cream. Combine with salad mixture, just to moisten. Serve on greens.

Cranberry Salad

Makes 14 servings

1 cup water
2 cups sugar
4 cups cranberries
2 cups miniature marshmallows, or cut large marshmallows

2 apples, diced
3 bananas, sliced
3 cups orange sections
½ cup pecans

Combine water and sugar; boil until thickened to a syrup. Add cranberries; cook until cranberries burst. Remove from heat; let stand 10 minutes. Chill. Add remaining ingredients to cranberries and chill thoroughly. Serve on lettuce leaf. Top with whipped cream dressing, if desired.

Pear Blush Salad

Orange Fruit Slaw

Orange Fruit Slaw

3 cups shredded cabbage

1 orange, peeled and sectioned

1 cup halved seedless red grapes

½ cup sliced celery

1 apple, cored and chopped

1 (8-ounce) carton orange yogurt

¼ cup toasted slivered almonds*

Combine cabbage, orange sections, grapes, celery, and apple in a large salad bowl. Mix in orange yogurt. Chill 2 to 3 hours. Just before serving, garnish with toasted slivered almonds.

*To toast almonds, spread on a baking sheet and place in a 350-degree oven for 5 to 8 minutes, stirring occasionally until lightly toasted.

Strawberry Nut Salad

Makes 8 to 10 servings

1 (6-ounce) package strawberry gelatin

1 cup boiling water

1 (10-ounce) package frozen sliced strawberries, thawed but undrained

1 (20-ounce) can crushed pineapple, drained

3 medium bananas, peeled and mashed

½ cup walnuts, coarsely chopped

1 (16-ounce) carton sour cream

In a large bowl dissolve gelatin in boiling water. Fold in strawberries, pineapple, mashed bananas, and nuts. Pour one-half of mixture into an 8x12-inch pan. Refrigerate until firm. Stir sour cream until smooth, then spread on set gelatin. Gently spoon remainder of gelatin mixture (which has been at room temperature) on top. Refrigerate.

Apple Pomegranate Salad

Makes 20 servings

14 red delicious apples

Juice of 2 lemons

2 stalks celery, diced

4 large pomegranates

3 cups cranberry sauce

1 cup grenadine

Fresh kiwis

Fresh cranberries

Core the apples and set in a large bowl of water that has the juice of 1 lemon added. Dice apples into ½-inch cubes. Remove peel and white pulp membranes from pomegranate seeds. Mix apples, celery, pomegranate seeds, cranberry sauce, and grenadine and refrigerate for 1 hour before serving. Garnish with kiwi slices and cranberries.

Fruit and Yogurt Parfait
Makes 20 parfaits

1 quart blueberry yogurt

1 quart peach yogurt

1 quart raspberry yogurt

1 (16-ounce) box Muselix cereal

4 cups raspberries

4 cups strawberries, quartered

4 cups blueberries

Raspberries, for garnish

Mint sprigs, for garnish

In tall parfait-style glasses alternate yogurt, Muselix cereal, and berries to fill each glass. Garnish top with whole raspberries and a sprig of mint.

Blueberry Salad
Makes 10 to 12 servings

1 (6-ounce) box raspberry gelatin

2 cups boiling water

1 (8-ounce) package cream cheese

1 (15-ounce) can blueberries, with syrup

1 (15-ounce) can crushed pineapple, drained

2 cups heavy cream

Red leaf lettuce

Fresh blueberries

Dissolve raspberry gelatin in 2 cups boiling water. Stir in cream cheese until melted and well incorporated. Add blueberries and crushed pineapple. Whip cream and fold ¾ of it into gelatin mixture, reserving ¼ of the whipping cream for garnish. Spread mixture into 9x13-inch pan and refrigerate until set. Cut into squares.

When ready to serve, wash lettuce and dry thoroughly. Wash blueberries and set aside. Place lettuce leaf on salad plate, then square of blueberry salad. Garnish with fresh blueberries and a dollop of whipped cream.

Molded Fresh Cranberry Salad
Makes 8 servings

2 cups water

¾ cup sugar

1 (12-ounce) package fresh cranberries

1 (6-ounce) package orange gelatin

1 (8.25-ounce) can crushed pineapple, with juice

½ cup chopped celery

Salad greens, for garnishing

1 (8-ounce) carton sour cream, for garnishing

8 orange slices, for garnishing

In a medium saucepan, bring water, sugar, and cranberries to a boil. Boil 5 minutes. Remove from heat and stir in gelatin until dissolved. Add crushed pineapple, including its juice, and celery. Pour into 8 single-serving-sized molds. Refrigerate until firm, at least 6 hours. Unmold on salad greens. Garnish each serving with a dollop of sour cream and an orange slice.

Fruit and Yogurt Parfait

Fruit Dip

Makes 20 servings

2 (8-ounce) tubs soft-style strawberry cream cheese

1 (14-ounce) jar marshmallow crème

2 tablespoons orange juice

2 tablespoons lemon juice

In a mixer bowl, beat together cream cheese, marshmallow crème, and fruit juices. Beat until smooth. Refrigerate before serving. Serve with fresh fruit.

Famous Fruit Salad Dressing

⅓ cup sugar
1 teaspoon flour
1 egg yolk
½ cup canned pineapple juice or orange juice

2 tablespoons lemon juice
1 teaspoon celery seed (optional)
½ cup heavy cream, whipped

In small saucepan, combine sugar, flour, egg yolk, and pineapple juice; stir until smooth. Cook over low heat until thickened, stirring constantly. Add lemon juice and celery seed; chill. Fold in whipped cream just before serving. Store dressing in refrigerator.

Mandarin Salad

8 cups salad greens (any favorite variety), torn into pieces
2 to 3 ribs celery, cut diagonally
1 (8-ounce) can mandarin oranges, drained
2 to 3 green onions, chopped diagonally, including tops

1 cup grapes, any variety (seeded grapes should be halved and seeds removed)
½ cup pecans, coarsely chopped
Dressing (below)

Clean and dry greens thoroughly. Toss all ingredients, except dressing, together. Just before serving, toss with dressing, using just enough to moisten lightly.

Dressing

2 tablespoons sesame seeds, toasted
3 tablespoons sugar or honey
1 teaspoon salt

Dash pepper
¼ cup salad oil
2 tablespoons vinegar

Mix all ingredients together thoroughly. Dressing should be stored in refrigerator. Shake well before using.

Note: To toast sesame seeds, measure seeds into pie pan or baking sheet and place in 350-degree oven for about 10 minutes, stirring occasionally, until golden but not brown.

Fresh Mozzarella and Tomato Salad

Makes 20 servings

2 pounds fresh mozzarella balls

2 pounds roma tomatoes

¼ cup fresh basil leaves

¼ cup olive oil

1 teaspoon crushed red pepper

Cut the mozzarella balls into ¼-inch thick slices. Slice the tomatoes into ¼-inch thick slices. Separate large basil leaves from the stems. Lay 5 leaves on top of one another and carefully cut the leaves into fine strips; repeat with remaining basil. Add the crushed red pepper to the olive oil and set aside to steep. Using a large serving platter, alternate slices of tomato with slices of mozzarella, working in concentric circles. When the platter is full, drizzle the olive oil and red pepper mixture over the tomatoes and the mozzarella. Finally, sprinkle the shredded basil on top as a garnish. Hold for a maximum of 2 hours before service.

Grapefruit and Avocado Salad

Makes 20 servings

Salad

5 large oranges

3 grapefruit

5 ripe avocados

3 (11.5-ounce) cans mandarin oranges

2 heads butter lettuce

Dressing

1½ cups vinegar

1½ cups oil

1½ cups sugar

1½ cups ketchup

2 teaspoons salt

1½ teaspoons garlic powder

1 tablespoon finely chopped white onion

Combine all ingredients for dressing in a jar and shake well. Chill one hour. Shake again just before serving.

To prepare salad, peel and section oranges and grapefruit. Peel, pit, and slice avocados. Open cans of mandarin oranges and drain. Arrange butter lettuce leaves on plates. Arrange avocado and fruit on top of lettuce. Drizzle dressing over salad just before serving.

Fresh Mozzarella and Tomato Salad

Sugar Pea Salad

Sugar Pea Salad

Makes 6 to 8 servings

1¼ pounds sugar peas
1 cup fresh mushrooms, sliced thin
½ cup finely chopped red bell pepper
1 cup bean sprouts, rinsed and drained
8 ounces cooked shrimp
¼ cup olive oil

1 tablespoon soy sauce
2 tablespoons lemon juice
1 teaspoon brown sugar
Leaf lettuce, for garnishing
2 tablespoons sesame seeds

Cut blossom end from peapods and place in bowl; add mushrooms, red bell pepper, bean sprouts, and shrimp. In a separate bowl combine olive oil, soy sauce, lemon juice, and brown sugar. Pour over vegetables and stir to coat. Cover and refrigerate for several hours, stirring occasionally. To serve, spoon onto lettuce leaf and sprinkle with sesame seeds.

Snowpea Cucumber Salad

Makes 20 servings

16 cucumbers
¼ cup sesame seeds

2 cups snowpeas, stemmed
1 recipe Ginger Dressing (see below)

Halve the cucumbers and remove the seeds with a spoon. Slice into ½-inch slices diagonally. Put the cucumber slices, sesame seeds, and snowpeas into a bowl. Mix in the Ginger Dressing and serve immediately.

Ginger Dressing

⅓ cup powdered ginger
2 tablespoons garlic powder
¼ cup sugar
2 cups salad oil

½ cup rice wine vinegar
1 cup honey
2 tablespoons sesame oil
Salt to taste

Mix dry ingredients together. Pour in half of the salad oil, mix thoroughly. Add vinegar and mix well. Slowly add half of the remaining salad oil, whisking the whole time. Add honey and mix well. Slowly add the remaining salad oil and the sesame oil. Adjust flavor with salt.

Sarah's Salad

Makes 8 servings

1 head iceberg lettuce
3 strips bacon
½ (10-ounce) package frozen peas
¼ teaspoon sugar
½ teaspoon salt

¼ teaspoon white pepper
2½ ounces Swiss cheese, cut in strips
⅔ cup chopped green onion
¼ cup mayonnaise
¼ cup salad dressing (such as Miracle Whip®)

Wash and drain lettuce; dry thoroughly. Dice bacon and sauté until crisp; drain on paper towels. Run hot water over frozen peas and drain. Into salad bowl, tear lettuce into bite-sized pieces. Sprinkle with sugar, salt, and pepper. Add peas, Swiss cheese, green onion, mayonnaise, and salad dressing. Chill. Toss when ready to serve and garnish with bacon.

Note: Ingredients may be layered, if desired, with mayonnaise spread on top as last layer. Cover tightly and refrigerate overnight.

Waldorf Salad

Makes 20 servings

½ cup walnuts, coarsely chopped
3 cups diced celery
7 cups diced Fuji apples*
1 cup raisins

Dressing

3 cups heavy cream
¾ cup sugar
1 teaspoon vanilla extract
¼ cup sour cream

In a large clean bowl whip the cream using an electric mixer. Gradually add the sugar as the cream whips.

Just before the cream reaches the soft peak stage, add the vanilla. Continue whipping until the cream is at the soft peak stage.

Add the sour cream and whip until incorporated. Cover and place the bowl in the refrigerator until ready to toss the salad.

Toss the apples, walnuts, celery, and raisins in a bowl. Mix in the whipped cream and serve immediately.

*Chef's tip: Fuji apples do not brown as quickly as other cut apples. But you should, nonetheless, work quickly to dice them just before combining with the whipped cream dressing.

Sarah's Salad

Spinach Salad
and Herbed Croutons

Spinach Salad

Makes 4 to 5 servings

1 pound fresh spinach
½ cup salad oil
1 clove garlic, slivered
¼ cup vinegar
¼ cup lemon juice
½ teaspoon salt
Dash pepper, grated
2 tablespoons grated Parmesan cheese
2 hard-cooked eggs, sliced
6 slices crisp-cooked bacon, crumbled
Herbed Croutons (optional)

Herbed Croutons

¼ cup grated Parmesan cheese
1 tablespoon oregano
1 tablespoon garlic powder
1 tablespoon basil
½ teaspoon salt
½ teaspoon freshly ground pepper
1 loaf dry bread, cubed (15 to 20 cups)
3 tablespoons oil

Wash spinach; dry thoroughly and discard stems. Tear in pieces into salad bowl. Chill. Combine salad oil and garlic; refrigerate one hour. Discard garlic. Heat oil with vinegar, lemon juice, salt, pepper, and Parmesan cheese. Toss spinach with dressing. Garnish with eggs and bacon. Add croutons, if desired.

For croutons: In small bowl, mix Parmesan cheese, oregano, garlic powder, basil, salt, and pepper; set aside. In large bowl, toss bread cubes with oil, then toss with cheese-herb mixture until well mixed. Spread on ungreased cookie sheet. Bake at 225 degrees for 1 hour or until crisp and lightly golden, stirring occasionally. Cool and store in plastic bags in cool place. Will keep about 1 month. *Makes 15 to 20 cups of croutons*

Green Salad

Makes about 12 servings.

Greens

1 large head crisped lettuce
7 green onions, chopped, including tops
¼ head red cabbage
¼ large head white cabbage
3 to 4 medium tomatoes, cut in wedges

Dressing

2 tablespoons mayonnaise
1 tablespoon chopped parsley
Dash garlic salt
Juice of 1 lemon (3 tablespoons)
2 tablespoons vinegar
Salt and pepper
1 teaspoon paprika
½ cup heavy cream

Combine dressing ingredients and let stand for at least 30 minutes. Toss greens in a separate large bowl. Pour dressing over greens. Do not mix, but toss lightly just before serving. Garnish with tomato wedges. Dressing should be stored in refrigerator.

Five-Way Crab Salad

Makes 4 to 5 cups salad

8 ounces imitation crabmeat	3 hard-cooked eggs, peeled and chopped
½ cup sliced celery	½ cup mayonnaise
¼ cup chopped green onion	½ teaspoon seasoned salt
1 tomato, cubed	½ teaspoon prepared mustard
¼ cup sliced ripe olives	Salt and pepper to taste

Combine crabmeat with celery, onions, tomato, olives, and chopped eggs. Gently blend in mayonnaise and seasonings. Chill. Serve in any of the following ways:

Stuffed Avocado: Cut 4 avocados in half; remove pits. Scoop crab salad into center of cavity. *Makes 8 stuffed avocados*

Stuffed Tomato: Cut 6 to 8 tomatoes into 8 sections, leaving connected at bottom. Place each tomato on lettuce leaf and scoop crab salad into center of each. *Fills 6 to 8 tomatoes*

Croissant Sandwiches: Slice croissants and stuff with crab salad. *Makes 6 to 8 croissant sandwiches*

Crab Puffs: Cut tops off cocktail-size cream puffs (see page 268). Spoon crab salad into each puff and garnish with sprig of parsley. *Fills 20 to 24 puffs*

Entrée Salad: Line 6 large salad plates with green leafy lettuce. Place mound of shredded lettuce in center. Spoon crab salad on top of shredded lettuce. Garnish with lemon wedge, olives, tomato wedges, and parsley. *Makes 6 large salads*

Shrimp Salad

Makes 6 to 8 servings

3 (5-ounce) cans shrimp, or 1 pound cooked, fresh bay shrimp	Dressing (below)
	3 hard-cooked eggs, peeled and cut in wedges
1 cup chopped celery	1 avocado, peeled and cut in wedges
¼ cup sliced green olives with pimiento	¼ cup coarsely chopped cashews (optional)
2 tablespoons lemon juice	

Combine shrimp, celery, olives, and lemon juice. When ready to serve, toss dressing with salad. Garnish with hard-cooked eggs, avocado, and cashews.

Dressing

1 cup mayonnaise	1 teaspoon grated onion
⅓ cup chili sauce	

Mix ingredients together. Toss with shrimp salad. Dressing should be stored in refrigerator.

Five-Way Crab Salad

Lion House Dinner Rolls

Makes 1½ to 3 dozen rolls, depending on shape and size of rolls

2 cups warm water (110 to 115 degrees)

⅔ cup nonfat dry milk

2 tablespoons active dry yeast

¼ cup sugar

2 teaspoons salt

⅓ plus ½ cup butter, margarine, or shortening, divided

1 egg

4½ to 5 cups all-purpose or bread flour, divided

1 tablespoon vegetable oil

Combine water and dry milk powder in a large bowl of an electric mixer, stirring until milk dissolves. Add yeast and then sugar, salt, ⅓ cup butter, egg, and 2 cups flour. Mix on low speed until ingredients are wet. Increase mixer speed to medium and mix for 2 minutes. Add 2 cups flour; mix on low speed until ingredients are wet and then for 2 minutes at medium speed. (Dough will be getting stiff, and remaining flour may need to be mixed in by hand.) Add remaining flour, ½ cup at a time, until dough is soft, not overly sticky, and not stiff. (It is not necessary to use the entire amount of flour.)

Scrape dough off sides of bowl and pour oil all around sides of bowl. Turn dough over in bowl so it is covered with oil. Cover with plastic wrap and allow to rise in a warm place until doubled in size, about 1½ hours. Lightly sprinkle cutting board or counter with flour and place dough on floured surface. Roll out and shape as desired. Place on greased or parchment-lined baking pans. Cover lightly with plastic wrap. Let rise in a warm place until rolls are doubled in size, about 1 to 1½ hours.

Bake 15 to 20 minutes at 375 degrees F., or until golden brown. Melt ½ cup butter and brush rolls with melted butter while hot.

Chef's tip: To freeze shaped rolls for later use, simply double the amount of yeast used when making dough. After the first rise, shape rolls but do not allow to rise again. Place rolls on a baking sheet and immediately place in freezer. When dough is frozen solid, remove rolls from pan and place in a plastic bag, squeeze excess air out of bag, and seal. Rolls may be frozen for 3 weeks.

When ready to use, place frozen rolls on greased or parchment-lined baking sheet, all facing the same direction. Cover lightly with plastic wrap and let thaw and rise until doubled in size, 4 to 5 hours. Bake as above.

Potato Rolls

Recipe makes 2 dozen rolls and can be doubled nicely

½ cup warm water
2 tablespoons active dry yeast
1 tablespoon granulated sugar
1 cup milk
¾ cup shortening
½ cup granulated sugar

1 teaspoon salt
1 cup mashed potatoes (homemade or instant, instructions on package)
2 eggs, beaten
3 cups all-purpose flour

In a large bowl, combine water, yeast, and the 1 tablespoon sugar and set aside to proof. Scald milk in a small saucepan over medium heat. Remove from heat and add shortening, ½ cup sugar, and salt. Let cool. Once milk mixture is cool, add to yeast mixture, along with mashed potatoes, beaten eggs, and 1½ cups of the flour. Gradually add remaining flour until a soft dough forms. Cover bowl with plastic wrap and let rise until doubled, about 45 minutes. Roll out dough on floured surface, shape rolls as desired, and place on greased pans. Cover with plastic wrap and let rise until doubled in size, 30 to 40 minutes. Bake at 425 degrees for 15 minutes, or until golden brown. Turn out on cooling racks and brush with melted butter or margarine.

Refrigerator Rolls

Makes 4 dozen rolls

1 cup shortening, melted
½ cup sugar
4 eggs
2½ cups water

2 tablespoons dry yeast
2 teaspoons salt
7 cups flour

Note: You can use this recipe to make wheat rolls as well. Use 4 cups whole wheat flour and 3 cups white flour.

Mix melted shortening, sugar, eggs, water, yeast, and salt with 3 cups flour in a 5-quart bowl. Gradually add rest of flour, 1 cup at a time, beating on low speed to make a soft dough. Cover tightly and refrigerate overnight. Two to three hours before baking, remove from refrigerator. Roll out on lightly floured surface. For Parkerhouse rolls, cut with biscuit cutter in circles; fold in half and place on greased cookie sheets. Allow to rise until double in bulk, about 45 minutes. Bake at 375 degrees for 15 minutes.

Out-of-This-World Rolls

Makes 3 dozen small rolls

2 tablespoons active dry yeast	3 eggs
¼ cup warm water	1 cup warm water
½ cup granulated sugar	1½ teaspoons salt
½ cup shortening	4 to 5 cups all-purpose flour

Combine yeast and the ¼ cup warm water in a small bowl and set aside to proof. In a large mixing bowl, cream together sugar and shortening until light and fluffy. Add eggs, one at a time, mixing after each addition. Add softened yeast, 1 cup warm water, salt, and enough flour to make a soft dough. Mix well. Cover bowl with plastic wrap and let dough rise 1 hour. Punch down, let rise again for 40 to 45 minutes. Shape as desired and place on greased baking sheets. Cover with plastic wrap and let rise until doubled in size, about 40 minutes. Bake at 350 degrees for 15 minutes. Dough will keep in the refrigerator up to 5 days after second rise and shaping. Take out 3 hours before baking. Allow to rise for about 3 hours and bake as above.

Lion House Wheat Rolls

Makes 4 dozen rolls

1 package (2¼ teaspoons) active dry yeast	1 cup all-purpose flour
3 cups lukewarm water	6½ cups whole wheat flour
1 cup quick-cooking rolled oats	6 tablespoons shortening
¼ cup molasses	1½ tablespoons salt
6 tablespoons nonfat dry milk	

Dissolve yeast in ¼ cup of the lukewarm water and set aside. In a large mixing bowl, combine remaining 2¾ cups water, oats, molasses, and dry milk powder; add half of the white flour and half of the whole wheat flour, one cup at a time, beating well after each addition. Add dissolved yeast, the remaining flour, shortening, and salt. Mix well, then knead until dough is smooth and elastic, about 5 minutes. Place in a covered bowl in a warm area until dough has doubled in bulk, about 1 hour. Knead for one minute to force out air bubbles. Pinch off and shape into 1¼-inch pieces and place on greased cookie sheets 1½ inches apart. Cover with plastic wrap and let rise until doubled in size, about 30 to 40 minutes.

Bake at 375 degrees for 12 to 15 minutes.

Angel Biscuits

Makes 18 biscuits

1 package (2¼ teaspoons) active dry yeast
¼ cup warm water
5 cups all-purpose flour
1 teaspoon salt
¼ cup sugar

2 teaspoons baking powder
1 cup shortening
2 cups buttermilk
3 tablespoons butter, melted

Preheat oven to 400 degrees F. and grease a baking sheet.

Dissolve yeast in warm water and set aside. Stir together flour, salt, sugar, and baking powder. Cut in shortening with a pastry cutter or two knives. Add yeast to the buttermilk, and then add to mixture. Mix well with a fork, wooden spoon, or your hands. Turn dough onto a floured surface and pat to desired thickness. Cut biscuits with a round biscuit cutter or a glass cup. Dip biscuits in melted butter and place on greased pan. Bake 12 minutes, or until golden brown on top.

Chef's tip: You may bake these immediately or leave out 30 to 40 minutes before baking. They may also be frozen, unbaked, if covered with plastic wrap and then foil. To use, remove from freezer and allow to thaw completely. Remove plastic and foil and bake as instructed above.

Easy Cheesy Drop Biscuits

Makes 12 biscuits

1¾ cups all-purpose flour
2 tablespoons sugar
2½ teaspoons baking powder
1 teaspoon salt

1 cup shredded sharp or medium cheddar cheese
1 egg, beaten
¾ cup milk
⅓ cup vegetable oil

Preheat oven to 400 degrees F. Lightly grease a jelly roll pan or line it with parchment paper.

Mix together flour, sugar, baking powder, salt, and cheese in a large bowl. Beat together egg, milk, and oil in another bowl. Add to dry ingredients all at once, stirring with a fork until just moistened. Spoon by heaping tablespoons onto prepared pan. Bake 15 to 20 minutes.

Chef's tip: This can also be baked as a loaf by greasing a 9x5-inch bread pan and pouring the batter into the pan. Bake 30 to 35 minutes or until a toothpick inserted into the center of the loaf comes out clean.

Angel Biscuits

Bread Sticks

Makes 24 to 36 bread sticks

2 cups warm water
1½ tablespoons dry yeast
4 tablespoons sugar, divided
1 tablespoon salt
¾ cup butter or margarine, softened

5½ to 6½ cups all-purpose flour, divided
1 tablespoon vetetable oil
1 to 2 cups grated cheese: Parmesan, Asiago, Swiss, ched-
    dar, or a mixture of your favorite flavors
Oregano or Italian seasoning, optional, for added flavor

Place water in large mixing bowl. Sprinkle yeast and 2 tablespoons sugar over the water. Stir to dissolve. Add salt, remaining sugar, butter, and half of the flour. Mix on low speed until smooth. Add remaining flour by ½ cup, mixing after each addition. Dough should be soft but not sticky. Remove dough from bowl and brush bowl with oil (so the dough doesn't stick or dry out). Cover bowl loosely with plastic wrap and allow dough to rise until double in size, about 45 minutes.

Place dough on floured surface and cut into 2 equal pieces; set one aside. Roll out half of dough to an 18x13-inch rectangle, about ½-inch thick. With a sharp knife or pizza wheel, cut 1-inch strips lengthwise and then cut them in half, making 9x13-inch bread sticks. Place strips on a greased or parchment-lined baking pan, leaving 1 inch between each piece. Repeat with reserved dough. Spritz dough strips lightly with water and sprinkle with grated cheese. Let rise 20 minutes and bake 15 minutes at 400 degrees F. Sprinkle with oregano or any Italian seasoning, if desired. Serve hot or at room temperature. They are best if eaten the day they are made.

Seasoned Bread Sticks

Makes 24 bread sticks

1 dozen Lion House Frozen Rolls, thawed and at room
    temperature
½ cup butter, melted
1 teaspoon poppy seeds

1 teaspoon sesame seeds
½ teaspoon fennel seeds
½ teaspoon caraway seeds
⅛ teaspoon celery seed, cumin, or dill weed

Place all seasonings in a small bowl and mix together. Set aside. On a lightly floured surface, unroll Lion House Rolls and cut each roll in half lengthwise using a very sharp knife or a pizza cutter. Place each piece on a greased or parchment-lined cookie sheet about ½-inch apart. Brush each piece with melted butter and generously sprinkle seed mix on the butter. Allow to rise until double in size (45 minutes to 2 hours, depending on how warm the rolls are when you start). The warmer the dough feels when unrolling them, the shorter the time they will take to rise. Bake in a 375-degree oven for about 10 minutes.

Chef's note: These are good with just the butter brushed on them, or add some Parmesan cheese or your favorite herb mixture.

Bread Bowls

Makes 6 bread bowls or 2 loaves French bread

½ cup warm water

2 tablespoons yeast

3 tablespoons sugar, divided

2 cups hot water

2 tablespoons salt

½ cup vegetable oil

5 cups all-purpose or bread flour, divided

1 egg white

1 tablespoon water

Preheat oven to 400 degrees F. Grease two 12x18-inch baking sheets and set aside.

Place warm water in a small bowl, sprinkle yeast on top, and stir in 1 tablespoon sugar; set aside. Place hot water, salt, 2 tablespoons sugar, and oil in a large bowl. Add 3 cups flour. Blend well. Add yeast mixture, stir well. Add the remaining 2 cups flour and stir well. Leave spoon in dough and let rise 10 minutes. Stir down and repeat 5 times.

For bowls: Divide dough into 6 equal pieces. Form bowl by slightly pulling top of dough toward the bottom and tucking it in until a round ball is formed. (It will be slightly flat where you have tucked in the dough.) Place bottom of dough on a greased baking sheet. Three bowls will fit on one sheet. Repeat with rest of dough. Whisk egg white and 1 tablespoon water together. Make 2 diagonal slits about ½-inch deep in the top of each bowl and brush with egg white mixture. Allow to rise 30 minutes. Place pan in oven. Squirt 5 sprays of water from a spray bottle into the oven. Bake 20 to 25 minutes. Cool completely. Cut the top off each bowl and remove most of the inside bread. Set to the side. To serve, ladle soup into bowl, set lid ajar over soup, and place scooped bread to the side.

For French loaves: Divide into 2 equal balls. Place one on a floured surface and roll out until it forms a 12x14-inch rectangle. Roll up like a jelly roll so you have a long loaf. Place on a greased baking sheet. Repeat with the remaining ball. Both loaves should fit on the same sheet. Make 3 diagonal slits about ½-inch deep on the top of the loaves. Brush with the egg white wash (see above). Allow to rise 30 minutes. Place pan in the oven. Before baking, squirt 5 sprays of water with a spray bottle into the oven. Bake 20 to 25 minutes.

Orange Rolls

Makes 18 rolls

1 recipe dough for Lion House Dinner Rolls, prepared
through first rise (see page 83)

½ cup butter, melted, plus additional butter for brushing
hot rolls

Zest of two oranges

¼ cup granulated sugar

1 recipe Orange Glaze (see below)

After dough for Lion House Dinner Rolls has completed the first rise, punch down and turn out onto a floured surface. Roll out dough into a rectangle about 18 inches long, 8 inches wide, and ¼ of an inch thick. In a small bowl, combine ½ cup melted butter and orange zest. Brush dough with orange butter and sprinkle the ¼ cup sugar on top.

With pizza cutter or very sharp knife, cut dough in half vertically to make two strips about 4 inches wide and 18 inches long. Make cuts through strips of dough every 2 inches, making about 18 pieces of dough.

Starting with short end, roll up one piece of dough with orange butter on the inside. Place on lightly greased baking sheet and cover with plastic wrap. Allow to rise until doubled in size, 1 to 1½ hours. Bake at 375 degrees for 12 to 15 minutes, or until light golden brown. Remove from oven and brush with melted butter. Allow to cool about 10 to 15 minutes, then drizzle with Orange Glaze.

Orange Glaze

1½ cups powdered sugar

2 tablespoons orange juice, squeezed from 2 oranges

2 to 4 tablespoons heavy cream, or 2 tablespoons half and
half

1 to 2 teaspoons orange zest (optional)

Place powdered sugar and orange juice in bowl and add half the amount of heavy cream. With spoon or mixer, stir until smooth. If icing is too thick, add more cream a little at a time. (The hotter the rolls are when frosted, the thicker the frosting needs to be.) If desired, add 1 to 2 teaspoons orange zest.

Polynesian Coconut Rolls

Makes 1 dozen rolls

1¾ cups coconut milk

1 cup water

6 tablespoons sugar

4 teaspoons cornstarch

12 Lion House Frozen Rolls, thawed

Combine coconut milk, water, sugar, and cornstarch in a small bowl, stirring well, until cornstarch is dissolved. Coat a 9x13-inch baking pan with cooking spray. Pour mixture into pan. Place thawed rolls on top of coconut mixture. Cover pan with plastic wrap and allow rolls to rise until doubled in size, about 1 to 1½ hours. Bake at 375 degrees for 20 minutes. These are best served hot.

Orange Rolls

Danish Pastry

Makes 24 large Danishes

½ cup warm water
2 tablespoons yeast
1 tablespoon sugar
1 cup butter or margarine, softened
2 cups warm milk
¾ cup sugar
1 teaspoon salt
2 eggs
8 cups flour
Sliced or slivered almonds
1 recipe Cream Filling
1 recipe Almond Filling
1 recipe Streusel Topping
1 recipe Almond Icing

Cream Filling

1 cup milk
1 egg yolk

½ teaspoon salt
⅓ cup sugar
2 tablespoons flour

Almond Filling

½ cup butter or margarine , softened
¾ cup sugar
½ cup oats
2 teaspoons almond extract

Streusel Topping

½ cup flour
½ cup sugar
½ cup butter

Almond Icing

1 cup powdered sugar
2 to 3 tablespoons milk or cream
1 teaspoon almond extract

Put ½ cup warm water in a bowl. Sprinkle yeast and 1 tablespoon sugar over water; set aside. Meanwhile, combine butter, milk, ¾ cup sugar, salt, and eggs in a large bowl. Stir in yeast mixture. Add flour and mix till well blended but do not overmix. Cover and let rise till double. Punch down. In the meantime, make Cream Filling, Almond Filling, Streusel Topping, and Almond Icing.

For Cream Filling: Heat milk in saucepan. Mix egg yolk into dry ingredients. Add a little warm milk to dry ingredients, then mix with heated milk and stir and cook till thick. Cover with plastic wrap and cool.

For Almond Filling: Mix all ingredients with fork, wire whip, or mixer till well blended.

For Streusel Topping: Mix all ingredients with fork until small crumbs form.

For Almond Icing: Combine powdered sugar with enough milk or cream to make slightly runny icing. Add almond extract.

Directions for assembling: Divide dough into 4 equal parts. On lightly floured board, roll out each part into a rectangle. Spread one-fourth Cream Filling on each; then one-fourth Almond Filling on each. Roll up jelly-roll fashion. Cut about 10 slashes through top with knife. Place each roll on greased cookie sheet. Sprinkle with Streusel Topping. Let rise in a warm place till double in bulk. Bake at 375 degrees F. for 20 minutes. Drizzle with Almond Icing and sprinkle with sliced or slivered almonds. Cut each into 6 pieces.

Creamy Cinnamon Rolls

Makes 20 servings

1 package Lion House Frozen Rolls, thawed and at room temperature

2 tablespoons butter, melted

⅔ cup brown sugar

½ cup walnuts or pecans, chopped

1 teaspoon cinnamon

½ cup cream, heavy or light

1 cup powdered sugar

1 tablespoon milk

Coat two 9-inch round baking pans with nonstick cooking spray. On an unfloured surface, unroll Lion House Rolls and pinch the edges together to form a rectangle without holes. Brush with butter. Combine brown sugar, nuts, and cinnamon. Spread evenly over dough. Roll up jelly-roll fashion from long side; pinch edges together and seal. Cut into 20 slices; place rolls cut-side down in prepared baking pans. Let rise until doubled in size, about 1½ hours. Pour cream over rolls. Bake at 350 degrees for 20 to 25 minutes. Mix powdered sugar and milk together; while rolls are warm, drizzle mixture on top.

Caramel Rolls

Makes 8 to 10 servings

1 dozen Lion House Frozen Rolls, thawed and at room temperature

½ cup butter, melted

1 cup brown sugar, packed

½ teaspoon cinnamon

1 (6-ounce) package cook-and-stir vanilla pudding mix (not instant)

3 tablespoons milk

½ cup chopped nuts (walnuts or pecans), optional

¼ cup sugar mixed with ½ teaspoon cinnamon

Coat a 9x13-inch pan or large Bundt pan with nonstick cooking spray. Cut 6 rolls lengthwise (once) then cut them the short way in thirds (so you have 6 pieces of dough from each roll). Place these pieces in prepared pan.

Combine melted butter, brown sugar, cinnamon, pudding mix, milk, and nuts. Stir until well blended. Pour ⅔ of this mixture over the dough pieces in the pan. Repeat the cutting process with the remaining 6 rolls and place these pieces on top of the first pieces. Pour remaining sauce over the dough pieces; sprinkle with the cinnamon-sugar mixture. Lightly cover with plastic wrap and allow to rise in warm place until doubled in size (45 minutes to 1 hour). Bake at 375 degrees for 30 minutes. Allow to cool 5 minutes, then invert onto large platter.

Cinnamon Rolls

Makes about 18 rolls

2½ cups water	1 tablespoon salt
½ cup vegetable oil	7 cups all-purpose flour
3 eggs	½ cup sugar
1 teaspoon vanilla	2 teaspoons ground cinnamon
½ cup nonfat dry milk	½ cup butter, melted
2 tablespoons active dry yeast	1 recipe Powdered Sugar Icing or Buttercream Frosting (see
1 cup granulated sugar	below)

Place water, oil, eggs, vanilla, and dry milk powder in the large bowl of an electric stand mixer and stir vigorously until milk is dissolved. Sprinkle yeast over liquid mixture, then add the 1 cup sugar, salt, and flour.

Put dough hook on mixer and mix for 10 to 15 minutes at low speed. The dough will be very sticky. Cover bowl with plastic wrap and let rise until doubled in size, about 1½ hours. Turn dough out onto a well-floured surface and roll out into a rectangle shape. Brush with melted butter. Sprinkle with sugar and cinnamon. Roll up rectangle lengthwise and cut into 1-inch slices. Grease a cookie sheet or line with parchment paper. Place rolls on cookie sheet, cover with plastic wrap, and allow to rise until doubled in size, 1 to 1½ hours.

Bake at 375 degrees for 12 to 14 minutes. After baking, let rolls cool slightly before frosting. Frost with Powdered Sugar Icing or Buttercream Frosting.

Note: If you want to make the dough a day ahead, mix dough according to directions. Instead of allowing dough to rise, place it in an oiled bowl, cover with plastic wrap, and refrigerate overnight. When ready to use, remove dough from refrigerator and follow directions for rolling out, rising, and baking. It will take longer for the shaped rolls to rise because dough will be cold.

Powdered Sugar Icing

2 cups powdered sugar	¼ cup half and half or evaporated milk
1 teaspoon vanilla	

Mix all ingredients together in a small mixing bowl and beat until light and well mixed.

Buttercream Frosting

3 cups powdered sugar	6 to 8 tablespoons cream or evaporated milk
½ cup butter, softened	1 teaspoon vanilla

Blend powdered sugar, butter, and 3 tablespoons of the cream in a large bowl with an electric mixer on low speed until combined well. Slowly add the rest of the cream, 1 tablespoon at a time, until creamy and smooth, but not at all runny. Add vanilla and mix again.

Crêpes

Makes 12 crêpes

3 eggs	3 tablespoons butter, melted
½ cup milk	¾ cup flour
½ cup water	½ teaspoon salt

Combine all ingredients in blender and process about 1 minute. Scrape down sides with rubber spatula and blend about 30 seconds more. Refrigerate for 1 hour. To cook, heat omelet pan, crêpe pan, or skillet over medium-high heat—pan should be just hot enough make a drop of water sizzle. Brush cooking surface lightly with melted butter. For each crêpe, pour in just enough batter to cover bottom of pan, tipping and tilting pan to move batter quickly over bottom. If crêpe has holes, add a drop or two of batter to patch. Cook until light brown on bottom and dry on top. Remove from pan and stack on plate.

Doughnut Balls

Makes 25

2½ cups flour	1 teaspoon vanilla
1 teaspoon baking powder	¼ teaspoon salt
2 eggs	1¼ cups vegetable oil for deep-frying
1½ cups sour cream	1 cup powdered sugar
2 tablespoons sugar	

In a large mixing bowl combine flour, baking powder, eggs, sour cream, sugar, vanilla, and salt until well blended. (The batter will be soft.) Heat oil in a deep skillet until oil is hot enough to fry a 1-inch cube of bread in 1 minute. Carefully place dough by tablespoonfuls into the oil. Fry doughnuts, a few at a time, for 3 to 5 minutes or until golden brown on all sides. Remove from pan with a slotted spoon. Drain on paper towels. When all doughnuts are cooked, pour powdered sugar into a plastic or paper bag. Add a few doughnuts at a time, close bag, and shake gently until doughnuts are well coated. Serve warm.

Baked Apple French Toast with Caramel Sauce

Makes 8 to 10 servings

1 loaf French bread, sliced in 1½-inch thick slices
6 eggs
1½ cups milk
½ cup sugar
1 tablespoon vanilla

6 medium apples, peeled and sliced (Fuji, Jonathan, or Granny Smith)
1½ teaspoons ground cinnamon
½ teaspoon ground nutmeg
3 tablespoons packed brown sugar
1 recipe Caramel Sauce (see below)

The night before serving, coat a 9x13-inch baking dish with nonstick cooking spray. Layer bread slices on the bottom of the pan. Combine eggs, milk, sugar, and vanilla in a large bowl; beat well and pour over bread slices. Place apple slices on top of bread. Sprinkle apples with cinnamon, nutmeg, and brown sugar. Cover with foil and refrigerate overnight. In the morning, preheat oven to 350 degrees F. Bake covered about 50 minutes; remove foil and bake 10 minutes more. Serve toast hot, topped with Caramel Sauce.

Caramel Sauce

½ cup packed brown sugar
¼ cup flour
½ cup butter, melted

½ cup milk
2 teaspoons vanilla

Combine all ingredients in a medium saucepan and cook over medium heat until thick, stirring constantly.

French Toast Triangles

Makes 20 servings

40 slices day-old Texas Toast style bread
5 eggs, slightly beaten
1½ cups heavy cream

2 teaspoons vanilla extract
¼ cup powdered sugar
Nonstick pan spray or butter substitute

In a medium bowl, mix the eggs, cream, vanilla, and sugar. Preheat a large skillet or electric skillet. Spray the skillet with the pan spray or for more flavor use a liquid butter substitute on the pan. Quickly dredge the Texas toast slices in the egg mixture and set them on the skillet.

Cook over medium heat until golden brown; turn and cook the second side. Cut each slice in half diagonally. Hold finished French toast in a warm oven until ready to serve. Sprinkle with powdered sugar immediately before service.

Note: Using slightly stale bread will make better French toast.

Soft Pretzel Sticks

Makes 24 servings

1 dozen Lion House Frozen Rolls, thawed
2 cups hot water (115 degrees)
2 tablespoons baking soda
⅓ cup butter, melted

Kosher or fine sea salt, to taste
¼ cup sugar
2 teaspoons cinnamon

Preheat oven to 400 degrees F. Mix the cinnamon and sugar together; place on a plate and set aside. Place rolls on a baking sheet and allow them to come to room temperature.

Unroll each roll. Fold each dough portion lengthwise into thirds, pressing edges down so they seal. Roll the folded dough on the counter with the palms of your hands to form a 12-inch-long rope. Press gently while rolling so dough will stay sealed. Repeat with each roll.

Cut each rope in half or, if you would like bite-size pieces, you can cut each rope into 4 or 5 pieces. Mix baking soda and hot water together and stir until the soda is dissolved. Dip each piece of dough into the water mixture, making sure it is completely covered. Remove immediately and place on a greased cookie sheet. Place 6 of the long pieces of dough on each cookie sheet. Put immediately into the oven. Bake 10 to 12 minutes or until dark golden brown. The soda will cause them to brown quickly; make sure they bake to suggested time so they aren't doughy.

Remove from oven and brush generously with melted butter. Sprinkle with kosher or fine sea salt for savory sticks, or roll in the cinnamon and sugar mixture for sweet sticks. Good at room temperature but delicious while warm.

Parmesan Bread

Makes 1 loaf or 6 servings

2 tablespoons active dry yeast
2 cups warm water
2 tablespoons sugar
2 tablespoons butter, softened

2 teaspoons salt
½ cup grated Parmesan cheese, divided
3½ cups plus 2 tablespoons all-purpose flour, divided

Sprinkle yeast over water in a large bowl. Let stand 3 to 4 minutes and stir to dissolve. Add sugar, butter, salt, all but 1 tablespoon Parmesan cheese, and 3 cups flour. Beat at low speed until smooth. Beat in remaining flour. Cover bowl and let rise 45 minutes. Stir bread down; beat 25 strokes with a wooden spoon. Pour into a greased, 2-quart ovenproof bowl and sprinkle with reserved Parmesan cheese. Bake 45 to 55 minutes at 375 degrees F., or until nicely browned.

Sun-dried Tomato Basil Bake

Makes 8 to 10 servings

8 Lion House Frozen Rolls, baked, cubed, and toasted
1 (8-ounce) jar sun-dried tomatoes in oil and herbs, drained, chopped; reserve oil.
½ cup diced onions
8 ounces mozzarella cheese, shredded
8 ounces Havarti cheese, shredded
½ cup Parmesan cheese, grated

1 ounce fresh basil, thinly sliced, divided
10 large whole eggs
2½ cups whole milk
½ cup heavy cream
1 teaspoon salt
½ teaspoon garlic salt
½ teaspoon seasoning salt (like Lawry's)
¼ teaspoon pepper

Oil a 9x13-inch glass pan or a 3½-quart baking dish with some of the oil from the sun-dried tomatoes. Heat 3 tablespoons of the reserved oil from the tomatoes in a nonstick skillet. Add onions and cook until translucent. Discard the remaining oil. Place the cheeses in a medium bowl and lightly toss with hands to combine. Place half of the cubed and toasted Lion House Rolls evenly in bottom of prepared baking dish. Sprinkle half of the onions and the oil from pan on the toasted rolls. Sprinkle with half the cheese mixture, chopped tomatoes, and basil. Repeat layers with remaining onions, cheese, tomatoes, and basil.

In a medium bowl, whisk eggs until blended. Add milk, cream, salts, and pepper, whisking until combined. Slowly pour egg mixture into baking dish over roll layers. Gently press down layered ingredients using the back of a wooden spoon until the rolls start to absorb the milk mixture. Let stand for 1 hour.

Preheat oven to 325 degrees F. Bake for 45 minutes or until the center is set and top is golden brown. Remove from oven and let stand 10 minutes before serving.

Onion Cheese Bread

Makes 8 to 10 servings

1 dozen Lion House Frozen Rolls
3 tablespoons butter
1½ cups chopped onion

2 to 3 cloves garlic
1 cup grated Parmesan cheese

Thaw frozen rolls overnight in the refrigerator. Remove rolls from refrigerator and allow them to come to room temperature (about 1½ hours), or take roll dough from freezer and allow them about 3½ to 4 hours to come to room temperature. Make the onion mixture about 30 minutes before the rolls are ready to use.

Onion Mixture: Melt 3 tablespoons butter in a large skillet over medium-high heat. Add onions and garlic and cook, stirring, until onion is translucent. Remove from heat and allow mixture to cool completely.

In a large bowl, tear thawed and unrolled rolls into 2-inch pieces. Add onion mixture and Parmesan cheese. Mix with hands until onions and cheese are mixed into the dough (about 5 minutes). Cover with plastic wrap and allow to rest 15 to 20 minutes.

Grease two cookie sheets. Divide dough in half and form two balls. Place on cookie sheets and allow to rise until doubled in size (35 to 45 minutes). Bake in a 350-degree oven for 35 to 40 minutes. Brush with butter while warm. Place on wire racks to cool. Makes two rounds.

Whole Wheat Bread and Lion House Raisin Bread

Whole Wheat Bread

Makes 2 loaves

1 package (2¼ teaspoons) active dry yeast

3 cups lukewarm water

1 cup oatmeal

¼ cup molasses

6 tablespoons nonfat dry milk

6 tablespoons shortening

5½ cups whole wheat flour

1½ tablespoons salt

2 cups white all-purpose flour

Directions for mixing with electric mixer: Soften yeast in 3 cups lukewarm water in a large mixing bowl. Add remaining ingredients and beat until dough forms a ball and leaves sides of bowl (part of flour may need to be mixed in by hand). Remove beaters, cover bowl, and let dough rise for 1 hour in a warm place, away from drafts. Punch down and shape into 2 loaves. Place in 2 well-greased 5x9-inch loaf pans; cover with a clean towel and let rise until almost doubled in size, about 45 minutes. Bake at 350 degrees for 30 minutes, or until a deep golden brown. Turn loaves out onto a wire rack to cool. Brush tops with melted butter.

Directions for hand mixing: Dissolve yeast in ¼ cup lukewarm water and set aside. Combine remaining 2¾ cups water, oats, molasses, and dry milk powder; add half the white flour and half the whole wheat flour, one cup at a time, beating well after each addition. Add softened yeast, remaining flour, shortening, and salt. Mix well; knead until dough is smooth and elastic, about 5 minutes. Place in a covered bowl in warm place until doubled in size. Knead 1 minute to force out air bubbles. Shape into 2 loaves. Place in 2 well-greased 5x9-inch loaf pans. Cover and let rise until doubled in size. Bake at 350 degrees for 30 minutes. Remove from pans to cool. Brush tops of loaves with melted butter.

Lion House Raisin Bread

Makes 2 loaves

1 recipe dough for Lion House Dinner Rolls, prepared
    through the addition of remaining flour (see page 83)

2 cups raisins

1½ teaspoons active dry yeast

¾ teaspoon ground cinnamon

¾ teaspoon nutmeg

Prepare dough for Lion House Dinner Rolls, stirring in raisins, yeast, cinnamon, and nutmeg at the same time that remaining flour is mixed into dough. Scrape down dough from sides of bowl. Pour a little oil around edge of bowl. Turn dough over once in bowl so dough is covered with oil. Cover with plastic wrap and allow to rise until doubled in size, 45 to 55 minutes. Shape into 2 loaves and place in greased 5x9-inch loaf pans. Allow to rise until dough is 1 inch above edge of pan, about 35 to 40 minutes. Bake at 350 degrees for 25 to 30 minutes, or until golden brown. Brush with melted butter after removing from oven; remove from pans and cool on wire rack.

Granary Bread

Makes 3 loaves

1½ tablespoons dry yeast
3½ cups warm water (110 to 115 degrees)
½ cup vegetable oil
½ cup honey
¼ cup molasses
1 tablespoon salt

1½ cups quick-cooking oats
1½ cups cracked wheat
½ cup wheat germ
½ cup soy flour
4½ cups whole wheat flour
2 cups white flour

Dissolve yeast in warm water in a large mixing bowl. Add oil, honey, molasses, salt, oats, cracked wheat, wheat germ, and soy flour. Beat well. Gradually add whole wheat and white flours to form a stiff dough. Turn onto a lightly floured surface and knead until smooth and elastic, 5 to 7 minutes. Place in a greased bowl; cover and let rise until double in bulk (30 to 40 minutes). Punch down, divide dough into thirds, and mold into loaves. Place in greased 4½x8-inch loaf pans. Let rise until doubled (30 minutes). Bake at 350 degrees for 30 minutes.

Jesse Evans Smith's 90-Minute Bread

Makes 2 loaves

2 cups warm water (105 to 115 degrees)
2 tablespoons active dry yeast
¼ cup granulated sugar

2 teaspoons salt
3 tablespoons vegetable oil
4 to 5 cups all-purpose flour

Grease two 5x9-inch loaf pans. Set aside. Pour water into a large bowl and sprinkle yeast over it. Sprinkle sugar and salt over yeast and wait until yeast bubbles and comes to the surface. Stir in oil. Add 2½ cups of the flour and whisk smooth with a wire whisk (or wooden spoon). Add 2 more cups of the flour and mix until dough gathers together in a ball. Sprinkle the remaining flour on work table. Turn dough onto it and knead in flour until the dough is no longer sticky but is elastic and slightly stiff, about 10 minutes. Divide dough into 2 loaves. Shape each loaf and place into greased bread pans; lightly cover with plastic wrap. Let dough rise until it peeks over the edge of the pan or doubles in bulk, about 45 minutes. Place in a 375-degree oven for 30 to 35 minutes, or until brown. Turn loaves out on a rack to cool. Brush tops with butter while hot.

Focaccia (Italian Flat Bread)

Makes 18 rolls or one 12x18-inch sheet pan

2 cups warm water
5¾ cups bread flour
2 teaspoons salt
¼ cup olive oil, plus a little more for brushing on bread

½ teaspoon garlic powder
¾ teaspoon oregano
1 tablespoon yeast

Place water in mixing bowl. Add flour, salt, oil, garlic powder, and oregano. Mix on low speed 30 to 45 seconds. Sprinkle yeast onto mixture and mix an additional 30 seconds. Mix 5 to 6 minutes on medium speed. Oil the top of dough and allow to double in size. Divide dough into 18 pieces for rolls and form into balls or make one ball for a sheet pan of bread. Brush with oil and allow to rest 30 minutes. Press out each ball by hand or spread the large ball onto a greased baking pan until it is very thin, like pizza crust. Brush top with oil and season as desired. Allow to rest 10 to 15 minutes. Bake 14 to 16 minutes in a preheated 450-degree F. oven or until lightly browned. Serve warm.

Quick and Easy French Bread

Makes 4 small loaves

2 cups hot water
2 tablespoons shortening
2 tablespoons granulated sugar
4 teaspoons salt
2 packages active dry yeast

1 cup lukewarm water
7 to 8 cups all-purpose flour
Evaporated milk
Coarse salt or sesame seeds

Combine the 2 cups hot water, shortening, sugar, and salt in a large bowl. Stir to melt shortening and dissolve sugar and salt. Set aside and cool to lukewarm.

Dissolve yeast in 1 cup lukewarm water. Add to cooled shortening-sugar mixture.

Mix in 4 cups of the flour and beat until well blended. Add remaining flour to make moderately stiff dough and knead until well mixed.

Cover and place in a warm spot to rise until doubled, about 1 hour.

Punch down and divide into 4 balls. Let rise for 10 minutes.

Roll each ball into a rectangle then roll up as a jelly roll. Shape and seal the ends. Score with kitchen shears or a sharp knife down the top of the loaf. Place on greased cookie sheets (2 per sheet), brush with evaporated milk, and sprinkle with coarse salt or sesame seeds.

Cover and allow to rise for 1½ hours, or until almost doubled.

Bake at 400 degrees for 25 minutes. Brush with melted butter, if desired, and remove to wire racks to cool.

Dilly Casserole Bread

Makes 1 round loaf

1 package (2¼ teaspoons) active dry yeast

¼ cup lukewarm water

1 cup cottage cheese, heated to lukewarm

2 tablespoons sugar

2 tablespoons finely chopped onion or 1 tablespoon dried minced onion

1 tablespoon butter or margarine, softened, plus additional butter for brushing hot bread

1 tablespoon dill weed

1 teaspoon salt

¼ teaspoon baking soda

1 egg

2 to 2½ cups all-purpose flour

Soften yeast in water in a small bowl and set aside. In a mixing bowl, combine cottage cheese, sugar, onion, 1 tablespoon butter, dill weed, salt, baking soda, egg, and softened yeast. Add flour, ½ cup at a time, to form a stiff dough, beating well after each addition. Cover and let rise in a warm place, until light and doubled in size, about 50 to 60 minutes. Punch dough down. Turn into a well-greased, 1½- to 2-quart round casserole dish. Cover and let rise in a warm place 30 to 40 minutes. Bake 40 to 50 minutes at 350 degrees F., or until golden brown. Brush with softened butter and sprinkle with salt.

Crunchy Onion Loaf

Makes 2 rounds

1 tablespoon dry yeast

¼ cup warm water (110 to 115 degrees)

1 envelope dry onion soup mix

2 cups water

2 tablespoons sugar

1 teaspoon salt

2 tablespoons grated Parmesan cheese

2 tablespoons shortening

1 egg yolk, beaten well

5 to 5½ cups flour

Cornmeal

1 egg white, beaten well

Soften yeast in ¼ cup water in a small bowl; set aside. Combine soup mix and 2 cups water in saucepan and simmer 10 minutes. Add sugar, salt, Parmesan cheese, and shortening. Cool to lukewarm. Pour in a large bowl and add egg yolk, softened yeast, and 2 cups flour. Beat 3 minutes. Add 1½ cups flour and beat until well mixed. Place 1 cup flour on countertop, turn dough out on it, and knead until smooth and elastic (5 to 7 minutes). If dough is sticky, add ½ cup flour and continue to knead until smooth. Place in greased or oiled bowl, cover and let rise until double in bulk (40 to 50 minutes). Punch down and divide in half. Shape into 2 round loaves. Place on greased baking sheet sprinkled with cornmeal. Cut several diagonal slashes on top of loaf and brush with slightly beaten egg white. Bake at 375 degrees for 30 minutes.

Dilly Casserole Bread

Rich Corn Bread

Rich Corn Bread

Makes 9 pieces

1 cup all-purpose flour
1 cup yellow cornmeal
1 teaspoon salt
4 teaspoons baking powder
4 eggs

½ cup sour cream
1 (14.75-ounce) can cream-style corn
2 tablespoons vegetable oil
1 cup shredded cheddar cheese

Preheat oven to 400 degrees F. Grease an 8x4-inch loaf pan or an 8x8-inch square pan and set aside. Sift together flour, cornmeal, salt, and baking powder and set aside. Beat eggs until light. Add sour cream, corn, and oil to eggs. Stir in dry ingredients and beat well. Pour into prepared pan and sprinkle with shredded cheese. Bake 30 minutes. Test for doneness by sticking a toothpick into the loaf or pan, just off center. If the toothpick comes out clean, the bread is done.

Chef's tip: If you like a little heat to your corn bread, stem, seed, and chop half of a jalapeño pepper and add it to the batter before pouring into the pan.

Johnny Cakes (Cornmeal Muffins)

Makes 12 muffins

2 cups yellow cornmeal
1 cup all-purpose flour
1½ teaspoons salt
1½ teaspoons baking powder
¾ teaspoon baking soda

1 cup packed brown sugar
4 eggs, beaten
1¼ cups sour cream
¾ cup butter, melted
2 cups frozen corn, thawed

Preheat oven to 375 degrees F. Coat 12 large muffin cups with nonstick cooking spray or line with cupcake papers and set aside. In a large bowl, whisk together cornmeal, flour, salt, baking powder, baking soda, and sugar. In a separate bowl, beat eggs and stir in the sour cream. Pour egg mixture, melted butter, and corn into the dry ingredients and fold together. Do not overmix. Scoop batter into prepared muffin cups and bake 18 to 22 minutes, or until a toothpick inserted near center comes out clean.

Nauvoo Café Bran Muffins

Makes 24 muffins

3 cups all-purpose flour
1 teaspoon salt
1 tablespoon baking soda
1¼ cups All-Bran® cereal
1¼ cups boiling water
1¼ cups dried cranberries
1¾ cups golden raisins

1¼ cups granulated sugar
¾ cup butter, softened
3 eggs
3½ cups Bran Flakes® cereal
1½ cups buttermilk
1¼ cups chopped walnuts

Preheat oven to 375 degrees F. Grease and flour muffin top pans or regular muffin tins for 24 muffins.

Whisk together flour, salt, and baking soda and set aside. Place All-Bran cereal in a small bowl and cover with boiling water. Stir gently to moisten all of the cereal then set aside. Place dried cranberries and golden raisins in a small bowl and cover with hot tap water then set aside.

In a large mixing bowl, beat sugar and butter together until soft. Add eggs and beat until fluffy. Add dry ingredients and moistened All- Bran and mix until incorporated. Add Bran Flakes. Turn mixer on low and slowly add the buttermilk. Mix until all ingredients are well incorporated.

Drain dried cranberries and golden raisins, then fold into the batter along with chopped walnuts.

Whole Wheat Muffins

Makes 12 muffins

1 cup whole wheat flour
1 cup white flour
½ cup packed brown sugar
½ teaspoon salt
4 teaspoons baking powder

⅓ cup shortening, melted
2 eggs, beaten well
1 cup milk
1 cup chopped walnuts

Preheat oven to 375 degrees F. Grease a 12-cup muffin tin or line with muffin papers. Combine flours, brown sugar, salt, and baking powder in a medium mixing bowl. Make a well in the mixture and add melted shortening, eggs, and milk. Mix until just moistened. Fold in chopped nuts. Spoon into muffin cups, filling ¾ full. Bake for 20 to 25 minutes.

Nauvoo Café Bran Muffins

Blueberry Muffins

Makes 20 muffins.

3½ cups all-purpose flour
½ cup sugar
5 teaspoons baking powder
½ teaspoon salt

2 eggs, well-beaten
1½ cups milk
⅔ cup oil
2 cups fresh blueberries*

Preheat oven to 400 degrees F. Grease muffin tins or line with paper cups. Sift flour, sugar, baking powder, and salt into a bowl; make a well in the center. In another bowl, beat together eggs, milk, and oil. Pour mixture into well and stir until moistened. Gently fold in blueberries.

Fill each muffin cup ⅔ full of batter. Bake 20 to 25 minutes.

Frozen blueberries may be substituted. Thaw and drain before using.

Oatmeal Apple Muffins

Makes 12 muffins

1 cup flour
3 teaspoons baking powder
⅓ cup packed brown sugar
1 cup quick-cooking oats
2 teaspoons ground cinnamon
1 teaspoon ground nutmeg

½ teaspoon salt
1 egg, beaten well
¾ cup milk
½ cup vegetable oil
1 cup raisins
1 apple, peeled, cored, and chopped

Preheat oven to 400 degrees F. Grease a 12-cup muffin tin or line with muffin papers. Mix together with a spoon the flour, baking powder, brown sugar, oats, cinnamon, nutmeg, and salt in a large bowl. In a separate bowl, combine beaten egg, milk, vegetable oil, raisins, and chopped apple. Fold wet ingredients into dry ingredients, mixing just to moisten. Spoon batter into greased muffin cups, filling ¾ full. Bake for 15 to 20 minutes until lightly golden and a toothpick inserted in the middle of one muffin comes out clean.

Buttermilk Scones

Makes about 60 to 100 scones, depending on size

4 cups buttermilk
2 packages (2 tablespoons) dry yeast
¼ cup lukewarm water
¼ cup sugar
2 eggs, beaten
2 tablespoons oil

1½ teaspoons salt
3 teaspoons baking powder
½ teaspoon baking soda
8 cups flour
Cooking oil or shortening for frying

Heat buttermilk until warm. Soften yeast in lukewarm water. In large bowl, combine buttermilk, sugar, eggs, oil, salt, baking powder, baking soda, and 4 cups flour. Add yeast; beat until smooth. Add remaining flour to make soft dough. Allow to rise, covered, until double in size. Punch down and place in refrigerator overnight.

When ready to fry, heat oil or shortening to 375 degrees F. Roll dough out on floured board. Cut into squares about 2x2 inches. Stretch each piece a little and drop into hot fat. Fry on one side until golden; turn and fry on other side. Drain on paper towels. Serve hot with honey butter. Dough will keep in refrigerator 3 to 4 days. Punch down from time to time and cover tightly with foil or damp cloth.

Honey Butter

½ cup butter, softened
½ cup honey

¼ teaspoon vanilla

Beat butter until it is broken up. Add the honey and the vanilla. Beat for 10 minutes, scraping mixture to the bottom twice during the mixing. (It is very important that this mix for the entire 10 minutes or it will separate.) Store, refrigerated, in a plastic container.

Raspberry Honey Butter

1 pound butter, unsalted
½ cup honey

½ cup raspberry preserves
1 teaspoon vanilla

Whip butter until light and fluffy. Add honey, raspberry preserves, and vanilla. Continue to whip until mixed.

Cranberry Nut Bread

Makes 1 large or 2 small loaves

2 cups flour
1 teaspoon baking powder
½ teaspoon baking soda
1 teaspoon salt
⅓ cup butter
¾ cup sugar

2 eggs
¾ cup orange juice
1 tablespoon grated orange peel
1 cup fresh or frozen cranberries (chopped, if desired)
½ cup chopped nuts

Preheat oven to 350 degrees F. Grease and flour 1 large 8x4-inch loaf pan or 2 small 7x3-inch loaf pans; set aside. In medium bowl, mix flour, baking powder, baking soda, and salt. In mixer bowl, cream butter until soft; add sugar. Beat until creamy; add eggs, orange juice, and orange peel. Beat until well mixed. Scrape down sides and bottom of bowl; add dry ingredients. Mix at low speed until blended, but do not overmix. Stir in cranberries and nuts by hand. Pour batter into prepared loaf pan or pans and bake 45 to 50 minutes for large loaf, less time for small loaves. Cool completely before slicing.

Orange Nut Bread

Makes 1 loaf

1 medium orange
1 cup raisins or dates
2 tablespoons melted butter or margarine
1 teaspoon vanilla
1 egg, beaten
2 cups flour

½ teaspoon salt
1 teaspoon baking powder
½ teaspoon baking soda
1 cup sugar
1 cup chopped nuts

Preheat oven to 350 degrees F. Grease well an 8x4-inch loaf pan. Set aside. Wash orange; squeeze juice. Pour juice into a one-cup measure; if there isn't enough juice to equal a full cup, add boiling water to make up the rest. Put orange rind and raisins through a chopper. (Raisins may be left whole if desired.) Combine butter, vanilla, and egg; pour onto chopped fruits. Sift dry ingredients together in a bowl and add to fruit mixture. Stir in nuts last. Pour into prepared pan. Bake 1 hour.

Note: If orange has a thick skin, remove as much of the white part under the skin as possible before grinding.

Cranberry Nut Bread

Banana Bread

Makes 2 loaves

6 large or 8 medium bananas, very ripe
4 eggs
2 cups sugar
¾ cup oil
4 cups flour

1 teaspoon baking soda
2 teaspoons salt
2 teaspoons baking powder
½ cup walnuts, chopped

Preheat oven to 325 degrees F. Prepare 2 large loaf pans by greasing and flouring well. Set aside. Peel bananas and place in a large mixing bowl; mix until bananas are mashed. Add eggs, sugar, and oil to the bananas and mix until well blended. In a separate bowl, mix flour, soda, salt, and baking powder. Add this mixture to the banana mixture. Mix together until the ingredients are blended. Add the nuts and mix briefly. (Overmixing causes tunnels and a coarse texture.)

Pour into prepared pans. Bake 50 to 60 minutes or until wooden toothpick inserted in center comes out clean.

Note: You can make smaller loaves if desired. Adjust baking time according to size; the smaller the loaf the shorter the baking time.

Zucchini Bread

Makes 10 to 12 servings

3 cups all-purpose flour
1 teaspoon baking soda
½ teaspoon baking powder
2 teaspoons ground cinnamon
3 eggs

1 cup vegetable oil
2 cups granulated sugar
1 tablespoon vanilla
2 cups grated zucchini
1 cup chopped walnuts

Preheat oven to 325 degrees F. Grease and flour an 8x4-inch loaf pan or two 7x3-inch loaf pans and set aside. In a large bowl, whisk together flour, baking soda, baking powder, and cinnamon and set aside. In a separate bowl, beat eggs with an electric mixer until light and foamy. Add oil, sugar, vanilla, and grated zucchini and mix well. Fold in flour mixture, stirring just until moist. Do not overmix. Fold in nuts.

Pour batter into prepared pan(s), about ⅔ full. Bake 45 to 50 minutes for large loaf or 35 minutes for smaller loaves, or until a toothpick inserted in center comes out clean. Turn loaves out onto wire racks to cool.

Lion House Pumpkin Bread

Makes 2 loaves

1½ cups vegetable oil
5 eggs
1 (16-ounce) can pumpkin
2 cups all-purpose flour
2 cups granulated sugar
1 teaspoon salt

1 teaspoon ground cinnamon
1 teaspoon nutmeg
1 teaspoon baking soda
1 (3-ounce) package vanilla instant pudding
1 cup chopped nuts

Preheat oven to 350 degrees F. Grease and flour two 9x5-inch loaf pans and set aside.

Beat oil, eggs, and pumpkin in a large mixing bowl. In a separate bowl, sift together flour, sugar, salt, cinnamon, nutmeg, and baking soda. Add dry ingredients to pumpkin mixture and mix until well blended. Stir in pudding mix and nuts. Pour into prepared pans and bake for 1 hour. Test for doneness by sticking a toothpick in the loaf, just off center. If the toothpick comes out clean, the bread is done. Turn loaves out onto wire racks to cool.

Applesauce Fruit Loaf

Makes 1 loaf

1 cup flour
¾ pound candied fruit mixture
½ cup chopped dates
¼ cup butter
½ cup sugar
1 teaspoon baking soda
¾ cup applesauce

¼ teaspoon cloves
½ teaspoon cinnamon
¼ teaspoon salt
1 egg, beaten
1 cup raisins
½ cup chopped nut meats

Preheat oven to 300 degrees F. Grease well an 8x4-inch loaf pan. Set aside. In a large bowl add flour to candied fruit and dates. In a large mixer bowl cream butter and sugar together. In a small bowl add soda to applesauce; combine with butter and sugar mixture, then add spices, salt, and egg. Combine this mixture with the fruit-flour mixture. Stir in raisins and nuts. Pour into prepared pan and bake for 1 hour or until wooden toothpick inserted in center comes out clean.

Aloha Bread

Aloha Bread

Makes 2 large loaves

1 cup butter
2 cups sugar
4 eggs
1 cup mashed bananas
4 cups flour
2 teaspoons baking powder

1 teaspoon baking soda
¾ teaspoon salt
1 (20-ounce) can crushed pineapple, drained
¾ cup chopped pecans
1 cup flaked coconut

Preheat oven to 325 degrees F. Grease 2 large 8x4-inch loaf pans; set aside. In large mixing bowl, cream butter and sugar. Add eggs; stir in bananas. In separate bowl, mix flour, baking powder, baking soda, and salt; add to banana mixture. Blend well, but do not overmix. (Overmixing causes tunnels and a coarse texture.) Add pineapple, pecans, and coconut; mix on low speed until blended. Pour into prepared pans. (Pans should be ⅔ full.) Bake 60 to 80 minutes.

Janell's Poppy Seed Bread

Makes 1 loaf

½ cup butter, melted
3½ tablespoons vegetable oil
2 eggs
½ cup milk
¾ cup granulated sugar
½ teaspoon vanilla

½ teaspoon almond extract
1 cup all-purpose flour
½ teaspoon salt
1 teaspoon baking powder
¾ teaspoon poppy seeds
1 recipe Orange Almond Icing (see below)

Preheat oven to 325 degrees F. Grease and flour an 8x4-inch loaf pan and set aside.

In a large mixing bowl, cream together butter, oil, eggs, milk, sugar, vanilla, and almond extract. In a separate bowl, whisk together flour, salt, baking powder, and poppy seeds. Add dry ingredients to cream mixture until well blended but not overmixed. Pour into prepared pan and bake for 45 minutes. Test for doneness by sticking a toothpick in the loaf, just off center. If the toothpick comes out clean, the bread is done. Turn loaves out onto wire racks to cool. Frost with Orange Almond Icing while still warm.

Orange Almond Icing

Makes enough icing for 1 loaf bread

1 tablespoon orange juice
¼ teaspoon vanilla

¼ teaspoon almond extract
¼ cup powdered sugar

Mix all ingredients in a small bowl until well blended.

Chocolate Zucchini Bread

Makes 2 loaves

2 cups all-purpose flour
½ teaspoon baking powder
1 teaspoon baking soda
1 teaspoon salt
½ teaspoon ground cinnamon
3 eggs
1 cup granulated sugar

1 cup brown sugar
1 cup vegetable oil
1 teaspoon vanilla
2 ounces melted unsweetened chocolate
2 cups grated zucchini
1 cup semi-sweet chocolate chips

Preheat oven to 325 degrees F. Grease and flour two 8x4-inch loaf pans and set aside.

Whisk together flour, baking powder, baking soda, salt, and cinnamon in a large bowl and set aside. In a separate mixing bowl, beat eggs with an electric mixer until light and foamy. Add the sugars, oil, vanilla, and melted chocolate and beat until creamy. Stir in grated zucchini. Mix in the dry ingredients until just incorporated. Do not overmix. Fold in chocolate chips. Pour equal amounts batter in each loaf pan and bake 45 to 50 minutes. Turn loaves out onto wire racks to cool.

Cherry Nut Bread

Makes 2 loaves

1 cup granulated sugar
½ cup vegetable oil
2 eggs
1 teaspoon vanilla
2¼ cups all-purpose flour

1 teaspoon baking powder
1 (8-ounce) jar maraschino cherries, chopped, juice reserved
½ cup chopped walnuts

Preheat oven to 325 degrees F. Grease and flour two 9x5-inch loaf pans and set aside.

In a large mixing bowl, cream sugar and oil; add eggs and beat well. Stir in vanilla. In a separate bowl, whisk together flour and baking powder. Measure out ½ cup of the reserved maraschino cherry juice. (If juice does not equal ½ cup, add enough water to make up the rest.) Alternately add flour mixture and cherry juice to sugar mixture until all is well blended. Fold in cherries and nuts. Pour into prepared pans and bake 55 to 60 minutes, or until toothpick inserted near center comes out clean. Turn loaves out onto wire racks to cool. Dust with powdered sugar when cooled.

Cherry Nut Bread, Chocolate Zucchini
Bread, and Janell's Poppy Seed Bread

English Wigs

English Wigs

Makes 24 buns

2 tablespoons dry yeast
½ cup warm water (110 to 115 degrees)
½ cup sugar
½ cup margarine, melted
1¾ cups warm milk
1 egg, beaten well
2 teaspoons salt

1½ teaspoons ground nutmeg
⅛ teaspoon ground cloves
⅛ teaspoon mace
5½ to 6½ cups flour
1 egg, for egg wash
Caraway seeds

Note: Serve these caraway-topped buns with hot spiced cider on Christmas Eve, or with raspberry jam as a Christmas-morning breakfast treat.

Dissolve yeast in warm water in a large mixing bowl. Stir in sugar, melted margarine, milk, beaten egg, salt, nutmeg, cloves, and mace. Add 3 cups flour and beat with electric mixer on low speed until smooth. Gradually add enough additional flour to make a soft dough. Turn out onto a lightly floured surface and knead until smooth and elastic, about 5 to 6 minutes. Place in greased bowl; cover and let rise until dough doubles in bulk, about 45 minutes. Punch down. Divide dough in half. Form 12 round buns and place on greased baking sheet. Repeat with other half of dough. Cut a deep cross on each bun with a sharp knife. Make an egg wash by beating an egg; brush over each bun. Sprinkle tops with caraway seeds. Cover and let rise until doubled, about 45 minutes. Bake at 375 degrees for 20 minutes.

Cheese Strata

Makes 8 to 10 servings

6 to 8 Lion House Frozen Dinner Rolls, thawed, baked and
    sliced
3 cups grated cheddar, Swiss, or Monterey Jack cheese
2 cups cooked, diced ham
6 eggs

3½ cups milk
2½ teaspoons dried onion flakes
½ teaspoon salt
¼ teaspoon dry mustard

Layer half of the sliced rolls on the bottom of greased 9x13-inch pan. Sprinkle 2 cups of the grated cheese over the rolls. Cover with diced ham. Top with the other half of the sliced rolls. In a medium bowl, beat eggs with milk, onion flakes, salt, and mustard. Pour over the rolls. Cover with plastic wrap and refrigerate overnight. Bake, uncovered, at 350 degrees for 40 minutes. Remove from oven, add remaining 1 cup cheese, and return to oven for 15 more minutes.

Chef's note: Instead of using ham, try cooked and crumbled sausage. Or try adding spinach, red and yellow bell peppers, or broccoli.

Broccoli Cheddar Rolls

Makes 2 dozen rolls

1 recipe dough for Lion House Dinner Rolls, prepared
through first rise (see page 83)
1 (10-ounce) bag frozen chopped broccoli, thawed and
drained
1 cup grated cheddar cheese
¼ cup dried minced onions

1 egg
1 teaspoon onion salt
2 tablespoons grated Parmesan cheese
2 tablespoons butter, melted
1 teaspoon Lawry's Seasoned Salt®

After dough for Lion House Dinner Rolls has completed first rise, turn out onto a floured surface. Roll out dough into a large rectangle, about ¼-inch thick. Mix broccoli, cheddar cheese, onions, egg, onion salt, Parmesan cheese, and Lawry's Seasoned Salt in a small bowl. Spread broccoli mixture over dough. Tightly roll up the dough jelly roll style. Using a little water on fingertips, pinch edge firmly to seal dough. Cut dough into 24 slices.

Place slices, cut side up, in cavities of muffin pans sprayed with cooking spray or place on greased baking sheets. Brush panned dough with melted butter. Cover with plastic wrap and let rolls rise until doubled in size, about 1 to 1½ hours. Bake at 375 degrees for 10 to 15 minutes. Remove from pan immediately to cool on a wire rack.

Cheesy Pull Apart Rolls

Makes 10 to 12 servings

1 cup butter, melted
1 cup grated Parmesan cheese
12 Lion House Frozen Rolls, thawed

Combine melted butter and Parmesan cheese in a shallow bowl. Cut thawed frozen rolls in half the short way. Roll each dough piece in the cheese and butter mixture. Place in a well-greased Bundt pan. Cover pan and allow dough to rise until it is doubled in size (35 to 40 minutes). Bake at 375 degrees for 20 to 25 minutes. After cooling for 10 minutes, invert onto serving platter.

Broccoli Cheddar Rolls

Breakfast Pizza

Lion House Pizza

Makes 6 to 8 servings

1 dozen Lion House Frozen Rolls
1¾ cups Italian sauce (your favorite flavor and kind)
12 ounces shredded mozzarella cheese

½ pound mild Italian sausage, browned and drained
¼ pound pepperoni slices
½ pound ground beef, browned and drained

Choose any of your favorite pizza toppings; those listed above are options. Other options are pineapple tidbits, green pepper, olives, ham, onions, etc.; use any or all.

Take rolls from bag and place on a greased 15x17-inch baking sheet. Cover with plastic wrap and allow to thaw overnight in the refrigerator, or thaw on the counter 2 to 3 hours. Unroll rolls and place flat on the pan, side by side; some may need to be turned a different direction so they all fit. Pinch together edges and press dough down so it makes one piece of dough. Gently press the dough up the sides of the pan slightly. Allow dough to come to room temperature. Spoon on sauce, spreading evenly. You may use less or more sauce depending on how you like your pizza. Sprinkle cheese on evenly and place the rest of the toppings on the cheese. Bake in a 375-degree oven 20 to 25 minutes. If your pizza has a lot of toppings, the baking time might be longer.

Chef's note: This recipe is fun and easy for kids to make their own pizza. Thaw roll dough as directed above. Unroll dough, leaving room between each roll. Cover dough with plastic and allow to come to room temperature about 1 hour. Have each child fold a roll in half the long way so the piece of dough is almost square. Press dough down and flatten so it is about 2½ inches by 2½ inches. Place the dough pieces on a greased baking sheet and let the child put the sauce and toppings on and bake. These bake for about 15 minutes.

Breakfast Pizza

Makes 12 servings

1 dozen Lion House Frozen Rolls, thawed
1 pound pork sausage, cooked and drained
2 medium potatoes, grated; or 2 cups frozen hash brown
    potatoes
½ cup chopped green or red bell pepper (optional)

½ cup chopped onion (optional)
1 cup grated Monterey Jack cheese
4 eggs
½ cup milk
½ teaspoon salt

Preheat oven to 375 degrees F. Unroll rolls and press each together to form a single crust. Place on a well-greased 18x13-inch jelly roll pan. Sprinkle pork sausage and grated potatoes over dough. If using, sprinkle chopped green or red pepper and onion over sausage and potatoes. Cover with grated cheese. In a small bowl, blend eggs, milk, and salt with a wire whisk and pour over top of cheese. Bake 20 to 25 minutes.

Chicken Cordon Bleu

Chicken Cordon Bleu

Makes 6 to 8 servings

4 boneless, skinless chicken breast halves

8 thin slices cooked ham

4 slices Swiss cheese, cut into strips about 1½ inches long and ½-inch thick

Salt

Pepper

Thyme or rosemary

¼ cup melted butter or margarine

½ cup cornflake crumbs

Cordon Bleu Sauce (below)

Cordon Bleu Sauce

1 (10.5-ounce) can cream of chicken soup

½ cup sour cream

Juice of 1 lemon (about ⅓ cup)

Place each chicken breast half between sheets of plastic wrap and pound with meat mallet to about ⅛-inch thickness.

On each ham slice place a strip of cheese; sprinkle lightly with seasonings. Roll ham and cheese jelly-roll style, then roll each chicken breast with ham and cheese inside. Tuck in ends and seal well. (Tie rolls if necessary, or fasten edges with toothpicks.) Dip each roll in melted butter, then roll in cornflake crumbs, turning to thoroughly coat each roll. Place rolls in 9x13-inch baking dish. Bake uncovered at 400 degrees for about 40 minutes, or until chicken is golden brown. Serve with Cordon Bleu Sauce, if desired.

For sauce: Blend ingredients and heat. Serve over chicken rolls, if desired.

Apricot Chicken

Makes 8 servings

2 tablespoons cornstarch

2 cups apricot nectar

1 envelope dry onion soup mix

2 frying chickens, cut up, or 8 chicken breasts

In saucepan, mix cornstarch in small amount of apricot nectar. Add remaining nectar and onion soup mix. Heat and stir until sauce thickens. Pour over chicken pieces that have been washed and dried and arranged in 9x13-inch baking dish. Bake covered at 350 degrees for 30 minutes. Uncover and bake about 30 minutes or until chicken is tender. Baste several times with sauce.

Lion House Chicken

Makes 8 to 10 servings

5 to 6 cups cubed bread for stuffing

1 medium yellow onion, diced

3 stalks celery, diced

1 cup sliced fresh mushrooms

1 cup butter

1 tablespoon rubbed sage

3 cups chicken stock

Salt and pepper to taste

8 to 10 boneless, skinless chicken breasts (7 ounces each)

2 cups bread crumbs

1 recipe Honey Dijon Sauce for Chicken (see below)

Toast cubed bread in oven at 300 degrees until crisp and lightly browned. Sauté onion, celery, and mushrooms in butter until onion is translucent. Add sage and chicken stock and bring to a low boil. Season with salt and pepper to taste. In large bowl, toss hot mixture with toasted bread cubes, adding enough liquid to make cubes soft but not soggy. Divide stuffing mixture into 8 to 10 equal parts.

Place each chicken breast between sheets of plastic wrap and pound to an even ½-inch thick. Bread one side of each chicken breast with crumbs, and hold chicken, breaded side down, in one hand. Put stuffing on top of the breast; fold over and secure with toothpicks. Bake at 350 degrees until cooked thoroughly, about 15 to 20 minutes. Test chicken with meat thermometer; internal temperature should be 155 degrees F. Drizzle Honey Dijon Sauce over cooked chicken.

Honey Dijon Sauce for Chicken

½ cup honey

⅓ cup Dijon mustard

2 cups mayonnaise

Mix honey, mustard, and mayonnaise together and chill.

Baked Chicken Supreme

Makes 8 servings

8 boneless, skinless chicken breast halves	¼ cup flour
¼ cup shortening	1 cup tomato juice
1 small clove garlic	1 (10.5-ounce) can tomato soup
⅓ cup chopped onion	1 cup sour cream
1½ teaspoons salt	¼ cup milk
½ teaspoon sugar	2 tablespoons grated Parmesan cheese
½ teaspoon oregano (optional)	4 cups hot, cooked rice

Preheat oven to 325 degrees F. Brown chicken breasts in shortening in a large frying pan over medium heat, using more shortening if needed. Remove from frying pan and place in a 9x9-inch baking dish. Pour off all but 2 tablespoons drippings from pan. Add garlic and onion to skillet; cover and cook until soft but not brown, about 5 minutes. Blend in salt, sugar, oregano, and flour. Add tomato juice and tomato soup; heat to boiling, stirring constantly. Remove from heat and blend in sour cream. Stir vigorously. Add enough milk to thin sauce a little. Add Parmesan cheese. Pour over chicken in baking dish. Cover and bake 45 minutes, or until meat is fork tender. Serve with cooked rice.

Note: Boneless, skinless breasts work best here, but unskinned, unboned pieces may be used. Or use all pieces from one chicken, or pieces desired from two chickens.

Savory Baked Chicken Breasts

Makes 8 servings

1 cup sour cream	1½ teaspoons sage
2 tablespoons lemon juice	1½ teaspoons garlic salt
8 boneless, skinless chicken breast halves	½ teaspoon black pepper
1 teaspoon salt	3 cups fine bread crumbs
1 teaspoon seasoned salt	½ cup butter or margarine, melted
1½ teaspoons paprika	

Note: Start this dish early in the day—or the night before serving—so chicken has time to soak up flavors from the simple marinade.

At least 4 hours before baking, combine sour cream and lemon juice in a small bowl. Place chicken breasts in a shallow bowl and pour mixture over chicken. Cover and refrigerate.

When ready to bake, preheat oven to 325 degrees and grease a 9x13-inch baking dish. Combine salt, seasoned salt, paprika, sage, garlic salt, and black pepper in a medium bowl. Mix in bread crumbs. Dip chicken breasts in crumb mixture to coat all sides. Arrange in baking pan. Drizzle melted butter over top. Cover with foil and bake for 2 hours. Remove foil and bake an additional 30 minutes to brown.

Chicken and Broccoli Bake

Makes 5 to 6 servings

4 chicken breast halves

3 (10-ounce) packages frozen broccoli, cooked according to package directions, or 2 pounds fresh broccoli, well trimmed and cooked until tender-crisp

1 (10.5-ounce) can cream of chicken soup

½ cup milk

¼ cup mayonnaise

¼ cup salad dressing (such as Miracle Whip®)

1 cup grated cheddar cheese

1 teaspoon lemon juice

½ cup bread crumbs

¼ cup grated Parmesan cheese

2 tablespoons butter or margarine, cut into small pieces

Cook chicken breasts in water just to cover for about 30 minutes. Remove chicken; cool, remove bones and skin, and dice meat.

Coat 9x9-inch pan with nonstick cooking spray. Layer broccoli in bottom of pan; place chicken pieces on top of broccoli. Mix soup, milk, mayonnaise, salad dressing, cheddar cheese, and lemon juice. Spread on top of chicken. Sprinkle with bread crumbs and cheese, and top with butter or margarine. Bake at 350 degrees for 30 minutes or 20 minutes on high in microwave.

Chicken Dijon

Makes 4 servings

4 boneless, skinless chicken breast halves

¾ cup water

¾ cup white grape juice

1 small onion, sliced

3 tablespoons lemon juice

1 chicken bouillon cube

12 whole peppercorns

1 teaspoon dried thyme

1 tablespoon honey

2 teaspoons Dijon mustard

1½ cups sliced fresh mushrooms

2 teaspoons flour

2 tablespoons water

4 sprigs fresh thyme, for garnishing

4 lemon slices, for garnishing

Place chicken breasts in a 12-inch skillet and add water, grape juice, onion slices, lemon juice, bouillon cube, peppercorns, and thyme. Cover and simmer 15 minutes or until chicken is no longer pink. Remove chicken and keep warm in serving dish. Strain pan liquids through a mesh sieve; discard solids and return liquid to pan. Add honey, mustard, and mushrooms. Bring to a boil and simmer 10 minutes. Make a paste of flour and water and stir into the sauce. Cook and stir over medium heat until slightly thickened. Spoon sauce over chicken. Garnish each breast with a sprig of thyme and a lemon slice, if desired.

Chicken and Cashews

Makes 4 to 5 servings

4 chicken breast halves
1 teaspoon sugar
4 tablespoons cornstarch, divided
½ teaspoon salt
¼ cup soy sauce
1 teaspoon vinegar

1 teaspoon Worcestershire sauce
3 tablespoons salad oil
2 cups hot chicken stock
2 teaspoons lemon juice
½ cup cashews
2 to 3 cups cooked rice

Bone and skin chicken breasts. Cover chicken bones and skin with cold water. Bring to a boil slowly and simmer for ½ hour or more. (Add a few slices of onion, carrot, and celery to improve flavor of the stock.) Strain and cool stock. Remove fat from surface.

Cut raw chicken into bite-sized pieces. Combine sugar, 2 tablespoons cornstarch, salt, soy sauce, vinegar, and Worcestershire sauce. Dredge chicken pieces in this mixture. Drain excess from chicken and save remaining mixture. In frying pan or wok, stir-fry chicken in hot oil until lightly browned and tender, about 10 minutes. Remove chicken from oil; drain excess oil from pan. Add remaining cornstarch and mixture drained from dredged chicken. Blend well, then add chicken stock to pan and bring to a boil, stirring constantly. Cook until thickened. Add lemon juice, then chicken pieces, and reheat. Do not boil. Adjust seasonings to taste. Add cashews. Serve over hot rice.

Note: *Chicken soup base or canned chicken stock may be used. Add water to desired consistency, if needed.*

Chicken with Satay Sauce

Makes 15 servings of 2 skewers each

Chicken

2½ pounds chicken breast, sliced ½-inch thick
Salt and pepper to taste
30 bamboo skewers soaked in water at least 1 hour

Satay Sauce

1 medium yellow onion, peeled and diced
3 tablespoons chopped garlic
2 tablespoons butter

1 (14-ounce) jar creamy peanut butter
1¾ cups rice wine vinegar
1 tablespoon soy sauce
2 cups water
1 cup cream
1 cup sugar
1 to 2 teaspoons red pepper flakes

Preheat oven to 350 degrees F. Slice the chicken breast into ½-inch strips. Thread 1 strip of chicken meat onto each skewer. Sprinkle with salt and pepper. Bake 5 minutes or until a thermometer reads 165 degrees F. Serve with Satay Sauce.

For sauce: Sauté onion and garlic in butter until translucent. Add peanut butter and stir until melted, being careful not to burn. Add vinegar and soy sauce and mix well. Stir in water and cream and return to a boil. Add sugar and mix well. Add red pepper flakes. *Makes 24 two-ounce servings of sauce*

Chicken and Wild Rice

Makes 6 servings

6 to 8 boneless, skinless chicken breasts	1½ teaspoons black pepper
6 cups flour	4 cups milk
2 tablespoons chili powder	2 cups oil
1 teaspoon cayenne pepper	1 recipe Sauce (see below)
1 teaspoon paprika	1 recipe Wild Rice (see below)
1 tablespoon salt	Diced bell peppers (optional)

Preheat oven to 375 degrees F. Divide the flour in half and place in 2 separate bowls. In the first bowl add chili powder, cayenne, paprika, salt, and pepper. Mix well. Place raw chicken breasts into the other bowl and coat evenly with flour, making sure to remove any excess flour. Pour milk into a third bowl. Transfer chicken breasts from flour into milk, one at a time. Remove and put each breast into seasoned flour to coat. Heat a large frying pan with oil on medium-high heat. Place each piece of meat in oil and cook approximately 2 minutes on each side or until golden brown. When browned, place chicken on a baking sheet and bake 20 to 25 minutes, until temperature of chicken reaches 165 degrees F. on meat thermometer.

Sauce

½ cup butter	1 tablespoon paprika
1½ cup diced onions	½ teaspoon Worcestershire sauce
¾ cup flour	½ teaspoon Tabasco® sauce
8 cups milk	1 lemon, juiced
1½ teaspoons cayenne pepper	Salt and pepper to taste

Melt butter and sauté onions until translucent. Add flour and stir until smooth. Let cook until slightly browned, about 5 minutes. Add milk, cayenne, paprika, Worcestershire sauce, and Tabasco sauce. Simmer over medium heat until thickened. Add lemon juice and salt and pepper to taste. Pour over baked chicken just before serving. Garnish with diced bell peppers, if desired.

Wild Rice

Makes 6 servings

1 tablespoon butter	3 cups water
1 cup white rice	½ teaspoon salt
½ cup wild rice	

Melt butter in saucepan. Add white and wild rice and stir over medium heat until white rice begins to brown. Add water and salt. Bring to a boil. Cover and reduce heat to low. Cook for 15 to 20 minutes or until tender. Serve with chicken.

Chicken Royale

Makes 8 servings

8 boneless, skinless chicken breast halves
2 tablespoons butter
¼ cup chopped onion
¼ pound fresh mushrooms
2 tablespoons flour
1 cup light cream

1 cup sour cream
1 teaspoon lemon juice
8 slices cooked ham
½ of small package stuffing mix, made according to package directions, or make 2 cups of your own stuffing, using any favorite recipe

Preheat oven to 325 degrees F. Using a meat mallet or rolling pin, flatten each chicken breast between pieces of plastic wrap to about ⅛-inch thickness. In large frying pan, melt butter; cook onion and mushrooms, covered, until soft but not brown, about 10 minutes. Remove from pan and reserve. In same pan, brown flattened chicken breasts; add more butter or cooking oil if needed. Remove chicken pieces from pan and reserve.

Add flour to pan drippings and blend well. Gradually add light cream and sour cream. Heat well but do not boil, stirring constantly until mixture thickens. Add reserved onion and mushrooms, and lemon juice. Adjust seasonings to taste.

Grease a 9x13-inch baking dish. Cut ham slices to fit chicken breasts, and place ham slices in baking dish. Top each ham slice with about ¼ cup stuffing; then cover with a chicken piece. Pour sauce mixture over all. Bake 30 minutes or until hot and bubbly and chicken is fork tender.

Swiss Chicken

Makes 8 servings

8 boneless, skinless chicken breasts
4 to 8 slices Swiss cheese
1 (14.5-ounce) can chicken broth

1 (10.75-ounce) can cream of chicken soup
½ cup dry stuffing mix

Preheat oven to 350 degrees F. Place chicken breasts in a 9x13-inch baking dish. Top each chicken breast with ½ to 1 slice of Swiss cheese, according to taste. In a medium bowl, blend chicken broth with cream of chicken soup with a wire whisk. Pour soup mixture over chicken and cheese. Sprinkle 1 tablespoon dry stuffing mix over each chicken breast. Cover pan with foil and bake 1 hour.

Chicken Wellington

Makes 10 servings

10 (6-ounce) butterflied chicken breasts
1 recipe Stuffing (see below)
5 sheets frozen puff pastry dough, thawed

1 egg yolk, beaten
1 recipe Mushroom Sauce (see below)

Preheat oven to 300 degrees F. Lay one chicken breast on a clean surface. Place 2 tablespoons stuffing in the center of the breast. Roll the breast around the filling. Cut a sheet of thawed pastry dough in half. Place the rolled breast atop one half of the sheet and fold dough over the top of the breast, sealing the edges with a small amount of water. Cut excess dough from around the chicken, forming a crescent. Pinch dough around the edges to seal. Brush with egg yolk. Repeat with remaining chicken breasts. Bake 30 minutes. Serve immediately with Mushroom Sauce.

Stuffing

2 tablespoons butter
½ medium onion, peeled and diced
2 cloves garlic, crushed
1 cup diced, cooked ham

1½ cups diced mushrooms
1 teaspoon salt
½ teaspoon pepper

Melt butter in a large skillet over medium heat. Add remaining ingredients and cook until onions are tender. Remove from heat and drain off excess liquid.

Mushroom Sauce

Makes 12 (2-ounce) servings

½ cup sliced button mushrooms
1 medium yellow onion, peeled and diced
2 tablespoons butter
2 tablespoons flour

1 cup water
1½ cups heavy cream
¼ cup chicken stock
Egg color, as needed

Sauté mushrooms and onions in butter in a medium saucepan over medium heat. Add flour and sauté for 2 minutes. Do not burn flour. Slowly add water, mixing into a paste. When all the water is added and mixed well, add the cream and chicken stock. Slowly bring to a boil, stirring constantly. Be careful not to burn. Add 3 drops egg color to make a light yellow sauce. Strain through a mesh wire sieve to smooth sauce.

Parmesan Ranch Chicken

Parmesan Ranch Chicken

Makes 6 servings

½ cup cornflake crumbs
½ cup grated Parmesan cheese
1½ ounces dry ranch dressing mix

6 boneless chicken breasts
¾ cup shredded Parmesan cheese
26 ounces marinara or spaghetti sauce

Preheat oven to 300 degrees F. In shallow bowl, combine cornflake crumbs, ½ cup Parmesan cheese and ranch mix. Coat both sides of chicken with mix. Place in 9x13-inch pan sprayed with nonstick cooking spray. Spray tops of chicken with nonstick cooking spray to keep moist. Bake 25 to 30 minutes. Just prior to serving, sprinkle with remaining Parmesan. Heat marinara sauce and serve over cooked pasta and chicken.

Chicken Crêpes

Makes 6 servings

2 cups chopped cooked chicken
½ cup grated cheddar cheese
1 (15-ounce) can pineapple tidbits, drained (reserve juice)
½ cup chopped almonds
1 (10-ounce) can cream of chicken soup

½ cup reserved pineapple juice
½ teaspoon dried thyme
½ teaspoon lemon pepper
12 crêpes (see recipe on page 96)
1 recipe Chicken Glaze (see below)

Preheat oven to 200 degrees F. Mix chicken, grated cheese, pineapple tidbits, and almonds with chicken soup and reserved pineapple juice in a large bowl. Add thyme and lemon pepper and mix thoroughly. Place ¼ cup of the mixture in center of each crepe and roll. Place crepes with seam side down in greased baking pan. Cover with aluminum foil and heat in oven for 30 minutes. When ready to serve, arrange 2 crêpes for each serving. Spoon Chicken Glaze over crêpes.

Chicken Glaze

4 tablespoons butter
4 tablespoons flour
3 cups chicken stock

½ teaspoon dried basil
½ teaspoon dried rosemary
½ teaspoon rubbed sage

Make a roux by melting butter in a heavy saucepan over medium-high heat until foamy. Stir in flour to make a golden, bubbly paste. Gradually add chicken stock and seasonings and cook until thickened, about 5 minutes.

Chicken Fajitas

Makes 6 servings

6 boneless, skinless chicken breasts

1 cup water

1 package fajitas seasoning mix

2 tablespoons vegetable oil

2 onions, sliced

1 green pepper, sliced in strips

1 red pepper, sliced in strips

12 flour tortillas

Sour cream, for garnishing

Salsa, for garnishing (see recipe below)

Guacamole, for garnishing (see recipe below)

Limes, for garnishing

Cut chicken breasts into strips. Combine water and seasoning mix in a medium bowl and marinate strips for 2 hours in the refrigerator. Heat oil in a 12-inch skillet over medium-high heat and sauté onions and peppers until crisp-tender. Remove vegetables from pan and set aside. Place chicken strips in pan, reserving marinade. Sauté chicken until light brown. Add leftover marinade to the pan and simmer for five minutes. Return vegetables to pan and heat to mingle flavors. Spoon mixture onto warm tortillas. Fold over and garnish with sour cream, salsa, guacamole, and a slice of fresh lime.

Salsa

Makes 3 cups

2 cups chopped tomatoes

½ cup chopped onion

1 (4-ounce) can diced green chilies

1 clove garlic, minced

½ teaspoon salt

¼ teaspoon black pepper

¼ teaspoon cumin

1 tablespoon vinegar

¼ teaspoon crushed hot red pepper (optional)

Mix all ingredients in a medium bowl until well blended. Cover and refrigerate for at least 2 hours before serving. Or place all ingredients in blender and process for just a few seconds. The salsa should still be a little chunky, not smooth. Can be refrigerated for up to 1 week.

Guacamole

Makes about 1⅓ cups

2 large ripe avocados

1 tablespoon finely chopped green onion

½ teaspoon salt

Dash oregano

1½ tablespoons lemon juice

Few drops red pepper sauce (optional)

Chopped jalapeño peppers (optional)

Skin avocados and remove pits. Place in small bowl and mash with a fork. Add green onion, salt, and oregano; mash together thoroughly. Add lemon juice and mix again. For hot guacamole, add red pepper sauce or jalapeño peppers according to taste.

Cold Chicken Salad on a Croissant

Makes 20 croissants

20 croissants

4 pounds boneless, skinless chicken breasts

2 tablespoons salt

½ cup diced onion

½ cup diced celery

¾ cup walnuts, chopped

1½ cups mayonnaise

Salt and white pepper to taste

Fill a large stockpot with water and 2 tablespoons of salt. Bring to a boil. Place the chicken breasts in the boiling water and cook until the juices run clear or the temperature registers 165 degrees F. on a meat thermometer.

Remove the pot from the stove. Remove the chicken from the pot and place in a large glass baking dish, spreading the chicken out to help it cool. Place the chicken breasts in the refrigerator for 4 hours or until the chicken is completely cooled.

In a large bowl combine the onion, celery, walnuts, mayonnaise, and salt and pepper. Mix with a large spoon. Cut the cooled chicken into strips. Mix the cut chicken with the ingredients already in the bowl. Season with additional salt and white pepper to taste. Chicken salad can be made up to 1 day in advance. Holding the salad any longer will bring out the unpleasant aftertaste of onion. Store in the refrigerator until ready to serve. Serve on a croissant.

Santa Fe Chicken

Santa Fe Chicken

Makes 8 to 12 servings

2 (8-ounce) packages cream cheese

1 cup green chilies

8 to 12 (7-ounce) boneless, skinless chicken breasts, butterflied

3 cups cornflake crumbs

Preheat oven to 350 degrees F. Mix cream cheese and chilies until soft. Bread one side of each breast with crumbs. Holding breaded side down in your hand, place one heaping tablespoon cream cheese mixture on chicken and wrap chicken around mixture. Bake on a large baking sheet until chicken is done, about 20 to 25 minutes.

Chicken Taco Pie

Makes 6 to 8 servings

1 cup chopped onion

2 tablespoons cooking oil

2 tablespoons taco seasoning (or to taste)

1¾ tablespoons chili powder

1 teaspoon salt

¼ teaspoon pepper

3 (10.5 ounce) cans cream of mushroom soup

1½ cups sour cream

3 cups cubed cooked chicken

6 to 8 corn tortillas, oiled and torn in pieces

1 cup shredded Monterey Jack cheese

Preheat oven to 350 degrees F. In skillet, cook onion in oil until tender but not brown. Add seasonings, cream of mushroom soup, and sour cream; heat and stir until smooth and warm. Add chicken. Grease a 2- to 3-quart flat casserole and cover bottom of pan with half of the torn-up oiled tortillas. Spread half the chicken mixture on tortillas. Top with additional oiled tortillas, then cover with remaining filling. Sprinkle with shredded cheese. Bake until hot and bubbly, about 10 minutes.

Thyme-on-Your-Hands Chicken

Makes 4 servings

1 (4- to 5-pound) chicken, quartered
1 lemon
2 tablespoons fresh thyme leaves, or 1 tablespoon dry
  thyme leaves

Kosher salt
Cracked black pepper

Preheat oven to 350 degrees F. Place chicken quarters in lightly oiled roasting pan large enough that pieces do not touch. Squeeze juice of one lemon over chicken and leave lemon peel in pan. Rub thyme leaves over chicken. Sprinkle with salt and pepper. Roast until chicken is cooked thoroughly, about 30 to 45 minutes.

Orange Chicken

Makes 6 to 8 servings

½ cup flour
2 teaspoons salt
¼ teaspoon pepper
6 to 8 chicken breasts, skin on
⅓ cup butter, melted
1 onion, thinly sliced

1 (6-ounce) can frozen orange juice concentrate
1 juice can water
¼ cup brown sugar
½ teaspoon nutmeg
2 tablespoons cornstarch

Preheat oven to 375 degrees F. Combine flour, salt, and pepper in plastic bag. Add chicken breasts and shake to coat well. Place chicken breasts in baking pan, skin side up and brush with melted butter. Bake 40 minutes. Remove chicken to 2-quart casserole and spread onions generously over surface. Combine orange juice, water, brown sugar, nutmeg, and cornstarch. Pour over chicken. Cover with foil, reduce oven temperature to 325 degrees F., and bake 30 minutes or until fork tender.

Thyme-on-Your Hands Chicken

Hawaiian Chicken

Hawaiian Chicken

Makes 4 to 6 servings

4 to 6 boneless, skinless chicken breasts
Flour
Salt
Cooking oil
1 (15.5-ounce) can pineapple chunks
½ cup honey
2 tablespoons cornstarch

¾ cup cider vinegar
1 tablespoon soy sauce
¼ teaspoon ginger
1 chicken bouillon cube
1 green pepper, cut in ¼-inch strips
2 to 3 cups hot, cooked rice

Preheat oven to 350 degrees F. Roll chicken pieces in flour and sprinkle with salt. Heat oil in a large skillet to almost smoking, add chicken breasts, and cook until golden brown. Turn over and brown other side. Remove from heat and transfer chicken to a 2-quart casserole, leaving drippings in the pan. Drain pineapple, reserve pineapple chunks, and pour juice into measuring cup. Add enough water to make 1½ cups. Add pineapple juice, honey, cornstarch, vinegar, soy sauce, ginger, and bouillon cube to drippings in pan; bring to a boil. Cook 2 minutes, stirring constantly. Pour over chicken pieces and bake uncovered 20 minutes. Add pineapple chunks and green pepper; bake 5 minutes longer. Serve with cooked rice.

Sweet and Sour Chicken

Makes 6 servings

6 boneless, skinless chicken breasts
1 teaspoon garlic salt
½ teaspoon black pepper
1 tablespoon vegetable oil
1 egg, beaten well
4 to 6 tablespoons cornstarch or flour

¾ cup sugar
½ cup cider vinegar
½ cup chicken stock
3½ tablespoons ketchup
1 tablespoon soy sauce

Sprinkle chicken with garlic salt and pepper. Refrigerate for at least one hour. Preheat oven to 325 degrees F. Heat oil in a 12-inch skillet over medium-high heat. Put beaten egg in a shallow dish; place cornstarch or flour in a second shallow dish. Dip chicken in beaten egg, then in cornstarch or flour. Place chicken in hot oil and brown on both sides. Place chicken in baking dish and set aside.

Prepare sweet and sour sauce by mixing sugar, vinegar, chicken stock, ketchup, and soy sauce in a medium saucepan and heating until sugar is dissolved. Pour over chicken. Bake uncovered for 1 hour. Turn chicken once or twice during baking time.

Roast Turkey

To buy: When buying turkeys under 12 pounds, allow about ¾ pound per serving. For turkeys 12 pounds and over, allow about ½ pound per serving.

To thaw: If the turkey is frozen, leave in original bag and thaw in refrigerator for 3 to 4 days. Cook as soon as thawed.

To roast: Remove plastic wrap; remove giblets and neck from body cavities. Rinse turkey inside and out, and pat dry with paper towel. Stuff turkey just before roasting—not ahead of time. Fill wishbone area first. Fasten neck skin to back with skewer. Fold wings across back with tips touching. Fill body cavity lightly. Tuck drumsticks under band of skin at the tail or tie together with heavy string, then tie tail. Place turkey, breast-side up, on rack in shallow roasting pan. Roast uncovered at 325 degrees F. Season turkey with favorite seasonings. When turkey begins to turn golden, cover with tent of foil to prevent over-browning.

Approximate Cooking Times for Ready-to-Cook Turkey

8 to 12 pounds: 3 to 4½ hours

12 to 16 pounds: 4½ to 5½ hours

16 to 20 pounds: 5½ to 6½ hours

20 to 24 pounds: 6½ to 7½ hours

Internal Temperature: 185 degrees

To serve: Remove turkey from oven and allow to stand about 20 minutes. Use drippings for gravy. Remove stuffing from turkey. Carve and serve. Refrigerate leftovers as soon as possible after serving.

Old-Fashioned Savory Stuffing

Makes enough stuffing for a 14- to 18-pound bird

4 cups diced celery	1½ teaspoons poultry seasoning
1 cup chopped onion	½ teaspoon sage
1 cup butter or margarine	½ teaspoon pepper
16 cups dry bread cubes	¾ to 1 cup hot broth or water
1 tablespoon salt	

Sauté celery and onion in butter in a large skillet. Combine with bread cubes and seasonings; toss lightly. Add enough broth to moisten as desired.

Giblet Stuffing: Add chopped, cooked giblets; use giblet broth as liquid.

Oyster Stuffing: Add 2 (8-ounce) cans oysters, drained and chopped.

Chestnut Stuffing: Add 1 pound fresh chestnuts. Prepare chestnuts by slashing shells with a sharp knife. Roast on baking sheet at 400 degrees for 15 minutes; cool. Peel and coarsely chop chestnuts; then add to stuffing.

Roast Turkey

Hot Turkey Salad Supreme

Makes 6 to 8 servings

2 cups diced cooked turkey
2 cups chopped celery
½ teaspoon salt
2 tablespoons minced onion
2 tablespoons lemon juice
1 cup mayonnaise

¾ cup grated cheddar cheese
1 cup crushed potato chips
½ cup slivered almonds
Leaf lettuce, for serving
Lemon wedges and parsley sprigs, for garnishing

Preheat oven to 350 degrees F. Mix turkey, celery, salt, onion, and lemon juice in a medium bowl. Fold in mayonnaise and spoon into a greased casserole dish. Sprinkle grated cheese on top, followed by crushed potato chips and slivered almonds. Bake for 15 minutes. Don't overbake; mayonnaise will break down. Serve on lettuce leaves and garnish with lemon wedges and parsley.

Pioneer Turkey Bake

Makes 6 servings

2 cups cubed cooked turkey
1 (6-ounce) package wild rice mix
½ cup chopped celery
2 tablespoons chopped onion
1 (4-ounce) can sliced mushrooms, drained

1 (10-ounce) can cream of chicken soup
1 teaspoon Worcestershire sauce
1¼ cups water
¼ cup slivered almonds

Preheat oven to 350 degrees F. Combine turkey with wild rice mix, including contents of seasoning packet. Add remaining ingredients and mix well. Pour into a 1½-quart casserole. Bake covered for 45 minutes.

Turkey Tetrazzini

Makes 8 servings

8 ounces spaghetti, broken in pieces
5 tablespoons butter or margarine
6 tablespoons flour
3 cups chicken or turkey broth
1 cup light cream
1 teaspoon salt

Pepper
1 cup fresh or canned mushrooms, including liquid
5 tablespoons minced green peppers
3 cups cooked cubed turkey
½ cup grated Parmesan cheese
½ cup shredded cheddar cheese

Preheat oven to 350 degrees F. Cook spaghetti in boiling salted water until just tender (do not overcook). Melt butter; blend in flour. Stir broth into flour mixture. Add cream. Cook until mixture thickens and bubbles. Add salt and pepper, cooked spaghetti, mushrooms, green peppers, and cooked turkey. Turn into individual baking dishes or into a 2- to 3-quart flat casserole. Sprinkle with cheeses. Bake 30 minutes or until bubbly and lightly browned.

Roast Turkey Breast Sandwiches with Apricot Cranberry Relish

Makes 20 sandwiches

Relish
Makes 20 (2-ounce) servings

3½ cups fresh cranberries

1 cup canned apricot nectar

1 cup sugar

2 tablespoons dried cranberries

2 tablespoons thinly sliced dried apricots

½ teaspoon pure vanilla extract

In a medium stainless steel saucepan, combine the cranberries, apricot nectar, and sugar and bring to a boil over moderately high heat. Reduce the heat to low, add the dried cranberries and apricots, cover and cook, stirring occasionally, until slightly reduced, about 20 minutes.

Drain the cranberries, reserving ¼ cup of the cooking liquid. Stir the vanilla into the reserved liquid. Add the drained fruits and let cool.

Sandwiches

40 slices whole wheat bread, toasted

4 pounds turkey breast, sliced

Salt and freshly ground white pepper to taste

80 scallions, green part only

40 romaine lettuce leaves

Spread 2 slices of the bread with about 1½ tablespoons each of the relish. Layer the turkey on the relish and season with salt and pepper. Top with the scallions, romaine lettuce, and the remaining bread.

The relish can be refrigerated for up to 1 week. The sandwiches can be refrigerated for up to 3 hours.

Rossini Tournedos

Makes 10 servings

5 pounds tenderloin of beef, center cut
Salt and pepper
Melted butter

1 recipe Bordelaise Sauce (see below)
1 recipe Bearnaise Sauce (see below)

Preheat oven to 450 degrees F. Cut raw beef into diagonal slices, about 1-inch thick, then cut each slice in half to make 2 small, thick steaks. Rub each slice with salt and pepper. Place in single layer in shallow roasting pan. Brush with melted butter. Bake 10 minutes (or to desired doneness), without turning. Serve both halves of the slice on dinner plate, with generous spoonful of Bordelaise Sauce on one half and Bearnaise Sauce on the other.

Bordelaise Sauce

Makes about 1 cup

2 tablespoons butter
1 onion, thinly sliced
2 tablespoons flour
1 cup beef broth
¼ teaspoon salt

⅛ teaspoon pepper
1 tablespoon chopped parsley
1 bay leaf, crushed
¼ teaspoon thyme

Heat butter in frying pan until golden brown. Add onion and cook until tender. Blend in flour and cook until a deep brown color. Remove from heat and stir in broth; stir and boil for 1 minute. Add salt, pepper, parsley, bay leaf, and thyme. Serve with Rossini Tournedos.

Note: For an excellent variation, add ¼ pound sliced mushrooms sautéed in 2 tablespoons butter.

Bearnaise Sauce

Makes 1 cup

½ cup apple juice
2 tablespoons white vinegar
2 small green onions, chopped
1 tablespoon crushed dried tarragon
¼ teaspoon pepper

3 egg yolks, beaten
½ cup butter, melted
2 teaspoons lemon juice
¼ teaspoon salt
Dash cayenne pepper

In small, heavy saucepan, combine apple juice, vinegar, onions, tarragon, and pepper. Boil until mixture is reduced by half, or to about ½ cup. Add gradually to egg yolks, stirring well to blend. Return to heat and cook until thickened and creamy, stirring constantly. Beat in butter, lemon juice, salt, and cayenne pepper. Serve with Rossini Tournedos.

Beef and Seven Vegetables

Makes 8 servings

1 tablespoon cooking oil

3 cups sliced cooked roast beef (about 1½x2-inch strips), or
    1½ pounds fresh lean beef, cut into strips

2½ cups thinly sliced carrots

1½ cups sliced green pepper

1½ cups sliced onion

2½ cups slant-cut celery

1 (4-ounce) can bamboo shoots, drained

4 cups beef stock, or 4 beef bouillon cubes and 4 cups
    water

½ to ¾ cup soy sauce

3 tablespoons cornstarch in ¼ cup cold water

15 cherry tomatoes

1 cup fresh or frozen snow peas, or broccoli florets

4 cups hot, cooked rice or Chinese noodles

Heat oil in frying pan. Add beef and brown lightly; remove meat. Add carrots and green pepper to pan; stir-fry for 1 minute. Add onions and celery; stir-fry for 1 minute. Add bamboo shoots. Remove vegetables and keep warm. Vegetables should remain crisp.

In heavy pot, bring soup stock and soy sauce to a gentle boil; thicken with cornstarch-water mixture. Add tomatoes, snow peas or broccoli, stir-fried vegetables, and meat; heat gently. Serve over rice or Chinese noodles.

Ginger Beef

Makes 6 to 8 servings

2 pounds beef round steak

2 cloves garlic

Dash of black pepper

1 (10-ounce) can beef broth

2 tablespoons cornstarch

¼ cup water

1 tablespoon soy sauce

¼ teaspoon crushed fresh ginger root

1 package frozen Chinese peapods or ¾ pound fresh
    peapods

2 to 3 cups hot cooked rice

Cherry tomatoes, for garnishing

Trim fat from meat, then cut meat into thin strips. Coat a 12-inch skillet with nonstick cooking spray. Peel garlic and make several cuts on end of each clove; cook and stir in skillet over medium heat until browned. Remove and discard. In skillet in which garlic has been browned, cook meat over medium-high heat until browned, stirring occasionally. Sprinkle beef with pepper. Stir in broth and heat to boiling. Reduce heat and simmer uncovered until meat is tender, 10 to 15 minutes. (Add small amount of water if necessary.) Mix cornstarch, water, and soy sauce in a small bowl; stir into meat mixture. Cook, stirring constantly, until mixture thickens and boils. Boil and stir 1 minute. Stir in crushed gingerroot and peapods. Cook, stirring occasionally, until peapods are crisp-tender, about 5 minutes. Serve over rice. Garnish with cherry tomatoes.

Beef and Seven Vegetables

Roulade of Beef

Makes 24 (8-ounce) servings

2 zucchini	2 carrots
2 onions	2 (5-pound) eye of round roasts
2 yellow squash	Salt and pepper to taste
2 red bell peppers	4 feet butcher's twine
2 green bell peppers	¼ cup vegetable oil

Preheat oven to 300 degrees F. Slice all vegetables lengthwise into ¼-inch strips (about the size and shape of a French fry). Reserve vegetables in refrigerator.

To prepare beef, first trim fat from roasts. Make a ¼-inch-deep cut down the length of each roast, running with the grain. Turn each roast so that the cut is ¼ inch above the cutting surface and begin to peel away the outside layer while rolling the beef away from the cut. Continue cutting and unrolling until you are left with a large sheet of meat. Place a layer of plastic wrap over the meat and use a mallet to tenderize and flatten it. (Tenderizing will help to expand the sheet of beef and smooth out any uneven spots left from cutting.) Season the beef with salt and pepper.

Arrange half the sliced vegetables in a pattern of colors on each sheet of beef so that they lie with the grain. Beginning at one edge, roll the beef so that the vegetables lie lengthwise in each roll. Placing the seam down, begin tying the beef with butcher's twine. Gently slide the string under each roll. Wrap the string around each roll and tie it tightly, placing one tie every 1½ to 2 inches.

Heat ¼ cup oil in large skillet or roasting pan. Brown beef rolls on all sides. Roast until rolls reach an internal temperature of 145 degrees F. Remove rolls from pan and allow to rest for 10 to 15 minutes.

In cooking pan, make sauce by bringing drippings to a boil and thickening with a mixture of cornstarch and water. Season to taste with salt and pepper. Slice the roulade across the grain to reveal the colorful spiral of vegetables. Top with the pan sauce and serve immediately.

New York Steak

Makes 5 servings

5 (6-ounce) New York steaks, cut by butcher
2 teaspoons salt

1 teaspoon white pepper
½ teaspoon garlic powder

Heat an electric or gas grill. Mix the salt, pepper, and garlic powder in a small bowl. Place the steaks on a large aluminum sheet tray. Sprinkle each steak with the salt mixture. Grill steaks only long enough to sear grill marks onto them. When the marks are seared on, turn the steaks 90 degrees to make a square grid on each steak. Do not grill the steaks long enough to completely cook them. Once marked, place each steak back on the tray. The steaks may be stored in the refrigerator for up to 4 hours before serving. Approximately 15 minutes before serving, heat an oven to 350 degrees F. Bake the steaks approximately 8 to 10 minutes, depending on how well done you prefer them.

Party Swiss Steak

Makes 8 to 10 servings

4 pounds beef round, top or bottom, cut about ½-inch thick
¾ cup flour, divided
4 to 6 tablespoons shortening
1 tablespoon salt
¼ teaspoon pepper
½ teaspoon thyme

2 cups water
1 cup chopped celery
1 cup chopped green pepper
2 (14.5-ounce) cans stewed tomatoes
½ pound mozzarella cheese, thinly sliced

Preheat oven to 325 degrees F. Cut meat into serving-size pieces. Place ½ cup of the flour in a shallow bowl. Melt shortening in a large skillet over medium heat. Dredge steaks in flour then brown in hot shortening. Remove meat to large Dutch oven or roasting pan. Blend remaining flour with hot drippings; add seasonings. Gradually blend in water. Add vegetables. Cook and stir until slightly thickened. Pour mixture over meat and bake 2½ to 3 hours, or until meat is tender. Top with slices of cheese. Return to oven just until cheese melts. Serve at once.

Savory Steak Italia

Makes 6 servings

1½ pounds round steak, ¾-inch thick, cut into 6 portions
3 tablespoons flour
1 teaspoon salt
¼ teaspoon oregano

¼ teaspoon pepper (or to taste)
1 (15.5-ounce) can spaghetti sauce with mushrooms
1 (9-ounce) package frozen Italian green beans
1 (6-ounce) can whole onions, drained

Preheat oven to 375 degrees F. Rub steaks with ⅓ of a mixture of flour, salt, oregano, and pepper; reserve remainder of mixture for sauce. In large skillet over medium heat, brown both sides of steaks in small amount of hot cooking oil. Remove browned pieces to shallow baking dish (about 11x7 inches). Heat sauce and remaining flour mixture to boiling, stirring constantly. Pour over steak; cover, and bake 45 minutes. Add vegetables; cover and bake another 45 minutes or until meat is tender.

Chateaubriand (Roast Beef Tenderloin)

Makes about 10 servings

5 pounds tenderloin of beef, center cut
Garlic (optional)
Salt

Soft butter, or 3 strips bacon
1 recipe Bordelaise or Bearnaise Sauce (see page 151)

Preheat oven to 450 degrees F. Trim excess fat or connective tissue from meat. Place meat in shallow roasting pan; rub with cut garlic and salt. Brush with soft butter or top with half strips of bacon. Bake 45 to 60 minutes (until meat is red to pink inside). Slit meat with tip of paring knife to check doneness. (Or use a meat thermometer and cook to desired doneness.)

Remove meat to warm platter and slice diagonally in about ½-inch-thick slices. Serve two slices per person, with Bordelaise Sauce or Bearnaise Sauce. Also good served with mushrooms that have been sliced and sautéed in butter.

Beef Tenderloin

Makes 5 servings

5 (5-ounce) filet mignon steaks, cut by butcher
2 teaspoons salt

1 teaspoon white pepper
½ teaspoon garlic powder

Heat an electric or gas grill. Mix the salt, pepper, and garlic powder in a small bowl.

Place the steaks on a large aluminum sheet tray. Sprinkle each steak with the salt mixture. Grill steaks only long enough to sear grill marks onto the meat. When the marks are seared on, turn the steaks 90 degrees to make a square grid on each steak. Do not grill the steaks long enough to completely cook them.

Once marked, place each steak back on the tray. The steaks may be stored in the refrigerator for up to 4 hours before serving.

Approximately 15 minutes before serving, heat an oven to 350 degrees F. Bake the steaks approximately 8 to 10 minutes, depending on how well done you prefer them.

Beef Wellington

Makes 6 to 8 servings

3½ to 4 pounds beef tenderloin
1 recipe Lion House Pie Crust (see page 216)

8 ounces liver sausage or liver paté
1 egg, beaten slightly

Place meat on rack in shallow roasting pan and roast uncovered at 425 degrees for 20 to 30 minutes, till rare to medium. Remove from oven and let stand for 30 minutes.

In the meantime, make Lion House Pie Crust for 9-inch double-crust pie. Roll dough into an 18x14-inch rectangle, ¼-inch thick. Spread paté on pastry, then place cooked tenderloin lengthwise, top side down, in center of pastry. Bring long sides of pastry up over bottom of tenderloin; brush with egg and seal the two sides together. Trim ends of pastry and fold over; brush with egg and seal.

Carefully transfer pastry-wrapped meat, seam side down, to baking sheet. Cut decorative shapes from pastry trimmings and arrange on top. Brush egg over all. Bake at 425 degrees for 30 minutes or until delicately browned. Let stand 10 minutes before carving.

Roast Beef and Yorkshire Pudding

Makes 8 servings

1 (5- to 7-pound) standing rib roast of beef
½ teaspoon salt

⅛ teaspoon pepper

Preheat oven to 325 degrees F. Wipe beef well with damp cloth. Rub the lean portion with salt and pepper. Insert oven-safe meat thermometer through outside fat into thickest part of muscle. Be careful that tip of thermometer does not touch bone. Place roast in shallow roasting pan and roast until internal temperature reaches 140 degrees for rare (about 20 minutes per pound), 160 degrees for medium (about 25 minutes per pound), or 170 degrees for well done (about 30 minutes per pound).

When roast is done, remove from oven to warm platter and increase oven temperature to 425 degrees F. Reserve meat drippings. Keep meat warm while making pudding and gravy. Let meat stand a while for easier slicing.

Yorkshire Pudding with Gravy

2 eggs
1 cup milk
1 cup sifted flour

½ teaspoon salt
Roast beef drippings
Roux (see page 20)

Preheat oven to 425 degrees F. Beat eggs, milk, flour, and salt until batter is smooth and creamy. Pour 2 tablespoons of the drippings into a 10-inch pie pan and tilt so drippings cover bottom of pan. Pour in batter. Bake about 25 minutes or until pudding is puffed and nicely browned. While pudding cooks, make gravy.

For gravy: Using the remaining meat drippings, add roux to thicken. Dilute with water or beef broth, if necessary, to reach desired consistency. When pudding is finished, serve immediately with roast beef.

Beef Enchiladas

Beef Enchiladas

Makes 12 enchiladas

Sauce

3 (8-ounce) cans tomato sauce

1 (14.5-ounce) can chili con carne without beans

1 (14.5-ounce) can kidney beans, ground

3 cups tomato juice

1 teaspoon basil

1 teaspoon chili powder

1 teaspoon oregano

½ teaspoon crushed red pepper

Mix all ingredients together in saucepan. Simmer on low heat for 30 minutes.

Filling

1 pound lean ground beef

½ cup tomato sauce

1 tablespoon taco seasoning

1 teaspoon crushed red pepper

2 teaspoons oregano

Dash Tabasco® sauce

12 corn tortillas

1 cup grated cheddar cheese, plus additional for topping

¼ cup ground onion

Preheat oven to 350 degrees F. Brown ground beef in skillet. Add tomato sauce, taco seasoning, red pepper, oregano, and Tabasco sauce. Mix thoroughly. Divide beef mixture evenly onto corn tortillas. Sprinkle cheese and ground onion over beef mixture; roll up tortillas. Place seam side down in baking dish. Pour sauce over top. Bake 30 minutes. Sprinkle with additional cheese just before serving.

Beef Goulash

Makes 4 to 6 hearty servings

2 pounds beef chuck, cut into cubes about 1½ inches square

2 tablespoons oil

2 large onions, chopped

½ cup canned tomato soup

2 bouillon cubes, or 2 teaspoons soup base

1½ cups water

1 tablespoon paprika

1 teaspoon vinegar

Cooked noodles

Brown meat in oil in skillet; remove from pan. Cook onions in same skillet until golden brown. Add meat, tomato soup, bouillon cubes, water, paprika, and vinegar; stir to mix. Lower heat and simmer about 2 hours or until meat is very tender. Serve with noodles. May also be cooked in a slow cooker, 6 to 8 hours on low heat.

Beef Pastries

Makes 6 servings

1 recipe Pastry for Double Crust Pie (see page 216)
1 pound lean ground beef
1 small can mushrooms, undrained
½ cup chopped onions
½ cup chopped celery

3 tablespoons sweet pickle relish
1 (10.5-ounce) can cream of mushroom soup
1 (10-ounce) can beef gravy, or about 1½ cups leftover gravy

Preheat oven to 500 degrees F. Roll out half of pastry dough and cut out 6 five-inch circles. Combine ground beef, mushrooms, onions, and celery. Cook in frying pan until meat loses its color; drain. Add pickle relish and soup. Place a large scoop of meat mixture in center of each pastry circle.

Roll out remaining pastry and cut out another 6 circles. Roll each of these circles a little larger than the first 6. Place over meat filling, moisten, and seal edges. Bake 10 minutes or until golden brown. Serve topped with beef gravy.

Party Lasagna

Makes 12 to 15 servings

1½ pounds ground beef
1½ tablespoons vegetable oil
1 clove garlic, minced
3 tablespoons parsley flakes, divided
1 tablespoon dried basil
2 teaspoons salt
1 (20-ounce) can stewed tomatoes

1 (6-ounce) can tomato paste
1 (10-ounce) package lasagna noodles
3 cups large curd cottage cheese
2 eggs, beaten well
½ teaspoon pepper
½ cup grated Parmesan cheese
1 pound mozzarella cheese, thinly sliced

Preheat oven to 375 degrees F. Brown ground beef in oil in a 12-inch skillet; drain off fat. Add garlic, 1 tablespoon parsley flakes, basil, and salt. Stir in tomatoes and tomato paste. Simmer uncovered until thick, about one hour, stirring occasionally.

Cook lasagna noodles as directed on package; drain and rinse in cold water. Mix cottage cheese with beaten eggs, pepper, 2 tablespoons parsley flakes, and Parmesan cheese. Place half of noodles in 9x13-inch baking pan. Spoon on half the cottage cheese mixture. Top cottage cheese with a layer of sliced mozzarella cheese, then spoon on a layer of meat mixture. Repeat layers, ending with layer of mozzarella on top. Bake 30 minutes.

Shepherd's Pie

Makes 6 servings

1 (10-ounce) can gravy, or about 1½ cups leftover gravy

1 cup cubed leftover roast lamb or beef

¾ cup sliced carrots, parboiled

½ cup chopped onions, parboiled

½ cup chopped celery, parboiled

½ cup frozen peas

Salt and pepper to taste

3 potatoes, boiled, drained and mashed; or 3 cups mashed potatoes from dehydrated potato flakes or granules

½ cup grated cheese

Preheat oven to 350 degrees F. Combine gravy, meat, carrots, onions, celery, and peas. Adjust seasonings to taste. Place mixture in 8x8-inch baking pan. "Frost" top with mashed potatoes; sprinkle with cheese. Bake until cheese melts and mixture bubbles, about 20 minutes.

Note: To use raw meat rather than leftover cooked meat, brown ½ pound lamb or beef cubes in a little cooking oil, then add water to cover; add carrots, onions, and celery after meat has simmered about 1 hour. Cook until meat and vegetables are tender. Thicken with about 2 tablespoons flour shaken with ½ cup cold water in ½-pint jar. Proceed as above.

Lion House Meat Loaf

Makes 8 to 10 servings

2 pounds lean ground beef

1 teaspoon salt

3 eggs, beaten slightly

¾ cup dry bread crumbs

1 recipe Meat Loaf Sauce (see below)

Preheat oven to 350 degrees F. Mix ground beef, salt, eggs, bread crumbs, and half the sauce until well blended. Mold into one large or two small loaf pans. Bake 1½ hours for large loaf or 1 hour for smaller ones. Remove from oven and allow to stand for about 10 minutes for easier slicing. Serve with remaining sauce.

Meat Loaf Sauce

½ cup chopped onion

2 tablespoons shortening

1 (10.5-ounce) can tomato soup

1 teaspoon Worcestershire sauce

Dash pepper

¼ cup water

Sauté onion in shortening until tender. Add soup, Worcestershire sauce, pepper, and water. Simmer a few minutes to blend flavors.

Stuffed Green Peppers

Makes 6 servings

6 green bell peppers
1 pound ground beef
1 small onion, chopped
½ cup chopped celery
1 (10½-ounce) can cream of mushroom soup
½ teaspoon dried oregano

½ teaspoon chili powder
½ teaspoon dried basil
½ teaspoon salt
1½ cups cooked rice
1 (10½-ounce) can tomato soup
1 (8-ounce) can tomato sauce

Preheat oven to 350 degrees F. Cut tops from green peppers; discard seeds. Cook peppers in small amount of boiling water for 5 minutes. Drain and arrange in a casserole dish; set aside. Brown ground beef and onion in a large skillet; drain off fat. Add celery, cream of mushroom soup, oregano, chili powder, basil, salt, and rice to ground beef. Mix well and spoon into green peppers. Combine tomato soup and tomato sauce in a small dish and pour over top of stuffed peppers. Bake 30 minutes.

Stir-Fried Beef and Peppers

Makes 4 to 6 servings

1 pound lean beef, cut in paper-thin strips (beef is easier to cut if partially frozen)
3 tablespoons soy sauce
1 tablespoon lemon juice
4 teaspoons cornstarch
¼ teaspoon sugar

⅛ teaspoon ground ginger
½ cup salad oil
½ pound mushrooms, thickly sliced
2 medium onions, quartered
2 small green peppers, cut in squares or strips
½ teaspoon salt

Combine meat strips with soy sauce, lemon juice, cornstarch, sugar, and ginger. Let stand while preparing vegetables.

Heat salad oil in large frying pan or Dutch oven. Stir-fry mushrooms, onions, green peppers, and salt until vegetables are tender-crisp, about 5 minutes. Remove vegetables from pan and reserve oil.

Stir-fry meat mixture in the hot oil a minute or two, until it loses its pink color. Add vegetables and stir until hot. Serve with cooked rice.

Stuffed Green Peppers

Zucchini with Ground Beef

Makes 8 servings, 2 stuffed shells each

8 medium zucchini
1 pound lean ground beef
1 medium onion, chopped
1 clove garlic
2 tablespoons chopped green pepper
1 tablespoon salad oil

Pinch each salt, rosemary, thyme, marjoram, pepper
½ cup grated Parmesan cheese
⅔ cup cracker crumbs
1 (8-ounce) can tomato sauce
½ cup water
1 bouillon cube

Preheat oven to 350 degrees F. Wash zucchini; boil in salted water 10 minutes. Cut lengthwise in halves and scoop out insides. Drain scooped-out portion and mash well. Sauté beef, onion, garlic, and green pepper in oil for 5 minutes. Stir with fork; add zucchini pulp, salt, herbs, all but 2 tablespoons cheese, and all but 2 tablespoons crumbs. Heap mixture into zucchini shells. Place in shallow baking dish. Heat tomato sauce, water, and bouillon cube until cube is dissolved. Pour over zucchini. Sprinkle with remaining cheese and crumbs. Bake 45 minutes, basting once or twice.

Sweet and Sour Beef

Makes 5 servings

1 pound tender lean beef, cut into thin strips (beef is easier to cut if partially frozen)
1 tablespoon cooking oil
1 recipe Sweet and Sour Sauce (see below)

1 green pepper, cut into ¼-inch strips
1 (15-ounce) can pineapple chunks, drained (reserve juice for sauce)
Hot cooked rice

Lightly brown in oil half of meat strips at a time. Add sweet and sour sauce and green pepper to meat strips; heat together until green pepper wilts but does not lose its color. Add pineapple chunks. Reheat and serve over cooked rice.

Sweet and Sour Sauce

2 tablespoons cornstarch
6 tablespoons sugar
Pineapple juice from above with water added to make 1½ cups

3 tablespoons vinegar
2 tablespoons soy sauce (or to taste)

Mix cornstarch with sugar. Add pineapple-water mixture, vinegar, and soy sauce. Boil together until thickened.

Beef Stroganoff

Makes about 5 cups, or 4 to 5 servings

1 clove garlic, cut in quarters
3 tablespoons olive oil or salad oil
1½ pounds lean round or sirloin steak, cut into thin bite-sized strips (1-inch long x ¼-inch thick)
¼ to ⅓ cup chopped onion
¾ to 1 teaspoon salt
⅛ teaspoon pepper

½ pound fresh mushrooms, washed and sliced
¼ cup flour
1½ to 2 cups milk
½ to 1 teaspoon paprika
1 cup sour cream
Hot cooked rice or cooked noodles

In heavy skillet, heat garlic in oil for a few minutes, then remove and discard garlic. Add meat to skillet; brown slightly. Add onion, salt, and pepper. Cover and cook slowly for 35 to 45 minutes or until meat is completely tender, turning occasionally. Add more oil or water during cooking, if necessary. Add mushrooms. Cover and cook gently until mushrooms are tender, about 10 minutes.

With slotted spoon, remove meat and mushrooms to top of double boiler. Blend flour into drippings in pan. Slowly stir in milk. Cook and stir over medium heat until mixture thickens. Sprinkle in paprika until sauce is a light pink color. Add sauce to meat and mushroom mixture in double boiler. Add sour cream. Mix and heat well before serving, but do not boil. Adjust seasonings to taste. Serve over rice.

Ground Beef Stroganoff

Makes 4 to 6 servings

½ cup chopped onion
1 small clove garlic, minced
1 tablespoon butter or margarine
1 pound ground beef
2 tablespoons flour
1 teaspoon salt

¼ teaspoon pepper
¼ teaspoon paprika
1 cup sliced mushrooms
1 (10.5-ounce) can cream of mushroom soup
1 cup sour cream
Cooked rice or noodles

Sauté onion and garlic in a little butter or margarine in hot skillet. Stir in meat, flour, and seasonings; sauté about 5 minutes or until meat loses its color. Add mushrooms, then soup; simmer about 10 minutes. Stir in sour cream and heat, but do not boil. Add a little milk if needed. Season to taste. Serve on hot rice or noodles.

Sweet and Sour Pork

Sweet and Sour Pork

Makes 8 to 10 servings

2 pounds lean pork loin, about ½-inch thick
2 tablespoons cornstarch
¼ cup soy sauce
3 tablespoons oil
2 cups chopped carrots
3 small onions, cut in quarters
1 green pepper, cut in strips

1 (20-ounce) can pineapple chunks, drained
3 tablespoons cornstarch
3 tablespoons brown sugar
2 cups pineapple juice
¼ cup vinegar
⅓ cup soy sauce
Cooked rice

Cut pork into 2-inch strips. Mix 2 tablespoons cornstarch and ¼ cup soy sauce. Marinate pork in this mixture for 1 to 2 hours or overnight, in refrigerator. Drain, reserving marinade. Stir-fry meat in hot oil until evenly browned and tender, about 10 minutes. Remove meat from pan. Stir-fry carrots and onions in same pan, using more oil, if necessary. Cover and cook on low heat until tender-crisp, about 10 minutes. Add green pepper and pineapple. Return meat to pan, then stir in marinade.

In the meantime, make sweet and sour sauce: Mix cornstarch and sugar in small saucepan. Add pineapple juice, vinegar, and soy sauce. Cook and stir until thickened and translucent. Pour over meat and vegetables; heat until flavors are blended, about 10 minutes. Adjust seasonings to taste. Serve over cooked rice.

Pork Chow Mein

Makes 4 to 6 servings

1 pound lean pork loin, cubed
Oil
1 cup chopped onion
1 cup slant-cut celery
½ cup canned sliced bamboo shoots
1 (2½-ounce) can mushrooms

1 cup bean sprouts
1 cup chicken stock
½ teaspoon sugar
2 tablespoons soy sauce
1½ tablespoons cornstarch
Chow mein noodles or hot cooked rice

Stir-fry cubed pork in oiled frying pan until browned and tender. Remove meat from pan.

Add vegetables and more oil, if necessary, and stir-fry for about 5 minutes. (Do not overcook—vegetables should be crisp.) Combine meat and vegetables; mix well.

Heat chicken stock, sugar, and soy sauce. Make a paste of cornstarch and a little cold water; stir into hot stock mixture. Cook, stirring constantly, until thickened. Pour over meat and vegetables. Allow time for flavors to blend before serving. Serve over chow mein noodles or rice.

Apple 'n' Orange Pork Chops

Makes 8 servings

8 pork chops, about ½-inch thick
Salt and pepper
1 tablespoon shortening
½ cup chopped onion
1 cup uncooked long-grain rice
1½ cups water

1 cup peeled and chopped tart apple
1 cup orange sections
1½ teaspoons salt
⅛ teaspoon pepper
⅛ teaspoon poultry seasoning (optional)

Preheat oven to 350 degrees F. Trim excess fat from pork chops; season lightly with salt and pepper. Brown quickly in shortening and remove from skillet. Pour from skillet all but 2 tablespoons of the drippings. Sauté onion in drippings. Add all remaining ingredients except pork chops; mix well. Pour into greased 9x13 casserole. Arrange chops on this mixture. Cover and bake 45 minutes.

Note: This recipe is also very good without apple or oranges.

Stuffed Pork Chops

Makes 6 servings

6 pork chops, cut 1-inch thick with pocket slit at butcher's
½ cup finely chopped onion
½ cup finely chopped celery
¼ cup butter
1 cup chicken stock
1 teaspoon salt
1 teaspoon poultry seasoning

1 teaspoon sage
3 cups ground dry bread crumbs, divided
½ teaspoon salt
½ teaspoon pepper
1 teaspoon paprika
1 (10.75-ounce) can cream of celery soup
⅓ can water

Preheat oven to 350 degrees F. Sauté onion and celery in butter. Mix in stock and seasonings. Remove from heat and mix in 2 cups of the bread crumbs until moistened. Stuff each pork chop with ½ cup stuffing. Mix together 1 cup fine bread crumbs, ½ teaspoon salt, pepper, and paprika. Coat each chop with bread crumb mixture. Place chops in shallow baking dish. Combine celery soup and water and pour over chops. Bake 1½ to 2 hours.

Pork Tenderloin with Balsamic Apple Sauce

Makes 8 to 10 servings of 3 slices each

Pork Tenderloin

3 (1- to 1½-pound) pork tenderloins

Salt and pepper to taste

2 tablespoons butter

1 recipe Balsamic Apple Sauce (see below)

Preheat oven to 350 degrees F. Sprinkle each tenderloin with salt and pepper and set in a bowl. Heat a large sauté pan over high heat until a small amount of water dropped on the pan sizzles. Add butter to the hot pan. Carefully place tenderloins in the pan so that it is filled but not crowded. If all 3 tenderloins do not fit at once, sear in batches. Sear each side of the loins until they have browned. Remove from the pan and place in a shallow baking pan.

Place the tenderloins in the oven for approximately 35 to 40 minutes or until a thermometer placed in the center of a loin reads 145 degrees F. If the pork is overcooked it will be dry and tough. Slice each tenderloin on the bias across the grain. Serve with Balsamic Apple Sauce.

Balsamic Apple Sauce

Makes 10 (2-ounce) servings

2 tablespoons clarified butter

3 Fuji apples, peeled and sectioned into 8 wedges each

6 tablespoons sugar

¾ cup balsamic vinegar

¾ cup heavy cream

¼ to ½ cup sugar

Cornstarch (if desired to thicken)

Heat a large sauté pan over high heat until a drop of water sizzles on the pan. Carefully pour the clarified butter into the hot pan. Place the apple wedges in the hot butter, being careful not to splatter the butter. Sauté the apples until they begin to brown, turning often so they do not burn. Sprinkle the 6 tablespoons sugar over the cooking apples and continue to cook until the sugar melts and begins to caramelize. Remove pan from heat. Using a pair of tongs, remove apples from pan and place on a platter until ready to serve.

Put the sauté pan with the apple juices and caramelized sugar back onto the stove and heat. Add the balsamic vinegar, stirring to dissolve the caramelized sugar. When the vinegar begins to boil, reduce heat and stir in the heavy cream. Taste the sauce, checking for sweetness. Some balsamic vinegars are more tart than others and you will have to judge how much more sugar to add to the sauce for your own taste. If more sugar is needed, add it in small amounts until the flavor is to your liking. Cook the sauce 2 to 3 minutes until it begins to thicken. Hold the sauce, covered, over a pan of simmering water until ready to serve. Place apples on tenderloins and drizzle with sauce.

Pork Tenderloin

Makes 6 to 8 servings

3 (1-pound) pork tenderloins
3 to 4 cloves garlic, minced
½ cup soy sauce
½ cup sugar

¼ to ½ teaspoon ground ginger
Red food coloring (optional)
Chopped green onions and sesame seeds, for garnishing

Place tenderloins in large glass baking dish. Combine garlic, soy sauce, sugar, ginger, and a drop or two of red food coloring in a small bowl; pour over meat. Cover with plastic wrap and refrigerate for several hours or overnight, turning a couple of times.

Preheat oven to 400 degrees F. Remove plastic wrap and bake, covered with foil, for about 40 minutes, or until meat thermometer registers 155 degrees F. When ready to serve, slice at an angle into serving pieces. Place on serving platter and pour marinade on top. Garnish with chopped green onions and sesame seeds.

English Sausage Rolls

Makes 12 sausage rolls

2 pounds bulk sausage
2 cups flour
½ teaspoon salt
4 teaspoons baking powder

1 tablespoon sugar
⅓ cup shortening
1 egg, beaten well
½ cup milk

Note: This recipe uses shortcake dough to wrap up the sausages, but pie dough will work as well.

Preheat oven to 400 degrees F. Form sausage into 12 patties and brown lightly in a large skillet. (Brown patties in batches to get even browning.) Drain off fat and pat patties with paper towel to remove grease. Sift flour, salt, baking powder, and sugar into a large mixing bowl; cut in shortening with a pastry blender or fork until mixture resembles coarse crumbs. Add egg and milk and stir just enough to moisten. Roll out on slightly floured board. Cut squares of dough and wrap around each sausage patty. Place on greased baking sheet and bake for 15 minutes, or until pastry is golden brown. Serve with ketchup or chili sauce.

Barbecued Spareribs

Makes 6 servings

4 pounds boneless pork spareribs
1 tablespoon salt
½ teaspoon black pepper
2 onions, chopped
2 tablespoons vinegar
1 teaspoon chili powder

2 tablespoons Worcestershire sauce
¾ cup water
½ teaspoon cayenne pepper
¾ cup ketchup
1 teaspoon paprika

Preheat oven to 350 degrees F. Sprinkle spareribs with salt and pepper. Place in roasting pan and cover with onions. Combine remaining ingredients and pour over meat. Cover and bake about 2 hours. Baste and turn ribs once or twice. Uncover last half-hour for browning.

Party Ham Roll-Ups

Makes 25 servings (recipe may be halved, if desired)

25 slices ham (about 5 pounds)
25 slices Swiss cheese (about 1½ pounds)

Cornbread Stuffing (see below)
Apricot Sauce (see below)

Preheat oven to 350 degrees F. Lay out ham and cheese slices. Spoon about ⅓ cup Cornbread Stuffing in center of each ham slice. Lay slice of Swiss cheese on top of stuffing. Roll up and secure with toothpick. Place in shallow baking dish. Bake 45 minutes. Spoon 2 or 3 tablespoons Apricot Sauce over each roll-up at serving time.

Cornbread Stuffing

1 (8x8-inch) pan of cornbread, baked according to package directions
1 cup finely chopped celery and leaves
4 tablespoons finely chopped onion

1 cup butter or margarine
½ cup apricot preserves
¼ cup water

Crumble cornbread into a large bowl; set aside. Cook celery and onion in margarine until soft. Stir in preserves and water. Toss mixture lightly with crumbled cornbread. Add more water, if desired, for a moister stuffing.

Apricot Sauce

1 tablespoon cornstarch
2 tablespoons brown sugar
1 cup water

1 cup pineapple juice
1 tablespoon butter
¼ cup apricot preserves

In small saucepan, mix cornstarch and brown sugar. Add water and pineapple juice; stir over medium heat until mixture boils and thickens. Stir in butter and preserves.

Buffet Ham

Makes about 16 servings

1 (7- to 8-pound) boneless ham, cut by butcher in ½-inch slices
Prepared mustard
1½ cups orange juice
1½ cups maple syrup
1 teaspoon allspice

½ teaspoon mace
½ teaspoon cinnamon
2 teaspoons paprika
1½ cups heavy cream
1½ cups half and half

Preheat oven to 350 degrees F. Spread one side of each ham slice generously with mustard. Arrange in large roasting pan, slices overlapping. In medium bowl, combine orange juice, syrup, allspice, mace, cinnamon, and paprika; pour over ham. Bake uncovered 30 minutes. Remove from oven and pour cream and half and half over ham. Return to oven and bake about 1 hour longer. Spoon hot sauce over each slice at serving time.

Ham with Pineapple Sauce

Makes 20 servings

1 (7- to 8-pound) ham, cut into 20 slices
3 cups pineapple juice
1½ cups brown sugar

1 cup water
2 to 3 tablespoons cornstarch

Preheat oven to 350 degrees F. Place ham slices in baking dish. Bake for 12 minutes. Reduce heat to oven's lowest temperature and cover baking dish with foil to keep ham moist. Meanwhile, bring pineapple juice and brown sugar to a boil. Dissolve cornstarch in water then add to boiling juice mixture, stirring until thickened.

When ready to serve, top each warm ham slice with 2 tablespoons of pineapple sauce.

Ham with Maple Syrup and Cider Glaze

1 cup maple syrup
½ cup sweet cider

Ham
Whole cloves

Preheat oven to 325 degrees F. Combine syrup and cider and set aside. Place ham in roasting pan, fat side up. Score fat with sharp knife, diagonally in two directions, forming diamond shapes. Stud points of diamonds with whole cloves. Brush entire surface with syrup and cider glaze. Bake 15 to 25 minutes per pound, basting occasionally with glaze.

Ham with Pineapple Sauce

Ham and Green Noodle Casserole

Makes 8 servings

1 cup sour cream
1 (10.5-ounce) can cheddar cheese soup
½ recipe Green Noodles (see below)
1½ cups cooked, diced ham
½ cup pitted ripe olives, sliced

1 (2.5-ounce) can mushrooms, drained
¾ teaspoon prepared mustard
¼ cup milk
⅛ teaspoon pepper
1 cup grated sharp cheddar cheese

Preheat oven to 350 degrees F. Combine sour cream and soup. Beat till smooth. Add remaining ingredients except cheese. Place in 8x8-inch baking pan or casserole. Sprinkle with grated cheese and bake 25 minutes.

Green Noodles

Makes about 1 pound noodles

1 (10-ounce) package frozen chopped spinach
2 eggs

½ teaspoon salt
2½ cups flour

Cook spinach according to package directions. Drain well, pressing out moisture with back of spoon. Force spinach through food mill or puree in blender. In mixing bowl, beat eggs and salt; beat in spinach purée. Add enough flour to make a firm dough. Knead thoroughly. Cut dough into 4 pieces and let rest 30 minutes.

On floured board, roll each piece of dough into a very thin 12-inch square. As each square is rolled, remove it to a kitchen towel and let dry about 1 hour. Cut into strips about ¼-inch wide. Cook noodle strips in large quantity of boiling, salted water 8 to 10 minutes. Drain and rinse thoroughly.

Ham-Cheese Strata

Makes 4 to 6 servings

8 slices firm white bread, crusts removed
4 slices sharp cheddar cheese
1 cup chopped cooked ham
4 eggs, beaten
2 cups milk

1 teaspoon finely chopped onion
Dash pepper
½ teaspoon salt
¼ teaspoon dry mustard

Arrange 4 slices bread in bottom of 8x8-inch baking pan. Cover with slices of cheese, ham, and remaining bread. Combine eggs, milk, onion, and seasonings; pour over sandwiches. Let stand 1 hour. Bake at 325 degrees for 1 hour or until lightly browned and puffy. Let stand a few minutes; cut into squares.

Ham Quiche

Makes 24 servings

3 (9-inch) frozen pie shells
4 cups half and half
9 eggs
1 teaspoon salt
½ teaspoon white pepper

2 teaspoons chopped fresh parsley
1 teaspoon chopped fresh thyme
2¼ cups shredded cheddar cheese
2¼ cups shredded Swiss cheese
1 cup diced ham

Preheat oven to 350 degrees F. Place the pie shells on an ovenproof baking sheet. Bake in the oven for 5 minutes or until the shells are just turning golden brown.

While the shells are baking, mix the half and half, eggs, salt, white pepper, parsley, and thyme in a large bowl. Stir for 1 minute to dissolve salt.

In another bowl mix the cheeses and ham. Once the shells are cooked, remove them from the oven and fill each with a third of the cheese and ham mixture. Pour one-third of the egg mixture into each shell. Place the quiche on baking sheets and set them in the oven. Reduce oven temperature to 275 degrees F. and bake for 40 minutes. When slightly shaken, the quiche should not seem fluid. Remove from oven and let sit for 5 minutes to set the custard. Cut each into 8 pieces and serve.

Quiche Lorraine

Makes 6 servings

1 (9-inch) unbaked pie crust (see page 216)
1 cup (4 ounces) shredded Swiss cheese
6 slices bacon, cooked and crumbled
1 cup minced ham
2 green onions, sliced and chopped
½ green pepper, chopped

5 eggs, slightly beaten
1 cup half and half
⅛ teaspoon grated lemon peel
½ teaspoon salt
⅓ teaspoon dry mustard

Preheat oven to 325 degrees F. Arrange cheese, bacon, and ham in bottom of unbaked pie crust. Sprinkle with green onions and green pepper. In medium bowl combine eggs, half and half, lemon peel, salt, and dry mustard. Pour evenly over cheese mixture. Bake 45 minutes or until set. Remove from heat and let stand about 10 minutes before serving.

Baked Salmon Steaks (facing page)
and Rice Pilaf (page 207)

Baked Salmon Steaks

Makes 6 servings

6 salmon steaks, about ¾-inch thick, washed well in cold running water
⅓ cup butter, melted

3 tablespoons fresh lemon juice (or more to taste)
½ teaspoon salt

Preheat oven to 350 degrees F. Arrange salmon steaks in single layer in shallow, greased baking pan. Combine butter, lemon juice, and salt; spoon over steaks. Bake uncovered 15 to 20 minutes, or until fish flakes easily with fork. Remove salmon to warm serving platter; keep warm. Pour pan drippings into warm serving dish; add more lemon juice if desired. Pass sauce to spoon over salmon.

Honey Garlic Variation

1 cup honey
3 cloves garlic

1 tablespoon soy sauce

Place ingredients in food processor and blend until garlic is well minced. Warm sauce. Brush over salmon steaks prior to baking.

Dill Lemon Pepper Variation

1 tablespoon dill weed
2 teaspoons lemon pepper

Butter

Mix dill weed and lemon pepper and sprinkle over salmon steaks; place thin pats of butter on steaks before baking.

Salmon Tetrazzini

Makes 6 to 8 servings

1 (15.5-ounce) can salmon
½ pound mushrooms, sliced
2 cloves garlic, minced
½ cup chopped green onions
¼ cup butter or margarine
¼ cup flour
1 cup chicken broth
1½ cups half and half

2 tablespoons lemon juice
½ teaspoon salt
⅛ teaspoon pepper
¼ cup grated Parmesan cheese
8 ounces spaghetti, cooked
3 tablespoons grated Parmesan cheese
Lemon slice and parsley for garnish (if desired)

Preheat oven to 375 degrees F. Drain and flake salmon, reserving liquid. Sauté mushrooms, garlic, and green onions in butter or margarine. Blend in flour. Gradually add chicken broth, half and half, lemon juice, and reserved salmon liquid. Cook, stirring constantly, until thickened and smooth. Add seasonings, ¼ cup grated Parmesan cheese, and salmon. Combine with spaghetti. Adjust seasonings to taste.

Turn into buttered 2½-quart casserole. Sprinkle with 3 tablespoons grated Parmesan cheese. Bake 20 to 25 minutes, until bubbly and slightly browned. Garnish with slice of lemon and sprig of parsley.

Grilled Salmon with Pineapple Raspberry Salsa

Makes 6 to 8 servings

Salmon

6 to 8 (8-ounce) salmon filets

Salt and pepper to taste

1 recipe Pineapple Raspberry Salsa (see below)

Heat an outdoor grill until hot. Sprinkle salmon filets with salt and pepper. Grill each filet only long enough to sear grill marks onto the salmon. Turn the salmon 90 degrees to make a square grid on each filet.

Once seared, place the filets on a flat baking tray and store in refrigerator until 20 minutes before serving. At that time, preheat oven to 350 degrees F. and bake filets for approximately 8 minutes. Top each serving with 3 to 4 tablespoons Pineapple Raspberry Salsa.

Pineapple Raspberry Salsa

Makes 8 (2-ounce) servings

1 cup diced fresh pineapple

⅓ cup diced red onion

¼ cup diced red bell pepper

¼ cup diced yellow bell pepper

2 teaspoons chopped cilantro

2½ tablespoons lime juice

1 teaspoon chopped jalapeño pepper

1 tablespoon raspberry vinegar

1 tablespoon olive oil

Salt to taste

Combine all ingredients and season to taste. Cover and refrigerate for at least 1 hour. Serve atop grilled salmon.

Lemon-Marinated Salmon

Makes 6 servings

2 pounds salmon steaks or fillets

1 cup water

½ cup lemon juice

⅓ cup sliced green onion

¼ cup vegetable oil

3 tablespoons snipped parsley

3 tablespoons chopped green pepper

1 tablespoon sugar

2 teaspoons dry mustard

⅛ teaspoon cayenne pepper

½ teaspoon salt

Place fish on greased rack in a large skillet or fry pan. Pour in 1 cup water. Cover with a lid and steam for 5 to 7 minutes, or until fish is done and flakes easily when tested with a fork. Remove from pan to a shallow dish. Place the remaining ingredients in a screw-top jar and shake vigorously to combine; pour over fish. Cover and chill several hours or overnight, spooning marinade over fish several times. Drain before serving. Serve cold.

Grilled Salmon with
Pineapple Raspberry Salsa

Crab Cakes with Chili Remoulade

Makes 20 servings

1½ pounds crabmeat, picked free of shells
1¼ cups dry bread crumbs, divided
⅓ cup mayonnaise
1½ tablespoons Dijon mustard
¾ teaspoon Tabasco® sauce

1¼ teaspoons salt
Pinch fresh ground black pepper
¾ cup flour
2 eggs, beaten
1 recipe Chili Remoulade (see below)

In medium bowl, combine the crab, ¼ cup of the bread crumbs, the mayonnaise, mustard, Tabasco sauce, salt, and pepper. Shape the mixture into sixteen ¾-inch thick cakes, using about a ¼ cup of the mixture for each. Dust the cakes with the flour and pat off the excess. Dip each cake into the eggs and then into the remaining bread crumbs.

In a large nonstick frying pan, heat about ½ inch of oil over moderate heat. When the oil is hot, add some of the crab cakes and fry until golden brown and crisp, 2 to 3 minutes. Turn the cakes and fry them until golden brown on the other side, about 2 minutes longer. Drain on paper towels. Repeat until all the crab cakes are fried. Serve with the Chili Remoulade.

Chili Remoulade

2 dried or canned chipotle chilies
½ cup boiling water
2 cups mayonnaise

4 teaspoons Dijon mustard
4 teaspoons lime or lemon juice
½ teaspoon salt

If using dried chilies, place in a small bowl, cover with the boiling water, and let soak 20 minutes. Stem and seed the chilies. Scrape the inside of each chili with a small knife to get the pulp. If using canned chilies, simply remove the seeds.

Put the chilies in a small bowl and stir in the mayonnaise, mustard, lime juice, and salt. Store in refrigerator until ready to serve.

Crab Tetrazzini

Makes 10 to 12 servings

8 ounces dry spaghetti, broken in pieces 3 to 4 inches long
2 (10.5-ounce) cans cream of mushroom soup
1½ cups milk
5 tablespoons butter

¼ cup chopped green pepper
1 cup grated cheddar cheese
½ cup grated Parmesan cheese
1 pound imitation crabmeat

Preheat oven to 350 degrees F. Cook broken spaghetti pieces in boiling salted water according to package directions; drain and set aside. Mix soup, milk, butter, and green pepper together in a large saucepan and warm over medium heat until butter is melted. Mix well. Add cooked spaghetti, cheddar cheese, Parmesan cheese, and imitation crabmeat. Pour into a 9x13-inch baking dish or large casserole dish. Cover and bake until bubbly, 30 to 40 minutes. If desired, sprinkle additional grated cheese on top of casserole near the end of baking time.

Crab Claws

Makes 40 servings

40 crab claws, purchased frozen
Water
1 tablespoon salt

Fill a medium saucepan with water and 1 tablespoon of salt; bring to a boil. Add the frozen crab claws and simmer for 2 minutes. Remove from the water and serve immediately.

Shrimp-Cheese Fondue

Makes 12 servings

3 (4.5-ounce) cans shrimp, deveined, or crab meat
3 cups white bread cubes
2 cups grated sharp cheddar cheese
9 eggs, lightly beaten
4½ cups milk

1½ teaspoons salt
¾ teaspoon dry mustard
3 teaspoons minced onion
¼ teaspoon pepper

Preheat oven to 350 degrees F. Layer shrimp, bread, and cheese in greased 2-quart casserole. Combine remaining ingredients and pour over layers in casserole. Bake about 1 hour, or until set.

Shrimp Creole with Rice

Shrimp Creole with Rice

Makes 6 servings

2½ tablespoons butter or margarine
½ cup chopped green pepper
⅓ cup chopped green onions, including tops
1 cup chopped celery
2 tablespoons flour
⅛ teaspoon paprika
2 cups reserved tomato liquid, heated
1 (28-ounce) can whole tomatoes, drained (reserve liquid)

1 small bay leaf
2 (5-ounce) cans shrimp, drained, or 1½ pounds fresh shrimp, cooked
1 tablespoon chopped parsley, or ¾ teaspoon dry parsley flakes
Salt to taste
Cooked rice

Melt butter in large frying pan or Dutch oven. Sauté green pepper, green onions, and celery until soft but not brown, 5 to 10 minutes on low heat. Add flour and paprika; blend well. Add hot tomato liquid; cook and stir until smooth and thick. Add whole tomatoes and bay leaf. Cover and simmer 30 minutes. Add shrimp and continue cooking until shrimp is heated, about 5 minutes. Add parsley. Adjust seasonings to taste. Serve immediately over hot cooked rice.

Seafood Newburg

Makes about 2 quarts, or about 10 servings

¼ cup minced onion
¼ cup minced green pepper (optional)
1 cup butter
1 cup flour
¼ cup chopped pimiento (optional)
1 tablespoon paprika
1 teaspoon salt

¼ teaspoon white pepper
Dash cayenne
4 cups milk, heated
1 cup light cream
2 tablespoons lemon juice
4 cups cooked seafood and fish*
Pastry shells, cooked rice, or crisp toast

Make a thick white sauce: In top half of a 3- or 4-quart double boiler placed over medium heat, sauté onion and green pepper in butter, covered, until soft but not brown, about 5 minutes. Blend in flour and seasonings. Add hot milk and stir until mixture is very thick. Add part of cream, to desired consistency. Fill bottom half of double boiler with water and bring to a boil. Place top half of double boiler (containing sauce) over boiling water. Cover and cook for about 10 minutes. Add lemon juice, seafood, and fish. Add more cream if necessary. Adjust seasonings to taste. Serve in pastry shells or over hot cooked rice or buttered toast.

Note: Sauce may be prepared and frozen up to a month in advance. Thaw overnight in refrigerator and reheat over boiling water, stirring frequently. If necessary, blend with whip or rotary beater until smooth. Then add seafood and lemon juice. Adjust seasonings to taste.

Use at least 2 cups shrimp, crab meat, lobster or scallops. The remainder may be flaked cooked white fish, such as cod, haddock, halibut, or sole.

Halibut au Gratin

Makes 6 servings

1 to 1½ pounds halibut

2 to 3 tablespoons each chopped onion, celery, carrot

¼ teaspoon salt

6 tablespoons butter or margarine

6 tablespoons flour

½ teaspoon salt

⅛ teaspoon white pepper

2½ cups milk

½ cup grated Parmesan cheese

2 cups shredded sharp cheddar cheese

¼ cup chopped pimiento (optional)

Preheat oven to 350 degrees F. Place halibut pieces in a single layer in a large frying pan; spread with chopped onion, celery, and carrot. Add ¼ teaspoon salt to small amount of water (about ½ cup) and pour into pan with fish. Cover and steam gently until fish flakes easily with fork, about 20 minutes. Turn fish halfway through cooking time. Remove fish from pan, scrape off vegetables, and when cool enough to handle, remove skin and bones; break fish into large chunks.

In the meantime, make a white sauce: Melt butter in small saucepan. Add flour, salt, and pepper; stir over medium heat until mixture foams. Add milk; stir occasionally until sauce is thick and smooth. Pour half the sauce into a 2-quart casserole or 9x9-inch shallow baking dish. Layer fish chunks over sauce, then Parmesan cheese, then cheddar cheese. Cover with remaining white sauce. Sprinkle with chopped pimiento. Bake 30 minutes or until hot and bubbly. Do not overcook or fish will be tough and dry.

Creamy Baked Halibut Steaks

Makes 4 large or 8 small servings

4 halibut steaks, about ¾-inch thick

Salt

Pepper

¾ cup thick sour cream

¼ cup dry bread crumbs

¼ teaspoon garlic salt

1½ teaspoons chopped chives, fresh or frozen

⅓ cup grated Parmesan cheese

1 teaspoon paprika

Preheat oven to 400 degrees F. Place steaks close together in shallow buttered baking dish; sprinkle with salt and pepper. Mix together sour cream, bread crumbs, garlic salt, and chives; spread over steaks. Sprinkle with Parmesan cheese and paprika. Bake uncovered 15 to 20 minutes, or until fish flakes easily with a fork.

Halibut au Gratin

Halibut Broil Amandine

Halibut Broil Amandine

Makes 6 servings

6 halibut steaks or fillets

1 cup chicken broth

2 tablespoons butter or margarine, melted

1 teaspoon dried thyme leaves

¼ cup butter or margarine

¼ cup sliced almonds

2 tablespoons lemon juice

Note: This cooking method works equally well for bass, cod, flounder, red snapper, shark, or orange roughy.

Preheat broiler in oven. Rinse fish and pat dry. Arrange in a single layer in a greased, broiler-safe baking pan. Pour broth around fish. Mix 2 tablespoons melted butter with thyme and brush half on fish. Place baking dish on broiler pan and place on oven rack about 3 to 4 inches from heat. Broil fish (do not turn), basting once or twice with remaining butter mixture. Broil 3 to 6 minutes for fish that is ½- to ¾-inch thick or 6 to 10 minutes for fish that is 1- to 1¼-inches thick. Melt ¼ cup butter in a small skillet. Add almonds and stir until nuts begin to brown. Remove from heat and add lemon juice. Pour over fish when ready to serve.

Broiled Fish Steaks or Fillets

Makes 8 servings

8 fish steaks or fillets, washed well in cold running water

Salt

Paprika

¼ cup lemon juice

½ cup butter or margarine, melted

¼ cup chopped parsley

Place fillets or steaks on well-greased baking sheet. Sprinkle with salt and paprika. Drip lemon juice and butter generously over fish. Broil about 6 inches from heat for about 10 minutes for each 1 inch of thickness, basting once with lemon and butter. When fish is firm and flakes easily, remove from broiler. Baste again with lemon and butter; garnish with parsley and serve immediately.

Roasted Root Vegetables

Roasted Root Vegetables

Makes 6 to 8 servings

1 large onion	1 teaspoon cracked black pepper
2 large carrots	1 teaspoon kosher salt
1 large potato	1 red bell pepper
2 large parsnips	1 green bell pepper
2 large turnips	1 tablespoon chopped fresh parsley
3 tablespoons canola oil	

Preheat oven to 375 degrees F. Thoroughly clean all vegetables. Peel onion and carrots. Slice or chop all vegetables into bite-sized pieces, keeping each separate. Combine hard root vegetables (carrots, potatoes, parsnips, and turnips) in a large mixing bowl. Add 2 tablespoons oil and ½ teaspoon pepper and ½ teaspoon salt. Toss well until vegetables are evenly coated. Spread vegetables out evenly in one layer on a large baking pan and place in oven. Toss remaining vegetables in remaining oil, pepper, and salt. When vegetables in oven are slightly tender, remove from oven and add remaining vegetables to pan. Return to oven and continue roasting until all vegetables are tender and begin to brown. Serve hot, garnished with chopped fresh parsley.

* Any combination of vegetables will work well. Use whatever you like. Other vegetables recommended are zucchini, yellow squash, any hard winter squash, or beets. Beets will tend to color the other vegetables, so keep them separate until served. Remember to add softer vegetables later to avoid overcooking.

Roasted Julienned Root Vegetables

Makes 20 servings

6 large parsnips	1 red bell pepper
6 rutabagas	¼ cup, plus 2 tablespoons olive oil
6 carrots	1 teaspoon salt
6 turnips	½ teaspoon white pepper
1 red onion	3 tablespoons chopped fresh parsley
1 green bell pepper	

Preheat oven to 375 degrees F. Wash all vegetables thoroughly. Peel the parsnips, rutabagas, carrots, turnips, and onion. Halve the bell peppers and discard the seeds. Cut the vegetables into ¼-inch sticks. Place the parsnips, rutabagas, carrots, turnips, red onion, and ¼ cup of the olive oil in a large mixing bowl, season with the salt and pepper and mix to distribute the oil. Spread these vegetables on a large baking pan and place in the oven. For best cooking results avoid stacking more than 2 layers high. Place baking sheet in the oven. In the same bowl mix the bell peppers and remaining olive oil. With a metal spatula turn vegetables every 20 minutes. After 30 minutes add the bell peppers. (Peppers require a shorter cooking time.) Continue turning and cooking until vegetables are lightly browned, about 1 hour, soft but not mushy. Check seasoning; add more salt and pepper if desired. Sprinkle with chopped parsley and serve.

Baked Summer Squash

Makes 4 to 6 servings

4 medium-sized yellow crookneck squash
Salt
1 small onion, finely chopped
2 tablespoons butter or margarine

½ cup cream
¼ cup crushed saltine crackers
Butter
Soft bread crumbs

Preheat oven to 400 degrees F. Slice squash and boil in salted water until tender. Drain well and mash. Sauté onion in butter until translucent but not brown, 5 to 10 minutes. Add to squash. Add cream and cracker crumbs. Pour into greased 1-quart casserole. Dot with butter and a few soft bread crumbs. Bake about 30 minutes or until firm.

Sautéed Summer Squash Medley

Makes 8 to 10 servings

1 small onion
4 small yellow summer squash
4 small zucchini
1 green bell pepper
1 red bell pepper
1 yellow or orange bell pepper
2 tablespoons olive oil

1 tablespoon fresh, chopped oregano
1 tablespoon fresh, chopped basil
1 teaspoon salt
½ cup pitted black olives, sliced
½ cup crumbled ricotta salata or ½ cup crumbled mildly herbed goat cheese
1½ teaspoons fresh squeezed lemon juice

Clean and slice vegetables. Heat oil in a sauté pan; sauté onion until transparent. Add squash, zucchini, and peppers; stir fry over medium heat for 4 minutes or until tender-crisp. Add oregano, basil, and salt. Toss with olives, cheese, and lemon juice.

Harvest Vegetable Bake

Makes 6 servings

1 head cauliflower
½ cup chopped celery
⅓ cup chopped onion
⅓ cup chopped green pepper
3 tablespoons margarine
1 tablespoon cornstarch

1 cup milk
1 cup grated Swiss cheese
¾ teaspoon salt
1 tomato, sliced
Paprika

Preheat oven to 350 degrees F. Break cauliflower into florets and cook in small amount of salted water until tender. Drain and pour into a shallow baking dish. In a small saucepan, sauté celery, onion, and green pepper in melted margarine until crisp-tender. Pour over cauliflower. In the same pan, combine cornstarch and cold milk and bring to a boil, stirring until thickened. Stir in Swiss cheese and salt. Pour sauce over vegetables. Top with sliced tomato and sprinkle with paprika. Bake 20 minutes.

Vegetable Medleys

Makes 4 servings

2 medium carrots
3 small zucchini
3 ribs celery

Water
2 tablespoons butter
Salt and pepper to taste

Peel carrots; wash and clean zucchini and celery. Slice vegetables diagonally. Place ¼ inch water and butter in saucepan and bring to a boil. Add carrots and simmer, covered, for 4 minutes. Add celery and simmer an additional 2 minutes. Add zucchini and continue cooking for an additional 5 minutes, or until all vegetables are tender-crisp. Season to taste with salt and pepper. Serve at once, retaining remaining liquid in serving dish.

Vegetable Medley 2

Combine cooked, sliced, small yellow summer squash with package of cooked green peas. Season with salt, pepper, and butter.

Vegetable Medley 3

Combine cauliflower, broccoli, and carrots. Season with salt, pepper, and butter.

Fresh String Green Beans

Makes 20 servings

5 pounds fresh green beans*
¼ cup butter
¼ teaspoon onion powder

1 clove garlic, peeled and crushed
Seasoned salt to taste

Break ends from beans. Beans should snap when broken; break in thirds. Place in vegetable steamer over boiling water, or cook in a pot of boiling water, until tender, about 5 to 6 minutes. Drain and place in serving dish. Melt butter; stir in onion powder and crushed garlic. Toss seasoned butter with green beans. Season to taste with your favorite seasoned salt. Serve immediately.

* To use frozen green beans, follow package instructions to cook beans. Then drain beans and continue following recipe.

Green Beans Parmesan

Serving size is about ½ cup

Ingredients	12 servings	25 servings
Bacon, diced	6 ounces	12 ounces
Finely chopped onions	¾ cup	1½ cups
Green beans, canned, cut	6 cups	1 No. 10 can
Salt*	¼ teaspoon	¾ teaspoon
Cornflake crumbs	½ cup	1 cup
Grated Parmesan cheese	½ cup	1 cup

Fry diced bacon until crisp; remove from fat and drain. Cook onions in bacon fat until tender, stirring constantly. Drain off most of bacon fat. Heat green beans; drain well. Add bacon, onions, salt, cornflake crumbs, and cheese to green beans; toss lightly until thoroughly mixed. Serve immediately.

*Amount of salt will depend on saltiness of canned beans.

Italian Green Beans

Makes 6 servings

4 slices thick bacon

2 tablespoons bacon drippings

1 green onion, chopped

1 tablespoon chopped green pepper

1 (14.5-ounce) can green beans, drained

1 (15-ounce) can seasoned tomatoes

½ teaspoon salt

Sauté bacon in hot frying pan until cooked but not crisp. Remove from pan. Measure 2 tablespoons drippings into frying pan. Add onion and green pepper; cook until soft but not brown, about 5 minutes. Add green beans, seasoned tomatoes, salt, and bacon pieces. Stir; cover and simmer for 20 minutes.

St. Nick's Green Beans

Makes 6 servings

1½ pounds fresh green beans

1½ cups water

½ teaspoon salt

6 slices bacon, cooked crisp and crumbled, drippings reserved

1 small onion, chopped

2 tablespoons flour

1 tablespoon vinegar

⅔ cup heavy cream

Cook beans in boiling, salted water until crisp-tender; set aside—do not drain off liquid. Using 2 tablespoons bacon drippings, sauté onion in a 12-inch skillet over medium-high heat until onions are translucent. Add flour and cook and stir about 1 minute. Stir in vinegar. Stir this mixture into beans and liquid, and cook until thickened. Just before serving, stir in cream.

Sesame Green Beans

Makes 4 servings

1 pound fresh green beans

1 tablespoon toasted sesame seeds

1 tablespoon soy sauce

2 tablespoons butter or margarine, melted

Wash green beans, snip ends, and cut into ¼- to ½-inch lengths. Cook in boiling salted water until just tender. Drain. In a separate pan, combine sesame seeds, soy sauce, and butter or margarine. Heat thoroughly and serve over green beans. This sauce is also good on cooked, well-drained spinach or asparagus.

Honeyed Onions

Makes 4 servings

1 (8-ounce) can tomato sauce

½ cup honey

⅓ cup butter or margarine

16 small, raw, whole peeled onions

In saucepan, combine tomato sauce, honey, and butter. Add onions and simmer slowly until tender. Let stand in syrup. Reheat (the more times the better) and serve. If syrup boils down, add a little water or tomato juice.

Holiday Creamed Onions

Makes 6 to 8 servings

6 or 7 onions, peeled and sliced
1 cup water
⅔ cup milk
2 tablespoons butter
2 tablespoons flour

1 egg yolk, beaten well
Salt and pepper to taste
Buttered bread crumbs*
¼ cup slivered almonds

Preheat oven to 350 degrees F. Cook sliced onions in water in a small saucepan over medium-high heat until tender. Drain onions, reserving liquid, and place onions in a casserole dish. Combine onion liquid with milk in saucepan and keep warm over low heat. In a separate saucepan, make a roux by melting butter over medium-high heat until foamy. Stir in flour and cook and stir until golden and fragrant, about 1 minute. Add roux to hot liquid and stir until thickened. Stir in beaten egg yolk and salt and pepper. Pour sauce over onions. Top with buttered bread crumbs and slivered almonds. Bake until heated through, about 10 minutes.

* To make buttered bread crumbs, combine 1 cup bread crumbs with 1 tablespoon of melted butter. Mix together until crumbs are coated.

Crumb-Topped Baked Onions

Makes 4 to 6 servings

18 to 20 small white boiling onions
1 chicken bouillon cube
¾ cup water
2 tablespoons butter or margarine, melted
½ teaspoon sage
¼ teaspoon pepper

1½ teaspoons cornstarch
1 tablespoon water
¼ cup croutons, slightly crushed
2 tablespoons grated Parmesan cheese
1 tablespoon chopped parsley

Preheat oven to 350 degrees F. Peel onions and arrange in single layer in 8- or 9-inch square baking dish. Crush bouillon cube, then stir in water and heat until cube is dissolved. Stir in melted butter, sage, and pepper. Pour over onions. Cover and bake 1 hour or until tender when pierced with a fork. Transfer onions to heated serving dish; keep warm.

Pour cooking juices into small saucepan. Blend cornstarch and 1 tablespoon water. Stir cornstarch mixture into cooking juices and cook, stirring, until sauce boils and thickens. Pour over onions. Combine croutons, Parmesan cheese, and chopped parsley; sprinkle evenly over onions.

Festive Beets

Makes 4 servings

1 (16-ounce) can diced beets
¼ cup sour cream
1 tablespoon tarragon vinegar or cider vinegar
1 teaspoon sugar

½ teaspoon salt
1 green onion, minced
Dash cayenne pepper

Warm beets in a small saucepan over medium heat; drain off liquid. Stir in sour cream, tarragon or cider vinegar, sugar, salt, onion, and cayenne pepper. Continue to heat slowly over medium heat. When hot, serve immediately.

Company Cauliflower

Makes 6 servings

2 teaspoons sesame seeds
1 medium head cauliflower
Dash salt

Dash pepper
1 cup sour cream
½ to 1 cup shredded cheddar cheese

Preheat oven to 375 degrees F. In shallow pan, toast sesame seeds on medium heat for 10 minutes or until browned, shaking pan occasionally. Rinse cauliflower and separate into small florets. Cook in 2-quart covered saucepan, in 1 inch boiling salted water, 8 to 10 minutes, or until tender; drain well. Place half the cauliflower in 1-quart casserole. Season with salt and pepper; spread with ½ cup sour cream and sprinkle with half the cheese; top with 1 teaspoon sesame seed. Repeat layers. Bake 15 minutes, or until heated through.

Broccoli Valhalla

Makes 6 servings

2 pounds fresh broccoli
3 large oranges, peeled and cut into chunks
4 tablespoons margarine

Wash broccoli and cut into 2-inch pieces. Cook in a small amount of salted water until crisp-tender; drain off water and set broccoli aside. Melt margarine in a 12-inch skillet over medium-high heat and sauté oranges for a minute or two. Add broccoli and heat to blend flavors.

Glazed Broccoli Amandine

Makes 6 to 8 servings

2 pounds fresh broccoli or 2 (10-ounce) packages frozen broccoli
¼ cup butter or margarine
2 tablespoons flour

1 cup light cream
1 tablespoon lemon juice
¼ cup grated Parmesan cheese
¼ cup slivered almonds

Wash and separate broccoli into spears. Steam in a small amount of salted water until crisp-tender. Drain off liquid and set broccoli aside.

In a small saucepan, melt butter over medium-high heat until foamy. Stir in flour to make a smooth paste. Add cream and lemon juice and stir until thickened. To serve, place broccoli in a serving dish. Pour sauce over broccoli and sprinkle with Parmesan cheese and slivered almonds.

Nutmeg Spinach Soufflé

Makes 6 servings

1 pound fresh spinach
2 tablespoons margarine
2 tablespoons flour
1 teaspoon salt
1 cup milk
4 egg yolks, beaten well

¼ cup chopped onion
⅛ teaspoon ground nutmeg
4 egg whites
¼ teaspoon cream of tartar
3 tablespoons grated Parmesan cheese

Preheat oven to 375 degrees F. Wash spinach; cook in small amount of salted water in a medium saucepan until tender. Drain; press out all excess water with paper towels or a clean dish towel. Chop spinach and set aside.

Make a roux by melting margarine in a heavy saucepan over medium-high heat. When margarine is melted and foamy, stir in flour and salt. Cook and stir until golden and fragrant, about 30 seconds to 1 minute. Gradually add milk, cooking and stirring until thickened. Gradually add beaten egg yolks. Stir in spinach, onion, and nutmeg. Remove from heat.

In a large clean bowl, beat egg whites and cream of tartar until stiff peaks form. Fold in spinach mixture. Pour into a greased soufflé dish or 1½-quart casserole dish. Sprinkle with Parmesan cheese. Bake for 50 minutes or until table knife inserted in center comes out clean.

Zucchini Boats

Spinach Supreme

Makes 8 servings

2 (10-ounce) packages frozen chopped spinach
2 cups cooked rice
2 cups grated cheddar cheese
4 eggs, beaten well
4 tablespoons margarine, softened

⅔ cup milk
¼ cup chopped onion
1 tablespoon Worcestershire sauce
2 teaspoons salt
1 teaspoon crushed rosemary

Preheat oven to 350 degrees F. Cook spinach according to package directions and drain well; set aside. In a large bowl, combine rice, cheese, beaten eggs, margarine, milk, chopped onion, Worcestershire sauce, salt, and rosemary. Stir in spinach and pour mixture into a greased casserole dish. Bake 35 minutes.

Zucchini Boats

Makes 6 servings

3 medium zucchini squash
1½ cups soft bread crumbs
¼ cup grated Parmesan cheese
1 egg, beaten well
2 green onions, minced

1 tablespoon minced parsley
½ teaspoon salt
Paprika
Grated Parmesan cheese

Preheat oven to 350 degrees F. Wash zucchini; cut off ends but don't peel. Cook in boiling, salted water for 7 to 10 minutes. Drain off water and cut zucchini in half lengthwise; carefully remove pulp with spoon, leaving shell intact. In a small bowl mash zucchini pulp with fork and mix with bread crumbs, Parmesan cheese, beaten egg, onions, parsley, and salt. Spoon mixture into zucchini shells and place in baking dish. Sprinkle with additional Parmesan cheese and paprika. Bake, uncovered, for 30 minutes.

Stuffed Zucchini

Makes 6 servings, ½ zucchini each

3 medium zucchini
1 (10-ounce) package frozen spinach, cooked
2 tablespoons flour
½ cup milk

Salt
⅓ cup shredded cheddar cheese
3 strips bacon, cut in half

Preheat oven to 350 degrees F. Trim off ends of zucchini; cook, drain, and cut in half lengthwise. Scoop out pulp; drain and chop pulp and add to cooked spinach. Blend flour and milk; cook and stir until thickened. Add spinach-zucchini mixture. Salt hollowed-out zucchini shells. Add creamed filling; top with cheese and bacon. Bake 20 minutes.

Cabbage Rolls

Makes 6 servings

1 pound lean ground beef
1 cup ground ham
¼ cup chopped onion
⅓ cup tomato sauce
½ cup cooked rice
½ teaspoon chili powder

⅛ teaspoon garlic powder
2 medium heads cabbage
1 cup tomato sauce
¾ cup grated sharp cheddar cheese
½ teaspoon seasoned salt

Preheat oven to 350 degrees F. Brown ground beef in a 12-inch skillet; drain off fat. Add ground ham, onion, ⅓ cup tomato sauce, rice, chili powder, and garlic powder; mix thoroughly. Core cabbage and remove 12 large outer leaves. Use remainder of cabbage for other recipes. Place leaves in boiling water in a medium saucepan and simmer for 5 minutes or until tender (leaves should be limp but not overcooked). Drain. Spoon meat mixture into center of each cabbage leaf. Fold up to make a tight roll and place seam-side down in a 9x13-inch baking pan. Mix 1 cup tomato sauce with grated cheese and seasoned salt. Pour over top of cabbage rolls. Or cover and refrigerate, then bake 30 minutes. Keep warm in oven set at 300 degrees until ready to serve.

Savory Cabbage

Makes 4 to 6 servings

1 medium head cabbage, shredded
½ teaspoon salt
Water
2 tablespoons butter or margarine

1 teaspoon finely chopped green onion
¼ cup heavy cream
Pepper

Cook cabbage in salted boiling water to cover until just tender. Drain well. In large skillet, melt butter; add onion, and cook for about 5 minutes or until onion is soft but not brown. Add cabbage and mix well. Pour cream over cabbage, and sprinkle with pepper. Serve at once.

Lemon-Parsley Turnips

Makes 6 servings

3 medium turnips
1 tablespoon butter
2 teaspoons freshly snipped parsley

1 teaspoon finely chopped green onion
1 teaspoon lemon juice

Peel and cut turnips into 2-inch strips, julienne style. Cook in small amount of boiling, salted water, until tender, about 10 minutes. Drain off water. Toss parsnips in a medium bowl with butter, parsley, onion, and lemon juice.

Deluxe Peas and Celery

Makes 6 servings

2 tablespoons butter
1 cup sliced mushrooms
½ cup bias-cut celery
2 tablespoons finely chopped onions

½ teaspoon salt
Black pepper to taste
¼ teaspoon savory salt
1 (10-ounce) package frozen peas, cooked and drained

Melt butter over medium-high heat in a 12-inch skillet. Sauté mushrooms, celery, and onions until softened and onions are translucent, about 8 to 10 minutes. Add salt, pepper, and savory salt. Stir in cooked peas and serve right away.

Almond Celery Casserole

Makes 4 to 6 servings

4 cups diagonally sliced celery
1 (10-ounce) can cream of celery soup
½ cup sour cream
1 cup sliced water chestnuts

½ cup shredded sharp cheddar cheese
½ cup slivered almonds
½ cup seasoned bread crumbs (stuffing mix)

Preheat oven to 350 degrees F. for Cook celery in lightly salted boiling water, just until tender-crisp. Drain well and add soup, sour cream, and water chestnuts. Pour into shallow 2-quart baking dish. Top with cheese, then almonds, then bread crumbs. Bake 30 minutes, or until hot and lightly browned.

Lemon Carrots and Apples

Makes about 8 servings

12 medium-sized carrots, cut in thin slices
½ teaspoon salt
1 teaspoon grated lemon peel

¼ cup butter or margarine
2 large tart apples, peeled, cored, and cut in ⅓-inch slices
2 tablespoons chopped parsley

Preheat oven to 375 degrees F. Place carrots in shallow 2-quart casserole. Sprinkle with salt and lemon peel; dot with butter. Bake, covered, until almost tender, about 30 minutes. Stir in apples. Cover and bake 10 to 20 minutes more, or until apples are tender. Stir well just before serving, and sprinkle with parsley.

Pineapple Carrots

Makes 4 servings

3 cups sliced carrots
1 cup pineapple chunks, unsweetened, canned or fresh
½ teaspoon seasoned salt

3 tablespoons orange juice
1 tablespoon butter or margarine

Preheat oven to 375 degrees F. Place carrots, pineapple, salt, and orange juice in 1½-quart casserole. Dot with butter, and cover. Bake 45 to 55 minutes.

Carrots Lyonnaise

Makes 6 servings

1 chicken bouillon cube
½ cup boiling water
6 medium carrots, peeled and julienned
2 tablespoons butter
2 medium onions, sliced

1 tablespoon flour
¼ teaspoon salt
Dash pepper
Pinch sugar
¾ cup water

Dissolve bouillon cube in boiling water in a medium saucepan. Add carrots; return to boiling, then reduce heat to a simmer and cook for 7 to 10 minutes, until crisp-tender. While carrots are cooking, melt butter in a small skillet over medium-high heat. Add sliced onions and sauté until translucent. Add flour, salt, pepper, sugar, and ¾ cup water. Stir until thickened. Stir in cooked carrots and the cooking water. Stir until all ingredients are blended. Serve hot.

Company Carrots

Makes 6 to 8 servings

2½ pounds carrots, peeled and cut in long, narrow strips
   (about 2-inch pieces)
½ cup mayonnaise
1 tablespoon prepared horseradish

1 tablespoon minced parsley
Salt and pepper to taste
½ cup fine cracker crumbs (Ritz®, for example)
3 tablespoons margarine

Preheat oven to 375 degrees F. Bring a small amount of salted water to a boil in a medium saucepan. Add carrot strips; return to boiling, then reduce heat to a simmer and cook carrots until crisp-tender. Drain carrots, reserving ¼ cup of liquid. Put carrots in a 1½-quart casserole dish and set aside. Combine carrot liquid with mayonnaise, horseradish, parsley, salt, and pepper. Mix well and pour over carrots. Sprinkle cracker crumbs on top and dot with margarine. Bake, uncovered, 20 minutes.

Pineapple Carrots

Cheese Sauce

Makes enough for 8 to 10 servings

3 tablespoons butter or margarine

3 tablespoons flour

1½ teaspoons prepared mustard

1½ cups milk

½ pound grated cheddar cheese

½ teaspoon salt

1 dash hot pepper sauce

1 tablespoon onion juice

1 tablespoon Worcestershire sauce

Melt butter; add flour and mustard, and blend. Add milk; stir over medium heat until thick. Stir in cheese, salt, hot pepper sauce, onion juice, and Worcestershire sauce. Stir until thick. Remove from heat. Serve on cauliflower, broccoli, or cabbage.

Noodles Romanoff

Makes about 16 servings

2 (8-ounce) packages noodles

3 cups large curd cottage cheese

2 cloves garlic, mashed

2 teaspoons Worcestershire sauce

2 cups sour cream

½ cup milk

1 bunch green onions, chopped

½ teaspoon Tabasco sauce

1 cup grated Parmesan cheese

Preheat oven to 350 degrees F. Cook noodles according to package directions. Drain. Combine with other ingredients. Pour into buttered 2- or 3-quart casserole. Bake until bubbly, about 15 minutes covered, then 15 minutes uncovered.

Note: Ingredients may be prepared ahead of time, then refrigerated. Allow an additional 15 minutes cooking time.

Confetti Risotto

Makes 20 servings

3 cups risotto, boiled

1 red pepper, diced

1 green pepper, diced

1 yellow pepper, diced

1 red onion, peeled and diced

¼ cup olive oil

Salt and pepper to taste

Boil the pasta according to directions on package. Clean and dice all the peppers and onion. Heat a sauté pan to sizzling. Add the oil and the peppers and onion. Sauté for 2 minutes only. Mix the risotto with the vegetables just before serving. Add salt and pepper to taste.

Oriental Rice

Ingredients	10 servings	20 servings
Bacon	¼ pound	½ pound
Onions, diced	1 cup	2 cups
Carrots, diced	½ cup	1 cup
Celery, diced	¾ cup	1½ cups
Green pepper, diced	¼ cup	½ cup
Cooked meat, diced	2 cups	4 cups
Soy sauce	3 tablespoons	6 tablespoons
Cold cooked rice	3 cups	6 cups

In large skillet, cook bacon until crisp; remove from skillet. Add onions and stir-fry one minute. Add carrots and stir-fry one minute. Add celery and green pepper and stir-fry one minute. Add meat and soy sauce and heat through. Break up cold cooked rice. Stir gently into meat and vegetables, taking care that each grain of rice is coated with oil and liquids that have formed in the pan. Heat through; add crumbled bacon and serve immediately.

Rice Pilaf (shown with Salmon Steaks on page 178)

Makes 10 (½-cup) servings

2 tablespoons butter
1½ cups uncooked rice
½ cup diced onion
¾ cup celery, diced

4½ cups hot chicken broth
2 tablespoons chopped parsley
6 tablespoons slivered almonds

Melt butter in hot sauté pan. Add rice, onion, and celery; stir and cook until slightly brown. Add chicken broth. Cover and simmer on low heat until moisture has been absorbed and rice is tender. Add parsley and almonds just before serving.

Hash Brown Quiche

Makes 8 servings

8 frozen shredded hash brown potato patties
½ cup butter, melted
1 cup cubed cooked ham
1 cup grated cheddar cheese

1 cup grated Swiss cheese
8 eggs
2 cups milk or cream
½ teaspoon salt

Preheat oven to 350 degrees F. Place hash brown potato patties in greased 9x13-inch pan. Pour melted butter evenly over the surface of potato patties and bake for 20 minutes. Remove from oven. Sprinkle potatoes with ham and cheeses. In a large bowl beat eggs. Add milk or cream and salt and stir well. Pour mixture over cheeses and ham. Bake 30 minutes, until puffy and golden brown.

Hash Browned Potatoes

Makes 10 servings

5 cups peeled and diced russet potatoes
1½ tablespoons butter

1½ teaspoons chopped fresh thyme
Salt and pepper to taste

Cook the potatoes in salted boiling water for 10 minutes or until tender. Remove from heat, drain, and set aside. Heat a large skillet until a drop of water sizzles. Add the butter and the potatoes. Add the fresh thyme, salt, and pepper. Cook the potatoes until they are browned on one side and then turn to brown the second side. Remove from heat and serve immediately. (Potatoes will be soggy if held.)

Potato Casserole

Makes 8 to 10 servings

5 large potatoes
3 tablespoons butter or margarine, melted
1 (10.5-ounce) can cream of chicken soup
1 cup sour cream
1 cup milk

3 tablespoons finely chopped green onions
¾ cup shredded sharp cheddar cheese
¾ cup cornflake crumbs or dry bread crumbs
2 tablespoons butter or margarine, melted
3 tablespoons grated Parmesan cheese

Preheat oven to 325 degrees F. Boil unpared potatoes until tender. Drain and peel; shred coarsely. Place in 2- or 3-quart casserole. Pour melted butter over potatoes. Mix together soup, sour cream, milk, green onions, and cheese. Pour evenly over potatoes. Do not mix. Toss crumbs with melted butter and Parmesan cheese; sprinkle on top of casserole. Bake 30 minutes.

Roasted Potatoes

Makes 10 servings

15 medium new potatoes, quartered
¼ cup butter, melted
1 tablespoon chopped fresh parsley,

1 tablespoon chopped fresh thyme
Salt and pepper to taste

Preheat oven to 350 degrees F. In a large bowl mix butter, parsley, thyme, and salt and pepper. Toss in the quartered potatoes until they are well coated. Spray a jelly-roll pan with nonstick cooking spray. Spread the potatoes evenly on the prepared pan.

Bake in preheated oven for 30 minutes or until the potatoes are tender. Reduce heat in the oven to 170 degrees F. or the lowest temperature your oven will go. Hold until ready to serve.

Potatoes au Gratin

Makes 10 to 12 servings

6 medium potatoes, peeled and diced
1 medium onion, chopped
½ green pepper, chopped fine
2 teaspoons salt
4 tablespoons margarine
½ cup flour

3½ cups milk
1¼ teaspoons salt
⅛ teaspoon black pepper
3 or 4 cups cubed cooked ham
1½ cups grated cheddar cheese

Preheat oven to 350 degrees F. Place potatoes, onion, green pepper, and 2 teaspoons salt in a large saucepan. Cover with water and bring to a boil. Turn off heat and let sit for 5 minutes, covered. Drain and spread potato mixture in a 9x13-inch baking pan; set aside.

Make a white sauce by melting margarine in a heavy saucepan over medium-high heat. When margarine starts to foam, stir in flour to make a roux. Cook and stir until fragrant and golden brown, about 30 seconds to 1 minute. Add milk, 1¼ teaspoons salt, and pepper; cook and stir until thickened. Reduce heat and stir in cubed ham and half of the grated cheese. After cheese has melted, pour sauce over potatoes. Top with remaining cheese. Bake 35 to 40 minutes.

Snow-Whipped Potato Boats

Snow-Whipped Potato Boats

Makes 6 servings

6 large baking potatoes
3 slices bacon, cooked crisp and crumbled
½ cup sour cream
½ cup milk

1 teaspoon salt
⅛ teaspoon pepper
4 green onions, chopped
½ cup grated cheddar cheese

Preheat oven to 400 degrees F. Wash potatoes and rub skins with vegetable oil. Bake for 1 hour, or until potatoes are fork-tender. Remove potatoes from oven and reduce oven heat to 350 degrees F. Cut a slice from top of each potato and scoop out pulp. In a medium bowl mash pulp with a fork, then stir in sour cream, milk, salt, pepper, and green onions. Whip until fluffy. Fill potato shells with mixture and sprinkle with grated cheese and crumbled bacon. Bake 10 minutes.

Potato Wedges

Makes 10 servings

5 cups Yukon gold Idaho potatoes, peeled
1½ tablespoons butter
½ teaspoon salt

¼ teaspoon white pepper
1½ teaspoons chopped fresh parsley

Cut the potatoes into uniform wedges. Cook the potatoes in salted boiling water for 10 minutes or until tender. Remove from heat, drain, and set aside. Heat a large skillet until a drop of water sizzles. Add the butter and the potatoes. Cook the potatoes until they are browned and crisp on one side and then turn to brown the second side. Once the potatoes are cooled, remove pan from heat and toss in salt, pepper, and fresh parsley until potatoes are evenly coated. (Potatoes will be soggy if held.)

Pineappled Sweet Potatoes

Makes 8 servings

6 medium sweet potatoes or yams, peeled
⅓ cup sugar
⅓ cup brown sugar
¼ teaspoon salt
2 tablespoons cornstarch

½ cup pineapple juice
½ cup orange juice
1 (13.5-ounce) can pineapple chunks, tidbits, or crushed
    pineapple, well drained
2 tablespoons butter

Preheat oven to 350 degrees F. Cook sweet potatoes in boiling salted water until tender. Cut into thick slices; arrange in shallow baking dish. In heavy saucepan, stir and blend well sugars, salt, and cornstarch. In small saucepan, bring fruit juices to a boil; gradually add to sugar mixture. Cook and stir until thickened. Add pineapple and butter; pour over sweet potatoes. Serve immediately, or place in preheated oven just until bubbly hot.

Southwest Egg Wrap with Homemade Salsa

Makes 6 to 8 servings

14 eggs
½ teaspoon salt
¼ teaspoon white pepper
1½ tablespoons olive oil
1 red bell pepper, julienned
1 green bell pepper, julienned
1 yellow bell pepper, julienned

1 small red onion, julienned
6 to 8 jalapeño flavored tortillas, warmed
14 to 16 slices bacon, cooked and drained
2 cups shredded cheddar cheese
2 tomatoes, diced
1 recipe Fruit Salsa (see below)

Beat eggs and season with salt and pepper. Cover and store this in the refrigerator until ready for service.

Preheat a sauté pan until a small amount of water sizzles in the pan. Carefully add the olive oil to coat the bottom of the pan. Add the peppers and onions to the hot pan. Sauté these only until the color of the peppers brightens slightly. Do not overcook them. Set these aside and keep warm.

Scramble the eggs in another hot sauté or nonstick pan. When you are ready to make the wraps, place a warmed tortilla in the center of a clean work area. Spoon in ½ cup of scrambled eggs, two strips of bacon, and 2 table-spoons of the pepper and onion mixture. Add approximately ¼ cup of the shredded cheddar cheese. Fold up the tortilla from the bottom, bringing the bottom two-thirds of the way up the center. Fold in each side approximately 1 inch. Roll the wrap up to complete the fold and set aside—keeping it warm—until you complete all the wraps. Serve the wrap whole or cut in half on a plate with Fruit Salsa (see below) as a garnish.

Fruit Salsa

Makes 10 (4-ounce) servings

1 cantaloupe, peeled and diced
1 honeydew melon, peeled and diced
1 red onion, peeled and diced
1 red bell pepper, diced
1 yellow bell pepper, diced
2 tablespoons fresh cilantro, chopped

2 tablespoons lime juice
1 jalapeño chili pepper, seeded and diced
3 tablespoons raspberry vinegar
½ teaspoon salt
3 tablespoons olive oil

Combine all ingredients in a glass bowl. Cover and refrigerate for at least 1 hour.

Mexican Quiche

Makes 6 to 8 servings

½ pound ground pork sausage

½ cup sliced green onion

2 cloves garlic, minced

1 (4-ounce) can diced green chili peppers, drained

2 cups grated American or cheddar cheese

2 tablespoons flour

1 cup light cream or milk

½ teaspoon hot pepper sauce

4 eggs, beaten well

1 (9-inch) pastry shell (see page 216), baked for 10 minutes in a 375-degree oven

Note: Instead of using a traditional pie crust, you can shape one 8-ounce can of Pillsbury® Refrigerated Crescent Dinner Rolls into a pie shell in the bottom of a 9-inch pie plate.

Preheat oven to 325 degrees F. In a 12-inch skillet, brown sausage, onions, and garlic over medium-high heat; drain off fat. Stir in chilies and set aside. Toss cheese and flour in a medium saucepan; pour in cream and cook and stir over medium heat until cheese is melted. Add hot pepper sauce. Gradually blend beaten eggs into hot cream mixture. Stir in meat mixture and pour into pastry shell. Bake 20 to 25 minutes, or until knife inserted 2 inches from pastry's edge comes out clean. Let stand 10 minutes before serving.

Vegetable Quiche

Makes 8 servings

1 (10-inch) unbaked pastry shell (see page 216)

4 cups cut-up fresh or frozen vegetables (carrots, broccoli, cauliflower, zucchini, or Italian green beans)

½ cup diced tomatoes

¼ cup chopped green onion

1½ cups grated Swiss cheese

4 eggs

1 cup half and half

½ cup sour cream

1 teaspoon salt

¼ teaspoon black pepper

¼ teaspoon dried oregano

½ teaspoon baking powder

Preheat oven to 400 degrees F. Bake pastry shell for 10 minutes. Remove from oven and let cool on wire rack. Reset oven to 325 degrees F. Blanch vegetables in small amount of water until crisp-tender. Drain off water and pour vegetables into bottom of pastry shell. Sprinkle with grated Swiss cheese. Beat together eggs, half and half, sour cream, salt, pepper, oregano, and baking powder. Pour over vegetables and cheese. Bake for 40 to 45 minutes. Insert a clean table knife into center of pie. If knife comes out clean, quiche is done. Quiche will be puffy and golden brown.

Oatmeal Crisp Pie Crust

Oatmeal Crisp Pie Crust

Makes 4 pie crusts

4⅓ cups all-purpose flour
⅔ cup rolled oats (not quick oats)
½ teaspoon baking powder
½ teaspoon salt
1 tablespoon packed brown sugar

1½ cups shortening
½ cup cold unsalted butter, cut into small pieces
1 egg
1 tablespoon vinegar
Ice water

Stir together flour, oats, baking powder, salt, and brown sugar in a large bowl. Cut in shortening with pastry cutter or 2 knives. Add small pieces of butter and set aside. Mix together egg, vinegar, and enough ice water to measure 1 cup. Add to flour mixture. Mix well. Divide into 4 balls. Wrap with plastic wrap and refrigerate until ready to use.

If the recipe calls for a baked pie shell, bake at 375 degrees F. for 15 to 18 minutes.

Old-Fashioned Pie Crust

Makes 4 (9-inch) pie crusts

4 cups all-purpose flour
1 teaspoon salt
1 cup lard

1 egg, beaten
1 tablespoon vinegar
Water

Place flour and salt in a medium bowl and mix together. Add lard and cut in with a pastry blender until the mixture is the size of small peas (or rub the flour and lard together between the palms of your hands).

In a 1-cup measuring cup, beat egg with a fork. Add vinegar to the egg and add water to make 1 cup. Stir slightly and pour over first mixture. With a fork stir together until all dry ingredients are stirred in.

If the recipe calls for a baked pie shell, bake at 375 degrees F. for 15 to 18 minutes.

Graham Cracker Pie Crust

Makes one 9-inch crust

16 graham cracker squares
3 tablespoons sugar

⅓ cup butter or margarine, melted

Place graham crackers in a plastic bag (8 at a time). Seal bag and roll with rolling pin to make fine crumbs. Pour into a medium bowl and repeat the process with remaining crackers. Add sugar and stir with a fork. Pour the melted butter on top of the crumb mixture. Stir until crumbs are moist. Pour mixture into a 9-inch pie pan and gently press crumbs into the bottom and sides of pan. This crust may be used either chilled or baked. If the recipe calls for a baked pie shell, bake at 375 degrees F. for 12 minutes.

Lion House Pie Crust

Makes 2 to 3 (9-inch) pie crusts

¼ cup butter

⅓ cup lard

¼ cup margarine

⅓ cup shortening

1 tablespoon granulated sugar

½ teaspoon baking powder

1 teaspoon salt

1 tablespoon nonfat dry milk

1½ cups pastry flour

1½ cups bread flour

½ cup plus 1 tablespoon cold water

In a medium bowl, cream together butter, lard, margarine, and shortening using an electric mixer. In a separate bowl, whisk together sugar, baking powder, salt, and dry milk powder; add to creamed butter mixture and mix briefly. Add pastry flour and beat until blended. Add bread flour and mix slightly. Pour in water and beat again just until water is blended.

Divide dough into 2 or 3 balls. Roll out each ball on a floured board. Line pie pan with dough and cut off excess dough. Flute edges. For recipes that call for baked pie crusts, prick holes in bottom with fork. Bake empty pie shell at 375 degrees F. for 15 to 18 minutes, or until light golden brown. Otherwise, fill unbaked pie shell and bake according to recipe.

Note: You may substitute 3 cups all-purpose flour for the pastry and bread flour called for in the recipe. Additionally, this dough may also be made by hand-cutting the fats into the dry ingredients. This recipe may be used to make the crust for any recipe in this book that calls for a single- or double-crust pastry.

Pastry for Double-Crust Pie

Makes 2 (9-inch) pie crusts

2½ cups all-purpose flour

¼ cup granulated sugar

½ teaspoon salt

1 cup butter-flavored shortening, chilled

1 egg, beaten

1 tablespoon vinegar

¼ cup ice water

In a medium bowl, mix together flour, sugar, and salt. Cut the shortening into the flour until pea-sized crumbs form. Carefully stir in beaten egg and vinegar. Gently sprinkle in water until dough starts to hold together. Shape dough into 2 balls.

If the recipe calls for a baked pie shell, roll out dough, press into pie pan, trim and flute edges, prick bottom of shell with a fork, and bake at 375 degrees F. for 15 to 18 minutes.

Helpful Tips for Making Pies

- For better sealing, brush edges of pie crusts with water just before putting on top crust.

- For a beautiful golden top, brush pie crust with milk, cream, half and half, or evaporated milk and sprinkle with sugar before baking.

- If your oven is large enough, bake 4 to 8 pies at a time and freeze in gallon freezer bags. When pies are frozen, stack them on top of each other. When needed, take prebaked frozen pie out of plastic bag and bake at 325 degrees F. for 35 to 40 minutes.

- Keep pie shells from shrinking by pricking bottoms with a fork before baking. You can also prevent shrinking by lining dough with aluminum foil. Pour 2 to 3 cups dried beans, wheat, or rice into foil-lined shell and bake for half the baking time. Lift out foil and contents and continue baking for remainder of baking time.

- Experiment with different pastry recipes for your pie crusts. You may find that you prefer one over another, or that one tastes best with fruit pies and another tastes better with cream pies.

Assembling and Baking Fruit Pies

To assemble a fruit pie, line a 9-inch pie pan with dough, pressing dough lightly against sides of pan and letting dough hang over edges of pie pan.

Spoon pie filling into unbaked shell. Brush edge of dough with water and place top crust on pie. Seal crusts together by gently pressing around the edge of pie pan. Cut excess dough from edge of pie. Crimp or flute edges if desired.

Butterscotch Cream Pie

Makes 1 pie

1 baked 9-inch pie shell (see page 216)
1⅓ cups sugar
2½ cups milk
¾ cup whipped cream
5 tablespoons cornstarch
3 egg yolks*

¼ teaspoon salt
1 teaspoon vanilla
2 tablespoons butter or margarine
1 cup heavy cream
¼ cup chopped nuts or toasted coconut, for garnish

Measure sugar into a heavy saucepan or skillet. Stir constantly over high heat until sugar is nearly melted. Reduce heat to medium and continue stirring until all sugar is melted and a light amber color. In the meantime, heat milk. Stir hot milk into melted sugar cautiously. Sugar will bubble and steam, then harden. Keep heat on low and stir occasionally until the hard sugar completely dissolves in the milk.

In a small bowl, add whipped cream to cornstarch gradually to make a smooth paste and then stir into hot milk mixture. Cook and stir until a smooth, thick pudding is formed. Let it boil a minute or two, stirring vigorously, then remove from heat. Place egg yolks in a small bowl and beat with a fork. Add salt, and then stir in some of the hot pudding. Stir egg mixture back into pudding and cook another 2 or 3 minutes. Remove from heat. Add vanilla and butter. Cool 5 minutes and then pour into baked pie shell. Chill 3 to 4 hours.

When ready to serve, whip the cream and spread over pie. Sprinkle with nuts or toasted coconut.

*Note: 2 whole eggs may be used, but filling may not be as smooth.

Buttermilk Pie

1½ cups sugar
1 cup buttermilk
½ cup Bisquick
⅓ cup margarine or butter, melted
1 teaspoon vanilla
3 eggs
Fresh fruit, for garnish
Caramel sauce, for garnish
Whipped cream, for garnish

Caramel Sauce

¼ cup butter
1½ cups brown sugar
½ cup heavy cream
2 tablespoons corn syrup
1 teaspoon vanilla

Preheat oven to 350 degrees F. Grease pie pan and set aside. In a medium bowl, combine sugar, buttermilk, Bisquick, butter, vanilla, and eggs. Stir until smooth. Pour into greased pie pan and bake 30 minutes, or until knife inserted in center comes out clean. Cool 5 minutes. Serve warm or cold with fresh fruit or caramel sauce and whipped cream.

For caramel sauce: In a heavy 2-quart saucepan, melt butter on high heat. Add brown sugar, heavy cream, and corn syrup. Bring to a boil, stirring frequently. Reduce heat to medium, until sauce thickens slightly, about 5 to 7 minutes. Remove from heat and add vanilla. Allow to cool in pan for 15 minutes. Drizzle over warm pie.

Peanut Butter Pie

Makes 2 pies

2 baked (9-inch) pie shells (see page 216)
¾ cup peanut butter
1½ cups powdered sugar
4 cups milk, divided
2 cups half and half
2 tablespoons butter

1¼ cups sugar, divided
3 egg yolks
¼ teaspoon salt
½ cup cornstarch
1½ teaspoons vanilla

In a medium bowl, mix together peanut butter and powdered sugar by hand. (This works best using the same technique as for cutting shortening into flour for pie dough.) Put a thin layer of peanut butter mixture in bottom of baked pie shells. Reserve some for garnishing tops of finished pies.

Place 3 cups milk in top of a double boiler and add half and half, butter, and ¾ cup sugar and stir. Cook until butter is melted and milk looks scalded.

In a bowl, whisk the egg yolks until well broken up; then add ½ cup sugar and salt and whisk together very well. Slowly add this mixture to the hot milk mixture, stirring constantly. Stir for approximately ½ minute and then allow to cook for 15 to 20 minutes. (This gives the eggs time to cook and start the thickening process. Undercooking at this point slows the finishing process down by as much as half an hour.)

Mix 1 cup milk and cornstarch together and slowly add to the hot mixture. Be careful to stir constantly or lumps will form. Continue stirring for at least 2 minutes and every 5 minutes for the next 15 to 20 minutes. When pudding is thick enough, stir in vanilla. Remove the whole double boiler from stove (the hot water will help keep the pudding hot while you assemble the pies).

Pour filling over peanut butter mixture in pie shells. Fill pies so the tops are a little rounded. Sprinkle reserved peanut butter filling on top. Gently pat the mixture so it doesn't fall off when serving. Chill well.

Coconut Cream Pie

Basic Cream Pie with Variations

Makes 2 pies

2 baked (9-inch) pie shells (see page 216)
4 cups milk, divided
2 cups half and half
2 tablespoons butter
1¼ cups granulated sugar, divided

3 egg yolks
¼ teaspoon salt
½ cup cornstarch
1½ teaspoons vanilla
Whipped cream, for garnish

Place 3 cups milk in top pan of a double boiler; add half and half, butter, and ¾ cup of the sugar and stir. Heat over medium-high heat until butter is melted and milk is scalded.

In a small bowl, whisk egg yolks well; add remaining ½ cup sugar and salt and whisk very well. Slowly add egg mixture to hot milk mixture, stirring constantly for about half a minute; allow mixture to cook for 15 to 20 minutes, stirring frequently. (This gives eggs time to cook and start thickening. Undercooking at this point can slow the finishing process by as much as half an hour.)

Mix 1 cup milk and cornstarch in a small bowl and slowly add to hot mixture, stirring constantly to avoid formation of lumps. Continue stirring for at least 2 minutes and then stir every 5 minutes for 15 to 20 minutes. When pudding is thick, stir in vanilla. Remove double boiler from stove. Pour half of the filling into each pie shell, rounding tops of pies. Cool on wire racks then chill in refrigerator 3 to 4 hours. When ready to serve, whip cream and spread over pie.

Coconut Cream Pie

Add 1 cup coconut (toasted, if desired) to pie filling with vanilla. Pour into baked shells. Chill 3 to 4 hours. When ready to serve, whip cream and spread over pie. Top each pie with another ¼ cup coconut.

Banana Cream Pie

Before pouring hot filling into pie shells, slice 2 bananas into each baked shell. Pour filling over bananas. Chill 3 to 4 hours. When ready to serve, whip cream and spread over pies.

Chocolate Cream Pie

Add 1 to 1⅓ cups semisweet chocolate chips to hot pudding. Stir until melted. Pour filling into pie shells. Chill 3 to 4 hours. When ready to serve, whip cream and spread over pies.

Pralines and Cream Pie

Add 1 cup caramel ice cream topping and 1 cup chopped pecans to basic filling. Pour into baked pie shells. Chill 3 to 4 hours. Top with sweetened whipped cream before serving.

German Chocolate Pie

To hot filling, add 1½ cups semisweet chocolate chips, 1 cup coconut, ½ cup chopped pecans, and ½ cup caramel ice cream topping. Stir until well blended. Pour into baked pie shells.

Tropical Isle Pie

To hot filling, add 1 cup coconut, ⅔ cup drained, crushed pineapple, and ⅔ cup drained mandarin oranges. Pour into baked pie shells.

Almond Coconut Pie

Makes 2 pies

2 (9-inch) chocolate ready crusts (purchase pre-made at your local store)

4 cups milk, divided

2 cups half and half

2 tablespoons butter

1¼ cups sugar, divided

3 egg yolks

¼ teaspoon salt

½ cup cornstarch

1½ teaspoons vanilla

1⅔ cups flaked coconut, divided

1⅔ cups slivered almonds, toasted and divided

1½ cups grated chocolate, divided

Whipped cream, for garnish

Place 3 cups milk in top of a double boiler and add half and half, butter, and ¾ cup sugar and stir. Cook until butter is melted and milk looks scalded.

In a bowl, whisk egg yolks until well broken up; then add ½ cup sugar and salt and whisk together very well. Slowly add this mixture to the hot milk mixture, stirring constantly. Stir for approximately ½ minute and then allow to cook for 15 to 20 minutes. (This gives the eggs time to cook and start the thickening process. Undercooking at this point slows the finishing process down by as much as half an hour.)

Mix 1 cup milk and cornstarch together and slowly add to the hot mixture. Be careful to stir constantly or lumps will form. Continue stirring for at least 2 minutes and every 5 minutes for the next 15 to 20 minutes.

When pudding is thick enough, stir in vanilla. Stir in ⅔ cup coconut and ⅔ cup almonds. Remove the whole double boiler from stove (the hot water will help keep the pudding hot while you assemble the pies).

Place ½ cup grated chocolate into bottom of pie shells. Pour filling over chocolate in pie shells. Fill pies so the tops are a little rounded. Cool at least 2 hours. Top with whipped cream and garnish with remaining chocolate, coconut, and almonds.

Almond Chocolate Pie

Makes 1 pie

1 graham cracker crust (see page 215) or baked (9-inch) pie shell (see page 216)

½ cup slivered almonds

1 (7-ounce) chocolate bar

½ cup half and half

18 large marshmallows

1 cup heavy cream

Preheat oven to 350 degrees F. Place almonds on a cookie sheet and bake for 5 to 7 minutes until light golden brown. Remove from oven. Be careful not to overcook; almonds will continue to brown after being removed from the oven.

Place chocolate bar, half and half, and marshmallows in top of a double boiler and heat until chocolate bar and marshmallows are melted. In a large bowl, whip the cream until stiff; fold cream and almonds into chocolate mixture. Pour into crust and refrigerate to cool. When cool, place in freezer. Remove from freezer 1 hour before serving.

Grasshopper Pie

Makes 1 pie

Crust

1½ cups finely crushed chocolate wafers (25 wafers)

6 tablespoons butter or margarine, melted

Filling

6½ cups miniature marshmallows

½ cup milk

¼ cup crème de menthe syrup

1 cup heavy cream

Few drops green food coloring (optional)

Whipped cream, for garnish

Chocolate curls, for garnish

For crust: Combine crushed wafers and melted butter. Spread evenly on bottom and sides of 9-inch pie pan. Chill about 1 hour.

For filling: In large saucepan, combine marshmallows and milk. Cook over low heat until marshmallows are melted. Remove from heat and cool, stirring several times while cooling. Add crème de menthe. Whip cream and fold into marshmallow mixture. Add food coloring, if desired.

Pour filling into crust. Chill 2 hours before serving. Garnish with whipped cream and chocolate curls.

Chocolate Angel Pie

Makes 1 pie

Meringue Shell

- 2 egg whites, room temperature
- ⅛ teaspoon salt
- ⅛ teaspoon cream of tartar
- ½ cup sugar
- ½ cup finely chopped nuts
- ½ teaspoon vanilla

Filling

- 1½ cups heavy cream
- 1 teaspoon vanilla
- 1 (8-ounce) milk chocolate bar with almonds

For meringue shell: Preheat oven to 300 degrees F. In a medium bowl, beat egg whites, salt, and cream of tartar until frothy. Gradually add sugar, beating until stiff peaks form. Fold in nuts and vanilla. Spread into a greased 9-inch pie pan, building up on sides of pan. Bake 50 minutes. Cool completely.

For filling: Whip cream with vanilla; set aside. Break up three-fourths of the chocolate bar into pieces and melt in top of a double boiler or microwave in a glass bowl. When chocolate is just lukewarm, fold into whipped cream and vanilla. Pile chocolate filling into cooled meringue shell. Grate remaining chocolate to garnish pie. Chill in refrigerator for 2 hours before serving.

Baked Alaska Pie

Makes 1 pie

1 baked (9-inch) pie shell (see page 216)
1 quart peppermint ice cream, slightly softened
2 to 3 tablespoons chocolate syrup
5 egg whites

1 teaspoon vanilla
½ teaspoon cream of tartar
⅔ cup sugar

Spoon ice cream into baked pie shell. Drizzle with chocolate syrup. Place in freezer until ready to use.

With an electric mixer, beat egg whites, vanilla, and cream of tartar until foamy. Gradually beat in sugar until mixture is stiff and glossy. Completely cover ice cream in pie shell with meringue, sealing well to edge of crust and piling high. (If desired, pie may be frozen up to 24 hours at this point.)

When ready to serve, bake pie at 500 degrees F. on lowest oven rack for 3 to 5 minutes, or until meringue is light brown. Serve immediately, or return to freezer until ready to serve.

Five-Step Black Bottom Pie

Makes 1 pie

Crust

36 gingersnaps
½ cup butter or margarine, melted
Dash salt

Filling

4 cups milk
4 tablespoons butter or margarine
½ cup cornstarch
1½ cups sugar
½ cup water

4 eggs, separated
2 teaspoons vanilla
2 squares unsweetened baking chocolate
2 envelopes (or 2 tablespoons) unflavored gelatin
½ cup cold water
1 cup sugar
1 teaspoon cream of tartar
2 teaspoons imitation rum flavoring
1 cup whipped cream, for garnish
Flakes of chocolate, for garnish

Step 1: Crush gingersnaps; roll fine and combine with ½ cup melted butter or margarine and salt. Mold evenly into 11-inch springform pan.

Step 2: Scald milk; add butter. Combine cornstarch and sugar; moisten with enough water to make a paste. Stir paste into scalded milk and cook until mixture comes to a boil, stirring constantly. Stir hot mixture gradually into slightly beaten egg yolks. Return to heat and cook 2 minutes. Add vanilla. Remove 2 cups of custard; add chocolate and beat well. Pour into crumb crust and chill.

Step 3: Blend gelatin with cold water; allow to sit a few minutes, then fold into remaining hot custard. Cool.

Step 4: Beat egg whites, 1 cup sugar, and cream of tartar into a meringue. Add rum flavoring and fold into custard from step 2.

Step 5: When chocolate custard has set, pour plain custard on top and chill until set. Serve with whipped cream and bits of chocolate for garnish.

Black Forest Pie

Makes 1 pie

1 unbaked (9-inch) pie shell (see page 216)

Filling

¾ cup butter or margarine

6 tablespoons unsweetened cocoa

1 cup sugar, divided

⅔ cup ground blanched almonds

2 tablespoons flour

3 eggs, separated

2 tablespoons water

Topping

⅓ cup sour cream

2 tablespoons sugar

½ teaspoon vanilla

1 cup canned cherry pie filling

Glaze

½ cup semisweet chocolate chips

1½ teaspoons shortening

For filling: Preheat oven to 350 degrees F. In a medium saucepan, melt butter or margarine; stir in cocoa and ¾ cup sugar. Remove from heat and allow to cool for 5 minutes. Add almonds and flour; stir well. Add egg yolks one at a time, stirring well after each addition. Stir in water. In a medium bowl, beat egg whites at high speed until foamy. Gradually add ¼ cup sugar, beating all the time, until soft peaks form. Fold chocolate mixture into egg whites just until blended. Pour mixture into unbaked pastry shell. Bake 35 to 45 minutes or until wooden toothpick inserted in center comes out clean. Cool 5 minutes.

For topping: In a medium bowl, combine sour cream, sugar, and vanilla. Spread over warm pie. Spoon cherry pie filling over the top and return pie to oven for 5 minutes.

For glaze: Melt chocolate chips and shortening over low heat in a small saucepan, stirring constantly. Drizzle over pie and refrigerate for at least 2 hours.

Macadamia Nut Cream Pie

Makes 10 servings

Crust

½ cup butter, softened	1 egg yolk
¼ cup sugar	½ teaspoon vanilla
¼ teaspoon salt	1 cup flour

Preheat oven to 325 degrees F. In a large bowl, cream together butter, sugar, and salt until light and fluffy. Beat in egg yolk and vanilla until well blended. Add flour all at once and beat at low speed just until flour is incorporated. Refrigerate dough at least 1 hour. Roll out dough on a lightly floured surface. Line a 12-inch pie tin with the pastry. Prick dough all around with fork. Bake 20 minutes or until pastry shell is golden brown.

Filling

1 envelope (1 tablespoon) unflavored gelatin	1 cup milk
⅓ cup water	1 cup diced macadamia nuts
3 egg yolks	½ teaspoon vanilla
⅓ cup sugar	1½ cups heavy cream, whipped and sweetened

In a large saucepan, sprinkle gelatin over water; let stand 5 minutes. Place over low heat and cook, stirring constantly, until gelatin dissolves. Remove from heat and set aside. In a small bowl beat egg yolks and sugar until thick and creamy. Heat milk in a medium saucepan to just below boiling point. Remove from heat. Stir 4 tablespoons hot milk into beaten egg yolk mixture. Return egg yolk mixture to milk in saucepan and cook, stirring constantly, until mixture thickens. Remove from heat, stir in macadamia nuts (reserve some for garnish), vanilla, and gelatin in water, and blend thoroughly. Set aside to cool. When cool, fold in whipped cream (reserve some for garnish). Pour filling into baked and cooled pastry shell. Refrigerate 30 minutes. Top with additional whipped cream that has been sweetened to taste with sugar, and garnish with diced macadamia nuts.

White Chocolate Macadamia Pie

Makes 1 pie

1 baked (9-inch pie) shell (see page 216)

Filling

1 (8-ounce) package cream cheese, softened

⅓ cup sugar

⅓ cup heavy cream, plus ¾ cup whipped soft

6½ ounces white baking chocolate, melted

½ teaspoon orange zest

⅔ cup chopped macadamia nuts, roasted

Ganache

¾ cup semisweet chocolate chips

½ cup heavy cream

Topping

3 cups sweetened whipped cream

1 to 2 tablespoons chopped macadamia nuts

For filling: Beat cream cheese and sugar with an electric mixer until smooth. Scrape bowl with a spatula and mix in ⅓ cup heavy cream. Add melted white chocolate, orange zest, and nuts and stir just until incorporated. Fold in the whipped cream. Spread into baked pie shell and level off with a rubber spatula. Freeze until solid, about 4 hours.

For ganache: Prepare 30 minutes to an hour before serving. Place chocolate chips in a metal mixing bowl and set aside. Bring cream to a simmer over medium heat. Pour simmering cream over chocolate chips and stir until melted. Set aside and allow to cool slightly. Spread warm ganache over top of the frozen pie, smoothing to the edges with a spatula.

For topping: Place sweetened whipped cream in a piping bag and pipe edges of pie with whipped cream or pipe rosettes onto each piece. Sprinkle with macadamia nuts. Refrigerate until ready to serve.

Note: If desired, you can prepare ganache ahead of time, then reheat before finishing pie. To reheat, place the ganache in the microwave on low power for no more than 10 seconds at a time. Stir after each warming, until ganache pours loosely but is not close to boiling. Be very careful when warming chocolate, as it will burn very quickly when heated in the microwave. If chocolate is scorched it is unusable.

Apricot Pineapple Pie

Makes 1 pie

Pastry for (9-inch) double-crust pie (see page 216)
1 (15.25-ounce) can apricot halves
1 (20-ounce) can pineapple tidbits

¾ cup sugar
¼ cup plus 2 tablespoons cornstarch
¼ teaspoon salt

Preheat oven to 375 degrees F. Drain apricots and discard ¼ cup apricot juice. Pour apricots and remaining juice into large mixing bowl. Cut apricots in half, making each piece ¼ of an apricot. Drain pineapple and discard ½ cup pineapple juice. Add pineapple tidbits and remaining juice to apricots. In separate bowl, mix sugar, cornstarch, and salt; pour on top of fruit. Mix well with rubber spatula.

Fill crust. Moisten edge of pie crust with water. Add top crust and seal. Brush with milk and sprinkle with sugar. Bake 45 to 50 minutes or until golden brown.

Pineapple Pie

Makes 1 pie

Pastry for (9-inch) double-crust pie (see page 216)
2 (20-ounce) cans pineapple tidbits in juice
1 cup sugar

3 tablespoons cornstarch
¼ teaspoon salt
1 drop yellow food coloring

Preheat oven to 375 degrees F. Pour pineapple into a bowl. Discard ¾ cup of the juice; keep the rest. Mix sugar, cornstarch, and salt together in a bowl; pour on top of pineapple. Mix well with a rubber spatula. Add food coloring and mix well.

Fill crust. Moisten edge of pie crust with water. Add top crust and seal. Brush with milk and sprinkle with sugar. Bake 45 to 50 minutes or until golden brown.

Lemon Truffle Pie

Makes 1 pie

1 graham cracker crust (see page 215)
or baked (9-inch) pie shell (see page 216)
3 tablespoons cornstarch
⅓ cup sugar plus ¼ cup sugar, divided
1½ cups water
5 tablespoons lemon juice
Zest from 2 lemons

4 egg yolks, beaten
1½ tablespoons butter
1 cup white chocolate chips
2 (8-ounce) packages cream cheese, room temperature
1 cup whipped cream
Toasted sliced almonds, for garnish

Mix cornstarch and ⅓ cup sugar in a medium saucepan; add water and stir. Stir in lemon juice and lemon zest. In a separate bowl beat egg yolks with a fork; add ¼ cup sugar and mix well. Add this mixture to the first and whisk together. Cook on medium heat, stirring constantly until mixture boils for one minute.

Remove from heat; add butter and stir until melted. Remove 1½ cups of liquid and reserve for top layer. Add white chocolate chips to remaining liquid and stir until they are melted and mixed in well. Cut the cream cheese in small cubes and add to the white chocolate mixture. Stir until well mixed and smooth. (You may need to use an electric mixer.)

Pour mixture into baked pie shell or graham cracker crust. Pour the reserved lemon sauce on top and chill at least 2 hours. Spread whipped cream over lemon filling. Garnish with toasted sliced almonds.

Lemon Cream Pie

Makes 1 pie

1¼ cups sugar
¼ teaspoon salt
6 tablespoons cornstarch
1½ cups boiling water
3 eggs, slightly beaten

6 tablespoons lemon juice
¼ teaspoon grated lemon rind
2 tablespoons butter or margarine
1 baked (9-inch) pie shell (see page 216)
1 cup heavy cream, whipped and sweetened

In 2- or 3-quart saucepan, combine sugar, salt, and cornstarch; blend well. Place over medium heat and add boiling water, stirring rapidly until smooth and thick. Bring to full boil to thoroughly cook cornstarch; remove from heat. In medium bowl, beat eggs slightly. Add small amount of hot pudding to eggs while stirring rapidly. Return egg mixture to hot pudding in saucepan and reheat, stirring constantly, just until smooth. Remove from heat; add lemon juice, rind, and butter. Pour into baked pie shell. Cover surface with plastic wrap to prevent skin from forming. Chill. Served topped with whipped cream.

Lemon Truffle Pie

Lime Chiffon Pie

Key Lime Pie

Makes 2 pies

2 graham cracker crusts (see page 215) or baked (9-inch) pie shells (see page 216)

2 envelopes (or 2 tablespoons) unflavored gelatin

1¾ cups sugar, divided

¼ teaspoon salt

6 eggs, separated

¾ cup lime juice

½ cup water

1 teaspoon lime zest

Few drops green food coloring

Whipped cream

Lime, thinly sliced for garnish

Mix gelatin, 1 cup sugar, and salt. Beat egg yolks, lime juice, and water; pour into a saucepan. Add gelatin mixture; stir constantly over medium heat until mixture boils. Stir in lime zest and food coloring. Pour into bowl (do not leave in aluminum pan) and refrigerate until mixture mounds when dropped from spoon. Beat egg whites until soft peaks form. Gradually add ¾ cup sugar and continue beating until stiff. Fold into lime mixture.

Pour into pie shells. Serve with whipped cream and garnish with thin slices of lime.

Lime Chiffon Pie

Makes 1 pie

1 baked (9-inch) pie shell (see page 216)

¼ cup sugar

1 envelope (or 1 tablespoon) unflavored gelatin

½ cup water

¼ cup lime juice

2 egg yolks

1 teaspoon lime zest

1 drop green food coloring, if desired

3 egg whites

¼ cup sugar

1 (8-ounce) tub frozen whipped topping, thawed

In a medium saucepan, combine ¼ cup sugar and gelatin. Add water and lime juice. Cook and stir over low heat until gelatin is completely dissolved. In a medium bowl slightly beat egg yolks. Gradually stir gelatin mixture into egg yolks and then return all of the egg yolk mixture to the saucepan. Bring to a gentle boil; cook and stir 2 minutes more. Remove from heat. Cool slightly. Stir in lime zest and food coloring. Cover and chill until mixture is the consistency of syrup, stirring occasionally.

In a medium bowl, beat the egg whites with an electric mixer on medium speed until soft peaks form. Gradually add ¼ cup sugar, beating on high speed until stiff peaks form. Fold egg whites into slightly thickened gelatin.

Fold whipped topping into gelatin mixture. If necessary, chill the filling until it mounds when spooned (about 1 hour). Spoon the filling into the baked pie shell. Cover and chill at least 4 hours (or overnight, if desired).

Pineapple Cream Pie

Makes 15 servings

Crust

> ¾ cup butter, at room temperature
> 1½ cups flour
> ½ cup chopped nuts

Pineapple Filling

> 1 (20-ounce) can crushed pineapple in juice, divided
> ⅓ cup cornstarch
> 4 egg yolks
> 1 tablespoon water
> 1 cup sugar
> ¼ teaspoon salt
> 2 cups whole milk
> 2 tablespoons butter or margarine
> 1 teaspoon vanilla

Cream Cheese Filling

> 1 (8-ounce) package cream cheese, softened
> ½ cup powdered sugar
> ½ teaspoon vanilla
> ⅓ cup finely chopped macadamia nuts
> ⅓ cup reserved drained pineapple

Topping

> 1 cup heavy cream
> ¼ cup powdered sugar
> Remaining pineapple, liquid squeezed out
> Chopped macadamia nuts

For crust: Preheat oven to 375 degrees F. Mix together butter, flour, and nuts in a medium bowl. Press into a 9x13-inch pan. Bake 15 minutes or until golden brown. Cool completely.

For pineapple filling: Measure 1 cup pineapple and juice, reserving remaining pineapple. Drain juice from measured pineapple. Combine cornstarch, egg yolks, and water in a small bowl. Combine sugar, salt, milk, and drained pineapple in saucepan. Cook over medium heat, stirring constantly, until mixture comes almost to a boil. Reduce heat to low. Add egg yolk mixture slowly, stirring constantly; continue to cook and stir until thickened. Add butter or margarine and vanilla. Remove from heat, cover with wax paper, and refrigerate for 30 minutes, stirring once or twice.

For cream cheese filling: Combine cream cheese and powdered sugar in a medium bowl. Beat with a fork until blended and smooth. Add vanilla, nuts, and ⅓ cup drained pineapple. Mix well. Spread over cooled crust. Top with pineapple filling.

For topping: In a small bowl, whip cream with powdered sugar until soft peaks form. Spread over pie and garnish with pineapple and nuts. (Make sure pineapple is well drained before placing on top of whipped cream.) Serve or refrigerate until ready to serve.

Apple Pie

Makes 1 pie

Pastry for (9-inch) double-crust pie (see page 216)
¾ to 1 cup granulated sugar
2 tablespoons all-purpose flour
½ to 1 teaspoon ground cinnamon

¼ to ½ teaspoon nutmeg
⅛ teaspoon salt
5 to 6 golden delicious apples, peeled, cored, and sliced
2 tablespoons butter or margarine

Preheat oven to 375 degrees F. Roll out pastry for bottom crust and line bottom and sides of pie pan. Roll out top crust, fold in half, and cut three ½-inch slits through both layers of crust, then set aside. In a large bowl, combine dry ingredients and stir. Place sliced apples on top of dry ingredients and stir. Pour apple mixture into bottom of crust. Dot with small pieces of butter.

Moisten edge of pie crust with water. Place top crust on pie and seal. Brush with milk, sprinkle with sugar, and bake 45 to 50 minutes or until apples test tender when a sharp knife is inserted into vent hole in top crust.

Note: A 30-ounce can of apple pie filling may be substituted for fresh apples, sugar, flour, and salt. Pour filling into pie crust. Sprinkle with cinnamon and nutmeg and dot with butter. Follow directions above for finishing pie.

Rhubarb Pie

Makes 1 pie

Pastry for (9-inch) unbaked double-crust pie (see page 216)
4 cups chopped rhubarb, frozen*
1¾ cups sugar
¼ cup flour

2 tablespoons cornstarch
¼ teaspoon salt
1 egg
1 drop red food coloring

Preheat oven to 350 degrees F. Place rhubarb in medium mixing bowl; let thaw 10 to 15 minutes. Drain liquid. In separate bowl, combine sugar, flour, cornstarch, and salt. Beat egg; blend with flour mixture. Add rhubarb and red food coloring; mix well.

Pour into unbaked pie shell. Roll out top crust; cut slits and place over filling. Seal; flute edges. Brush top with milk; sprinkle with sugar, if desired. Bake 45 minutes or until browned.

*Note: Four cups fresh rhubarb may be substituted for frozen rhubarb. Bake 50 to 55 minutes.

Caramel Apple Pie

Makes 1 pie

Pastry for (9-inch) double-crust pie (see page 216)

¾ cup granulated sugar, plus additional for dusting top crust

½ cup all-purpose flour

1 teaspoon ground cinnamon, plus additional for dusting top crust

½ teaspoon kosher salt

½ teaspoon nutmeg

8 apples, peeled, cored, and sliced

1 tablespoon vanilla

2 tablespoons unsalted butter

2 tablespoons cream

Caramel Sauce

¼ cup butter

1½ cups brown sugar

½ cup heavy cream

2 tablespoons corn syrup

1 teaspoon vanilla

For filling: In a large bowl, mix together sugar, flour, cinnamon, kosher salt, and nutmeg. Toss in apples and stir in vanilla. Set aside. Stir the apple mixture every 15 to 20 minutes while making the crust.

Once pastry dough is prepared, roll out pastry for bottom crust 3 inches larger than the pie pan. Ease pastry into pan and cut away so only ½ inch is overlapping the edge of the pie pan. Pour apple filling into prepared crust. Dot the butter over the apples. Brush cream around edges of pie crust.

Roll out pastry for top crust, fold in half, and cut three ½-inch slits through both layers of crust. Unfold crust and place over the apples. Trim away extra crust, leaving 1 inch overlapping. Crimp edges of pie. Brush cream over top and sprinkle sugar and cinnamon over top.

Cover the edges of the pie with foil. Bake at 375 degrees F. for 1 hour and 20 minutes, removing the foil from edges after 30 minutes and covering the whole pie with foil for the last 20 minutes. Pie should be light brown. Cool on a rack for 1 hour. While pie is baking, make the caramel sauce.

For caramel sauce: In a heavy 2-quart saucepan, melt butter on high heat. Add brown sugar, heavy cream, and corn syrup. Bring to a boil, stirring frequently. Reduce heat to medium, until sauce thickens slightly, about 5 to 7 minutes. Remove from heat and add vanilla. Allow to cool in pan for 15 minutes. Drizzle over warm pie.

Swiss Apple-Cherry Pie

Makes 1 pie

Pastry for 2-crust pie (see page 216)
4 tart apples
6 tablespoons butter or margarine
1 cup sugar
2 tablespoons flour

2 teaspoons cinnamon
½ teaspoon nutmeg
1 (21-ounce) can pitted sour red cherries, drained
½ teaspoon sugar
¼ teaspoon cinnamon

Pare, core, and slice apples. Melt 2 tablespoons butter and brush on bottom of pastry shell. Arrange a layer of sliced apples on bottom of shell. In a bowl, mix together sugar, flour, cinnamon, and nutmeg; then sprinkle about ¼ of this mixture over layer of apples. Arrange layer of cherries and sprinkle with ¼ of the sugar mixture. Repeat this step three more times, alternating with layers of apples and cherries, and ending with apples. Cover each layer of fruit with ¼ of sugar mixture, except last layer.

Dot top of last layer with remaining 4 tablespoons of butter. In a bowl, mix together ½ teaspoon sugar and ¼ teaspoon cinnamon. Place top crust on pie, then brush with cream or evaporated milk and sprinkle with cinnamon and sugar mixture. Cut vents in top crust. Bake at 425 degrees F. for 30 to 40 minutes. Serve warm with a scoop of vanilla ice cream.

Quick Swiss Apple Pie

Makes 1 pie

Pastry for (9-inch) double-crust pie (see page 216)
1 (21-ounce) can cherry pie filling
1 (21-ounce) can apple pie filling

½ teaspoon ground cinnamon
¼ teaspoon ground nutmeg

Preheat oven to 375 degrees F. Roll out pastry for bottom crust and line pie pan. Roll out top crust. Make 4 to 6 slits with a knife to vent; set aside. Discard ⅓ cup of juice from cherry filling and then spoon remaining juice and cherries into bottom of pie shell. Gently spoon entire can of apple filling over cherries. Sprinkle with cinnamon and nutmeg. Moisten edge of pie crust with water. Add top crust and seal. Brush with milk and sprinkle with sugar. Bake 35 to 45 minutes.

Swiss Apple-Cherry Pie

Deep-Dish Peach and Sour Cherry Pie

Makes 1 pie

Pastry for (9-inch) double-crust pie (see page 216)

Filling

4 cups sliced fresh peaches
2 cups sour cherries
⅔ cup granulated sugar
1 tablespoon lemon juice
¼ cup packed brown sugar
3 tablespoons cornstarch
¼ teaspoon ground cinnamon

Crumb Topping

1 cup all-purpose flour
½ cup rolled oats
⅔ cup packed brown sugar
½ teaspoon ground cinnamon
½ cup butter cut into ¼-inch pieces

Preheat oven to 400 degrees F. Prepare pastry and roll ¾ of the dough into a large round. Line a 9-inch deep-dish pie pan with pastry round, trim and flute edges, and set aside.

For filling: In a large bowl, toss peaches and cherries in granulated sugar and lemon juice. Let sit for 10 minutes to allow fruit to release juices. In a small bowl, mix ¼ cup brown sugar, cornstarch, and cinnamon. Add to fruit mixture and toss to coat. Pour filling into pastry and bake 30 minutes.

For crumb topping: Pulse flour, oats, ⅔ cup brown sugar, and cinnamon in a food processor several times to mix. Scatter the butter pieces over the top and pulse until it resembles small crumbs. Empty the crumbs into a large bowl and rub them between your fingers until you have large buttery crumbs. Refrigerate until ready to use.

Remove the pie from the oven and reduce the temperature to 375 degrees F. Spread the crumbs over the surface of the pie and press down slightly. Return the pie to the oven and continue to bake until the top is brown and the juices bubble thickly at the edge, 35 to 40 minutes. Cool for at least 2 hours before serving.

Note: The unused pie crust can be rolled out, cut into shapes and sprinkled with cinnamon sugar. Bake on a cookie sheet at 400 degrees F. for 8 to 12 minutes.

Fresh Peach Pie

Makes 1 pie

1 baked (9-inch) pie shell (see page 216)

3 cups water

1 cup granulated sugar

1 (3-ounce) package peach flavored gelatin

3 tablespoons cornstarch

4 cups sliced peaches

Whipped cream, for garnish

In a medium saucepan, bring water and sugar to a boil over medium-high heat. Mix gelatin and cornstarch together and gradually add to the boiling sugar water. Cook over medium-high heat, stirring constantly for 5 minutes or until mixture is clear and thickened slightly; remove from heat. Let stand at room temperature until cool and thickened like a heavy syrup. (Or refrigerate to cool, stirring often, so it doesn't set up too much.) Pour over fresh peaches and fold together gently.

Mound mixture in baked pie shell. Chill for at least 2 hours before serving. Top each slice with a dollop of whipped cream, if desired.

Pear Crisp Pie

Makes 2 pies

1 recipe Oatmeal Crisp Pie Crust (see page 214)

8 cups peeled, cored, and sliced pears (½-inch thick or thicker)

¾ cup granulated sugar

1 tablespoon lemon juice

3 tablespoons cornstarch

2 to 3 tablespoons chopped crystallized ginger

1 teaspoon ground cinnamon

½ teaspoon freshly grated nutmeg

Preheat oven to 400 degrees F. Roll out Oatmeal Crisp Pie Crust for 2 bottom crusts and line 2 pie pans. Roll out Oatmeal Crisp Pie Crust for 2 top crusts; fold each in half and cut three ½-inch slits through both layers of both crusts, then set aside.

In a large bowl, combine pears, sugar, lemon juice, cornstarch, ginger, cinnamon, and nutmeg. Toss well.

Pour half of mixture into each unbaked pie shell. Moisten edge of pie crust with water. Add top crust and seal. Brush tops with milk and sprinkle with sugar, if desired.

Bake 1 hour, or until top crusts are golden brown.

Very Berry Pie

Makes 2 pies

Pastry for 2 (9-inch) double-crust pies (see page 216)
1 (16-ounce) bag frozen boysenberries, thawed
1 (8-ounce) bag frozen blueberries, thawed
1 (8-ounce) bag frozen raspberries, thawed

1¾ cups granulated sugar
½ teaspoon salt
½ cup cornstarch

Preheat oven to 375 degrees F. Roll out pastry for 2 bottom crusts and line 2 pie pans. Roll out pastry for 2 top crusts; fold each in half and cut three ½-inch slits through both layers of both crusts, then set aside. Pour thawed berries and all their juices into a large mixing bowl. In a separate bowl, mix sugar, salt, and cornstarch and pour on top of berries. Mix well with rubber spatula.

Fill crusts. Moisten edge of pie crust with water. Add top crust and seal. Brush with milk and sprinkle with sugar. Bake 45 to 50 minutes, or until golden brown.

Blueberry Pie

Makes 1 pie

Pastry for (9-inch) double-crust pie (see page 216)
1 (16-ounce) bag frozen blueberries, thawed
1 cup granulated sugar

¼ teaspoon salt
4 tablespoons cornstarch

Preheat oven to 375 degrees F. Roll out pastry for bottom crust and line pie pan. Roll out pastry for top crust, fold in half, and cut three ½-inch slits through both layers of crust, then set aside. Pour thawed berries into a large mixing bowl. In a separate bowl, mix sugar, salt, and cornstarch; pour on top of berries. Mix well with rubber spatula.

Fill crust. Moisten edge of pie crust with water. Add top crust and seal. Brush with milk and sprinkle with sugar. Bake 45 to 50 minutes, or until golden brown.

Very Berry Pie

Cranberry Pie

Cranberry Pie

Makes 1 pie

1 baked (9-inch) pie shell (see page 216)
2½ cups fresh cranberries
1 cup water
¾ cup raisins
1 cup sugar

4 tablespoons cornstarch
½ cup chopped walnuts
2 tablespoons butter
Whipped cream, for garnish

In a medium saucepan, cook cranberries in 1 cup water over medium-high heat until cranberries pop. Add raisins. Combine sugar and cornstarch in a small bowl and stir into cranberry mixture. Cook and stir until mixture thickens and bubbles. Add nuts and butter and stir until butter melts.

Pour into baked pie shell. Cool. Serve topped with a dollop of whipped cream.

Two-Crust Cranberry Pie

Makes 1 pie

Pastry for (9-inch) double-crust pie (see page 216)
2 cups fresh cranberries
1 cup water
1 cup sugar

1¾ tablespoons cornstarch
¼ to ½ cup chopped walnuts
2 teaspoons butter or margarine

Preheat oven to 400 degrees F. Roll out pastry for bottom crust and line pie pan. Roll out pastry for top crust; fold in half and cut three ½-inch slits through both layers of crust, then set aside. In a medium saucepan, cook cranberries in water until cranberries pop. Strain and save the juice in pan. Mix sugar and cornstarch together and then add to juice. Cook mixture until it thickens and bubbles, stirring constantly. Stir in walnuts, cranberries, and butter.

Pour into pie shell. Moisten edge of pie crust with water. Add top crust and seal. Brush with milk and sprinkle with sugar. Bake 10 minutes. Reduce oven temperature to 350 degrees F. and bake 45 minutes, or until crust is nicely browned.

Fresh Strawberry Pie

Makes 1 pie

1 baked (9-inch) pie shell (see page 216)
4 cups diced ripe strawberries
2 cups granulated sugar
½ teaspoon salt
½ cup cornstarch

½ teaspoon lemon zest
2 tablespoons freshly squeezed lemon juice
2 cups halved ripe strawberries
½ cup fresh blueberries, divided
Whipped cream, for garnish

Place diced strawberries in a gallon-sized zipper-lock bag; seal well and knead bag to crush berries. Pour crushed berries into a large saucepan and combine with sugar and salt. Remove 1 cup of this mixture and blend with cornstarch in a small bowl; pour back into saucepan. Cook and stir strawberry mixture over medium-high heat until it comes to a boil. Reduce heat to medium and continue to stir and scrape the bottom of the pan until thick and clear. Stir in lemon zest. Place in a chilled, medium-sized bowl and cool in refrigerator, about 1 hour. Stir in lemon juice.

Place halved strawberries and ¼ cup of the blueberries in bottom of baked pie shell. Spoon chilled glaze over berries. Garnish with whipped cream and remaining blueberries.

Cherry Pie

Makes 1 pie

Pastry for (9-inch) double-crust pie (see page 216)
2½ tablespoons quick-cooking tapioca
⅛ teaspoon salt
1 cup granulated sugar

3 cups water-packed red sour cherries, drained, with juice reserved
6 drops red food coloring
¼ teaspoon almond extract
1 tablespoon butter

Preheat oven to 375 degrees F. Roll out pastry for bottom crust and line pie pan. Roll out pastry for top crust, fold in half, and cut three ½-inch slits through both layers of crust, then set aside.

Combine tapioca, salt, and sugar in a large bowl. Measure ½ cup of the reserved cherry juice and add to bowl, along with cherries, food coloring, and almond extract. Mix well. Let stand about 15 minutes and then pour into pie shell; dot with butter.

Unfold top pie crust and place over pie; press top and bottom crusts together around edge. Crimp or flute. Bake 45 to 50 minutes.

Fresh Strawberry Pie

Mini Pecan Pies

Mini Pecan Pies

Makes 24 mini pies

Pastry for double-crust pie (see page 216)
⅔ cup chopped pecans, divided
1 cup packed brown sugar
⅔ cup light corn syrup
2 teaspoons vanilla

¾ teaspoon salt
2 eggs
2 egg whites
Whipped cream, for garnish
24 pecan halves, for garnish

Preheat oven to 375 degrees F. Coat 2 muffin tins with nonstick cooking spray. Roll out pastry dough into a large rectangle. Use a round cookie cutter to cut out large circles. Press a dough circle into each muffin cup, lining the sides and bottom with dough. Divide ⅓ cup pecans among the pastry-lined muffin cups; set aside.

In a large bowl, stir remaining ⅓ cup pecans, brown sugar, corn syrup, vanilla, salt, eggs, and egg whites until well combined. Spoon filling into muffin tins. Bake 20 minutes. Cool in pan 10 minutes and then run knife around the pie crust to loosen. Carefully remove to cooling racks. Serve with a dollop of whipped cream and garnish with a pecan half.

Pecan Pie

Makes 1 pie

1 unbaked 9-inch pie shell* (see page 216)
3 eggs, slightly beaten
2 cups plus 3 tablespoons sugar
½ teaspoon salt

½ cup plus 1½ tablespoons dark corn syrup
½ teaspoon vanilla
1½ tablespoons butter, melted
1½ cups chopped pecans

Preheat oven to 350 degrees F. In a large bowl, slightly beat eggs and then add sugar and whisk together with a wire whisk. Add salt, corn syrup, vanilla, and butter. Mix well.

Arrange pecans in bottom of pie shell. Pour filling evenly on top of pecans and bake 50 to 60 minutes or until the filling is set. Allow to cool completely before cutting.

For easiest cutting, refrigerate until pie is completely cold. Carefully turn pie upside down and lay it on a cutting board. Use a knife that is as long as the pie is wide. Press the knife straight down through the pie to make the desired sizes. Carefully lift each piece of pie, turn it over, and place on a plate.

***Note:** Be sure to bake in a 9-inch pie shell; filling will bubble over edges and spill if an 8-inch shell is used.*

Chocolate Chip Walnut Pie

Makes 1 pie

1 unbaked (9-inch) pie shell (see page 216)

2 eggs

½ cup pastry flour

⅓ cup granulated sugar

⅓ cup packed dark brown sugar

¾ cup butter, melted and cooled

1 cup semisweet chocolate chips

1 cup chopped walnuts

Preheat oven to 350 degrees F. Beat eggs with an electric mixer until foamy. Add flour and sugars and mix well. Stir in cooled melted butter. Fold in chocolate chips and walnuts. Pour into unbaked pie shell.

Bake 45 minutes, or until golden brown and set in the middle. Cool on a wire rack. Serve warm.

Chocolate Chip Pie

Makes 1 pie

Chocolate pie shell

2 cups walnuts, chopped

4 eggs

6 tablespoons plus 1 teaspoon sugar

1 cup brown sugar

2½ tablespoons corn syrup

1 cup flour

¾ pound semisweet chocolate chips

1½ cups butter

Preheat oven to 350 degrees F. Chop walnuts and set aside. In a large mixing bowl, beat together eggs. Add sugar, brown sugar, and corn syrup. Add flour, chocolate chips, and chopped nuts.

Melt butter. Cool so it is still melted, but not too hot and add to mixture. Scoop into chocolate pie shell. Bake for 50 minutes.

Caramel Chocolate Pecan Pie

Makes 1 pie

1 unbaked (9-inch) pie shell (see page 216)

1 cup pecan pieces

1 cup semisweet chocolate chips

½ cup caramel ice cream topping

1 (8-ounce) package cream cheese

1 cup dairy sour cream

½ cup sugar

1 teaspoon vanilla

3 eggs

Cocoa powder, for garnish

Preheat oven to 350 degrees F. In the unbaked pie shell, sprinkle the pecan pieces and chocolate chips. Drizzle the caramel topping over the top; set aside while you make the filling.

In a medium bowl, beat the cream cheese until soft. Add the sour cream, sugar, and vanilla and mix until smooth. Add the eggs, beating on low speed until just combined. Pour into the prepared crust. Bake 45 minutes, until the center appears set. Cool and then chill at least 1 hour. Dust with cocoa powder.

Chocolate Chip Walnut Pie

Hurray for the Pumpkin Pie

Makes 1 pie

1 unbaked (10-inch) pie shell (see page 216)

First Layer

⅔ cup milk chocolate chips

1 cup granulated sugar

2 tablespoons butter or margarine

½ cup light corn syrup

¾ teaspoon vanilla

½ cup evaporated milk

¾ cup chopped macadamia nuts

Second Layer

1 (8-ounce) package cream cheese, softened

¼ cup granulated sugar

½ teaspoon vanilla

1 egg, beaten

Third Layer

1 (15-ounce) can pumpkin

1½ cups melted vanilla ice cream

3 eggs, beaten

⅓ cup packed brown sugar

⅓ cup granulated sugar

½ teaspoon ground ginger

¼ teaspoon salt

1¼ teaspoons ground cinnamon

½ teaspoon nutmeg

¼ teaspoon ground cloves

Topping

½ cup heavy cream

1 tablespoon powdered sugar

1 (8-ounce) package cream cheese, softened

1 cup sugar

¼ cup milk chocolate chips

1 tablespoon margarine or butter

⅓ cup crushed macadamia nuts

Line pie pan with pastry; trim and flute edges. Set aside while preparing first layer.

For first layer: Place milk chocolate chips in a small bowl and set aside. In a heavy saucepan, over medium heat, cook the sugar, butter or margarine, corn syrup, evaporated milk, and vanilla. Bring to a boil and stir continuously for 6 minutes. Remove from heat. Pour ⅓ cup plus 1 tablespoon of this hot caramel mixture over chocolate chips. Stir until smooth. Pour into bottom of pastry-lined pie pan; pat down with back of spoon. Stir macadamia nuts into remaining caramel mixture and allow to cool slightly before spreading over the chocolate.

For second layer: Beat cream cheese with an electric mixer on medium speed until smooth. Beat in sugar. Add vanilla and the beaten egg and beat until light and smooth. Chill for 20 minutes and then spread over first layer.

For third layer: Preheat oven to 450 degrees F. Combine pumpkin, melted ice cream, beaten eggs, brown sugar, sugar, ginger, salt, cinnamon, nutmeg, and ground cloves in a medium bowl and mix thoroughly. Pour over second layer. Bake 15 minutes. Reduce oven temperature to 350 and bake 50 minutes. Remove from oven and cool on a wire rack.

For topping: Once pie has cooled, beat together heavy cream and powdered sugar until stiff and then set aside. In another bowl, cream the cream cheese and sugar until smooth and fluffy. Fold in the whipped cream. With a cookie scoop, dollop topping around edges.

Melt the chocolate chips with butter or margarine in the microwave on high power in 30-second increments, stirring after each time, until mixture is melted. Cool slightly and then drizzle chocolate over the pie and whipped topping. Sprinkle with crushed macadamia nuts.

Rich Pumpkin Pie

Makes 1 pie

1 unbaked (9-inch) pie shell (see page 216)
1 (15-ounce) can pumpkin
2 tablespoons flour
½ teaspoon cinnamon
Pinch nutmeg
Pinch ginger
Pinch cloves

½ teaspoon salt
½ cup brown sugar
2 eggs
2 tablespoons corn syrup
1 cup milk
½ cup evaporated milk

Put pumpkin, flour, cinnamon, nutmeg, ginger, cloves, salt, and brown sugar in a large bowl. Blend together. Slowly add eggs, corn syrup, milk, and evaporated milk. Mix well.

Pour into unbaked pie shell. Let sit 60 minutes and then bake at 375 degrees F. for 60 minutes or until a knife inserted in the center comes out clean.

Pumpkin Pie

Makes 1 pie

1 unbaked (9-inch) pie shell (see page 216)
1½ cups canned pumpkin
½ teaspoon ground cinnamon
½ teaspoon nutmeg
¼ teaspoon ground ginger
¼ teaspoon allspice
½ cup granulated sugar

⅓ cup packed brown sugar
1 teaspoon salt
1½ tablespoons cornstarch
2 eggs
1 cup evaporated milk
1 cup water
Whipped cream, for garnish

Preheat oven to 375 degrees F. Place pumpkin in a large mixing bowl. In a separate bowl, mix cinnamon, nutmeg, ginger, allspice, granulated sugar, brown sugar, salt, and cornstarch. Add to pumpkin and mix until blended. Add eggs and evaporated milk and mix until blended. Add water and mix well. Pour into unbaked pie shell and bake 50 to 60 minutes, or until knife inserted near center comes out clean.

Cool on a wire rack. Top with whipped cream before serving.

Pumpkin Cream Cheese Pie

Makes 1 pie

1 unbaked (9-inch) pie shell (see page 216)

1 (8-ounce) package cream cheese, softened

¾ cup granulated sugar

½ teaspoon salt

1 teaspoon ground cinnamon

½ teaspoon nutmeg, plus more for garnish

½ teaspoon ground cloves

½ teaspoon ground ginger

2 eggs

1 (15-ounce) can pumpkin

1 teaspoon vanilla

½ cup pecan halves, for garnish

Whipped cream, for garnish

Preheat oven to 350 degrees F. In a large bowl, beat cream cheese, sugar, salt, and spices until fluffy. Add eggs, one at a time, beating well after each. Beat in pumpkin and vanilla. Pour into pie shell. Bake 55 minutes, or until knife inserted near center comes out clean. During last 15 minutes of baking, place pecan halves around edges for garnish.

Cool on a wire rack and then chill in the refrigerator for 3 to 4 hours. Serve with a dollop of whipped cream and a sprinkle of ground nutmeg.

Lemon Almond Tart

Makes one 8-inch tart

Pastry

  1¾ cups flour
  ⅓ cup sugar
  Pinch of salt
  ½ cup unsalted butter, softened
  1 teaspoon finely grated lemon zest
  3 egg yolks
  2 tablespoons water

Filling

  1½ cups ricotta cheese
  ½ cup sugar
  3 eggs, well beaten
  1 tablespoon finely grated lemon zest
  ¾ cup finely chopped blanched almonds
  3 tablespoons sliced almonds
  Powdered sugar, for garnish

For pastry: In a large bowl, combine the flour, sugar, and salt. Stir to combine. Make a well in the center and add the butter, zest, egg yolks, and water. Work the flour into the center with a fork or your fingers until a smooth dough forms. Wrap in plastic wrap, flatten slightly, and then refrigerate for 20 minutes. (If it gets too cold you will need to let it warm a little to make it easier to roll out.) Make filling while dough is chilling.

For filling: Place ricotta and sugar in a medium bowl and mix together with electric mixer. Add eggs gradually, beating well after each addition. Add the zest, beating briefly to combine. Stir in chopped almonds. Set aside.

Preheat oven to 350 degrees F. Brush an 8-inch fluted tart pan with melted butter. Roll out the pastry on a lightly floured surface and line the pan, trimming away the extra pastry. Pour the filling in the pastry and smooth the top. Sprinkle with sliced almonds and bake 55 to 60 minutes or until lightly golden and set.

Fresh Berry Tart

Makes 1 tart

Pastry

6 tablespoons sugar

⅔ cup margarine

1½ tablespoons cream

1 egg yolk

½ teaspoon almond extract

1¼ cups cake flour

Filling

3 cups strawberries*, blueberries, blackberries, boysenberries, or Marion berries

1 (3-ounce) package cream cheese, room temperature

4 tablespoons sugar, divided

½ (8-ounce) container frozen whipped topping, thawed in the refrigerator

For pastry: Preheat oven to 350 degrees F. Place sugar and margarine in a medium bowl and cream together. Add cream, egg yolk, and almond extract and mix till well blended. Add cake flour and mix until the dough comes together and leaves the sides of the bowl clean. Remove dough from bowl and wrap in plastic wrap. Refrigerate 30 minutes.

Roll dough out until it is 1½ inches larger than 9-inch tart pan. Transfer dough to tart pan, gently easing into the bottom and up the sides. Press slightly into the sides of the pan, letting the excess hang over the edges. Roll rolling pin over the top edge of the tart pan to seal and cut off the extra dough. Place a piece of aluminum foil that is slightly larger than the tart shell on top of the dough, gently pressing it against the bottom and sides. Pour 1½ cups baking beads, dry beans, or rice on top of the foil (this prevents the dough from rising during baking). Bake 15 minutes. Remove foil by bringing the corners together and lifting the bundle off. Return crust to the oven and bake for 10 minutes or until golden brown. Allow to cool completely before filling.

For filling: Rinse berries and dry by placing on a double layer of paper towels with another layer on top. Beat cream cheese and 1 tablespoon sugar until smooth. Add whipped topping and mix until well blended. Spread filling in tart shell, arrange berries on top of filling and sprinkle with 3 tablespoons sugar.

Note: Cut strawberries in half or in quarters.

Fruit Tarts

Makes 20 tarts

20 prepared tart shells

8 ounces bittersweet chocolate, melted

1 recipe Basic Pastry Cream (see below)

Seasonal fruit

Cook the tartlets according to directions on the box. When the tartlet shells are cooled, brush each with the melted chocolate. Spoon in pastry cream to just below the edge of the shell. Decorate each tartlet with slices of seasonal fruit. Suggested fruits include berries, kiwi slices, peach slices, edible flowers, and mandarin orange slices. Tartlets can be refrigerated up to 6 hours before service.

Basic Pastry Cream

Makes enough cream to fill 20 tartlet shells

3¾ cups sugar

¾ cup plus ½ tablespoon cornstarch

½ teaspoon plus ⅛ teaspoon salt

10 cups milk

15 egg yolks, beaten

10 tablespoons butter

5 teaspoons vanilla extract

Mix sugar, cornstarch, salt, and milk together in a heavy saucepan until sugar is dissolved. Bring to a boil over medium-high heat, stirring constantly. Cook 2 minutes, until thick and smooth. Remove a spoonful of the cream mixture and stir into beaten egg yolks. Add egg mixture to cream and cook until mixture begins to boil again. Stir constantly. Remove from heat. Add butter and vanilla extract, stirring until butter is melted. Cover with plastic wrap. Place wrap so that it touches the pudding. This will prevent a film from forming. Refrigerate. Pastry cream can be thinned by adding lightly whipped cream once the pastry cream has cooled. It can also be flavored with lemon curd.

Lion House Cheesecake

Makes about 12 to 14 servings

Crust

  1½ cups finely crushed graham cracker crumbs

  3 tablespoons sugar

  6 tablespoons butter, melted

Filling

  3 (8-ounce) packages cream cheese, softened

  1 cup sugar

  2 teaspoons lemon juice

  3 eggs

  ¾ teaspoon vanilla

Topping

  2 cups sour cream

  3 tablespoons sugar

  ½ teaspoon vanilla

Preheat oven to 300 degrees F.

For crust: Thoroughly mix graham cracker crumbs, sugar, and melted butter. Press firmly onto bottom of a 10-inch springform pan; set aside while preparing filling.

For filling: In a large mixing bowl, beat cream cheese until smooth; add sugar a little at a time. Add lemon juice. Add eggs, one at a time, beating after each addition. Mix in vanilla and combine thoroughly. Pour into crust; fill to within ½ inch of top to allow room for topping. Bake 55 to 60 minutes or until the center does not move when the pan is gently moved.

For topping: When cheesecake is almost finished baking, beat sour cream with a wire whisk; add sugar and vanilla and mix well. Pour over completely baked cake and bake an additional 10 minutes.

Cool completely. Refrigerate until ready to serve. Top with desired fruit topping or serve plain.

Note: All cheesecakes can be baked, cooled, and frozen for an easy dessert later.

Easy Cherry Cheesecake

Makes 18 to 24 servings

  2 cups graham cracker crumbs

  ½ cup margarine or butter, melted

  1 (8-ounce) package softened cream cheese

  2 tablespoons milk

  1 cup powdered sugar

  ½ teaspoon vanilla

  2 cups whipped topping (1 envelope whipped topping mix, such as Dream Whip, prepared according to directions)

  1 (16-ounce) can cherry pie filling

In 9x13-inch pan, mix graham cracker crumbs with melted margarine. Level well with fork, then press firmly in bottom of pan. Combine cream cheese, milk, powdered sugar, and vanilla; mix until smooth. Fold in whipped topping. Spread over cracker crumbs. Cover with chilled cherry pie filling. Chill 2 hours.

Black Forest Cheesecake

Makes 10 to 12 servings

½ (18-ounce) package Oreo® cookies

3 (8-ounce) packages cream cheese, softened

1 cup sugar

3 eggs

¾ teaspoon vanilla

1 teaspoon almond extract

⅓ cup maraschino cherry juice

⅓ cup diced maraschino cherries

2 cups sour cream

3 tablespoons sugar

½ teaspoon vanilla

½ cup chocolate chips

Preheat oven to 300 degrees F. Crush whole Oreo cookies, including frosting centers, to make 2 cups of fine crumbs. Press evenly into the bottom of a 10-inch springform pan.

Whip cream cheese in a mixer bowl; gradually add sugar; then add eggs one at a time. Stir in vanilla, almond extract, and maraschino cherry juice. Fold in maraschino cherries. Pour filling into crust. Bake 60 minutes. Whip sour cream; add sugar and vanilla. Put ½ of sour cream topping on cheesecake; set remaining half aside. Melt chocolate chips and stir into the remaining sour cream topping. Then swirl this mixture into the topping already on the cheesecake. Return to oven and bake for 10 more minutes. Cool before removing sides from springform pan. Refrigerate until ready to serve.

Grasshopper Cheesecake

Grasshopper Cheesecake (shown on facing page)

Makes 16 servings

Crust

- 1½ cups slivered almonds
- ¼ cup powdered whey
- 2 tablespoons sugar
- ¼ cup butter, melted

Ganache

- 4½ ounces bittersweet baking chocolate
- ¼ cup heavy cream

Filling

- 3 (8-ounce) packages cream cheese, softened
- ¾ cup sugar
- ¾ cup sour cream
- 1 teaspoon peppermint extract
- Green food coloring, as desired
- 4 eggs
- Whipped cream, for garnish
- Chocolate sauce, for garnish

Preheat oven to 350 degrees F.

For crust: Place almonds in food processor fitted with an S-blade. Process until almonds are a medium-fine texture. Add whey and sugar and pulse once. Place almond meal in a bowl and drizzle melted butter into it. Mix with your hands until it feels slightly squishy. Press into the bottom of a 10-inch springform pan. Bake 12 to 15 minutes, or until lightly browned and slightly pulling away from the sides of the pan. Remove from oven and let crust cool while you make the ganache.

For ganache: Melt chocolate with cream in the top of a double boiler over simmering water. Whisk well to make a smooth, shiny ganache. Spread evenly over the crust and set aside.

Reduce oven temperature to 325 degrees F. Place a pan of water on bottom rack of oven.

For filling: In a mixing bowl, beat cream cheese until smooth, scraping down the sides of the bowl often. Beat in sugar and sour cream and mix well. Add peppermint extract and food coloring. Add eggs, one at a time, beating after each addition until very smooth and creamy.

Pour the mixture into the chocolate-coated crust. Place cake in the oven, on the rack above the pan of water. Bake 1 hour. Turn off oven and prop the door open to cool cake slowly for 1 hour so the cake will not crack.

Remove from oven and chill at least 2 hours. Remove sides of pan and slice into 16 even pieces. Garnish with whipped cream and a drizzle of chocolate sauce.

Peppermint Cheesecake

Makes 12 to 14 servings

Crust

½ (18-ounce) package Oreo cookies

Filling

3 (8-ounce) packages cream cheese, softened

1 cup sugar

3 eggs

¾ teaspoon vanilla

1 teaspoon peppermint extract

2 drops red food coloring

Topping

2 cups sour cream

3 tablespoons sugar

½ teaspoon vanilla

Peppermint candies, crushed, for garnish

Preheat oven to 300 degrees F.

For crust: Crush whole Oreo cookies, including frosting centers, to make 2 cups fine crumbs. Press evenly onto bottom of a 10-inch springform pan and set aside.

For filling: In a large mixing bowl, beat cream cheese until smooth. Gradually add sugar and then add eggs, one at a time, beating well after each addition. Stir in vanilla, peppermint extract, and red food coloring. Pour filling into crust and bake 55 minutes.

For topping: When cheesecake is almost finished baking, beat sour cream with a wire whisk; add sugar and vanilla and mix well. Spread on top of completely baked cheesecake and return to oven. Bake 10 more minutes.

Cool before removing sides from springform pan. Garnish with crushed peppermint candy. Refrigerate until ready to serve.

Lemon Cheesecake

Makes 10 to 12 servings

1½ cups finely crushed graham cracker crumbs

3 tablespoons butter or margarine, melted

3 (8-ounce) packages cream cheese, softened

1 cup sugar

3 eggs

¾ teaspoon vanilla

⅓ cup lemon juice

1 pint sour cream

3 tablespoons sugar

½ teaspoon vanilla

1½ teaspoons lemon zest

Lemon slices, for garnish

Preheat oven to 325 degrees F. Mix together graham cracker crumbs and butter or margarine. Press firmly into bottom and sides of a 9- or 10-inch springform pan.

In a large mixer bowl beat cream cheese; gradually add sugar. Add eggs one at a time. Stir in vanilla, then stir in lemon juice. Pour filling into crust. Bake 60 minutes. Whip sour cream; add sugar, vanilla, and lemon zest. Spread on top of cheesecake and return to oven. Bake for 10 more minutes. Cool before removing sides from springform pan. Garnish with lemon slices. Refrigerate until ready to serve.

Pumpkin Cheesecake

Makes 12 to 14 servings

Crust

    1½ cups finely crushed graham cracker crumbs

    3 tablespoons butter, melted

Filling

    3 (8-ounce) packages cream cheese, softened

    1 cup sugar

    3 eggs

    ¾ teaspoon vanilla

    1⅓ cups plus 2 tablespoons pumpkin

    ¾ teaspoon cinnamon

    ¼ teaspoon nutmeg

    ¼ teaspoon ginger

    ¼ teaspoon cloves

    ½ teaspoon salt

Topping

    2 cups sour cream

    3 tablespoons sugar

    ½ teaspoon vanilla

    Dash of nutmeg, for garnish

Preheat oven to 300 degrees F.

For crust: Mix graham cracker crumbs and melted butter and press firmly onto bottom of a 9- or 10-inch spring-form pan and set aside.

For filling: In a large mixing bowl, beat cream cheese until smooth. Gradually add sugar and then eggs, one at a time, beating well after each addition. Stir in vanilla. In a separate bowl, combine pumpkin, cinnamon, nutmeg, ginger, cloves, and salt. Mix well and fold into cream cheese mixture. Pour filling into crust. Bake 55 minutes.

For topping: When cheesecake is almost finished baking, beat sour cream with a wire whisk; add sugar and vanilla and mix well. Spread on top of completely baked cheesecake and return to oven. Bake 10 more minutes.

Cool before removing sides from springform pan. Garnish with a sprinkle of nutmeg. Refrigerate until ready to serve.

Harvest Apple Crisp

Makes 12 to 15 servings

10 cups peeled and sliced apples

1 cup granulated sugar

1 cup plus 1 tablespoon all-purpose flour, divided

1 teaspoon ground cinnamon

½ cup water

1 cup quick-cooking rolled oats

1 cup packed brown sugar

¼ teaspoon baking powder

¼ teaspoon baking soda

½ cup butter, melted

Preheat oven to 350 degrees F. Place the sliced apples in a 9x13-inch pan. Mix granulated sugar, 1 tablespoon flour, and ground cinnamon together, and sprinkle over apples. Pour water evenly over all; set aside. In a large bowl, combine oats, remaining 1 cup flour, brown sugar, baking powder, baking soda, and melted butter. Stir to combine and then crumble evenly over the apple mixture. Bake 45 minutes, or until top is golden brown and apples are tender. Serve warm or cold, with whipped cream or ice cream.

Peach Crisp

Makes 12 to 15 servings

Topping

1 cup butter, cold
1 cup brown sugar
1 cup flour

1 cup oatmeal
¼ teaspoon baking powder

In a large bowl mix together butter, brown sugar, flour, oatmeal, and baking powder just until the butter is broken up and ingredients are mixed. Mixture should be crumbly. Set aside.

Filling

½ teaspoon cinnamon
¼ cup brown sugar
2 tablespoons cornstarch

2 (30-ounce) cans sliced peaches, drained
1 teaspoon lemon juice

Preheat oven to 350 degrees F. In a small bowl mix together cinnamon, brown sugar, and cornstarch. Set aside. In a large bowl, combine peaches and lemon juice. Stir in cinnamon and sugar mixture. Place in a 9x13-inch pan. Crumble crisp topping on top. Bake 25 to 30 minutes or until golden brown. Serve warm or cold, with whipped cream or ice cream.

Pear and Cherry Crisp

Makes 8 servings

1 (16-ounce) package frozen unsweetened pitted tart
   red cherries, thawed and drained (set juice aside), or 1
   (16-ounce) can pitted tart red cherries (water-packed)
⅓ to ½ cup granulated sugar
2 tablespoons all-purpose flour
1 teaspoon orange zest

½ teaspoon ground cinnamon
3 to 4 medium pears, peeled, cored, and thinly sliced
   (3 cups total)*
½ cup granola or streusel
2 tablespoons butter, melted
Vanilla ice cream (optional)

Preheat oven to 375 degrees F. If using canned cherries, drain cherries, reserving ½ cup of the juice. In a large mixing bowl, combine frozen or canned cherries and reserved juice; add sugar and toss to coat. Let stand for 5 minutes.

In a small bowl, combine flour, orange zest, and cinnamon. Sprinkle over cherries and toss to mix. Add sliced pears and toss to mix. Transfer mixture to an ungreased 2-quart square baking dish. Combine granola and butter and sprinkle over filling. Bake 30 minutes, or until pears are tender. If necessary, to prevent overbrowning, cover with foil the last 5 to 10 minutes. Serve warm with ice cream.

Note: Canned, sliced pears may be used in place of fresh pears, if desired.

Puff Pastry

Makes about 12 large cream puff shells

1 cup flour

¼ teaspoon salt

½ cup butter (or ¼ cup shortening and ¼ cup butter)

1 cup boiling water

4 eggs

Sift flour with salt. Combine butter (or butter and shortening) with boiling water in saucepan; keep on low heat until butter is melted. Add flour all at once, stirring vigorously until mixture forms a ball and leaves sides of pan. Cook about 2 minutes until mixture is very dry. Remove from heat.

Add unbeaten eggs one at a time and beat well after each addition. Continue beating until mixture forms a thick dough. To make cream puffs, cocktail puffs, or puff shells follow directions below.

To make cream puffs: Preheat oven to 425 degrees F. Drop dough by tablespoonfuls, about 2 inches apart, onto baking sheet lined with wax paper. Bake about 10 to 15 minutes. Reduce heat to 400 degrees F. and bake 5 to 10 minutes, then reduce heat to 375 degrees F. for another 5 to 10 minutes. Bake about 30 to 40 minutes total, or until beads of moisture no longer appear on the surface. Do not open oven door during early part of baking. Remove from oven and place on wire racks to cool.

When cool, cut a slit in side of each puff; remove doughy centers if necessary. Fill with a cream filling such as pudding, sweetened whipped cream, or with any other favorite cream filling.

To make cocktail puffs: Follow directions for baking cream puffs, except drop by small teaspoonfuls onto baking sheet lined with wax paper. Bake for a total of about 20 to 30 minutes. Fill with any savory filling. Makes 4 to 5 dozen small puffs.

To make puff shells: Drop dough by tablespoonfuls into deep hot fat (375 degrees F.). Fry 10 to 15 minutes, turning often, or until a good crust forms. Drain well, then cut top off each shell. Fill hot shells with creamed fish, poultry, meat, eggs, or vegetables. Or cool the shells and fill with a salad mixture, such as chicken salad. Replace tops before serving.

To make eclairs: Prepare puff pastries as directed. Instead of dropping dough onto baking sheets, force it through a decorating tube in strips about 1-inch wide and 4-inches long. Bake about 25 minutes. Fill as for cream puffs. Frost with your favorite chocolate frosting.

Cream Puffs and Eclairs

Chocolate Party Puffs

Makes 20 servings of 3 puffs each

60 cocktail-sized pastry puffs, purchased or homemade according to directions on page 268

4 cups vanilla ice cream

4 cups heavy cream, whipped

1 tablespoon sugar, or to taste

1 teaspoon vanilla, or to taste

1 cup chocolate syrup

1 (16-ounce) jar maraschino cherries, well drained

Make cocktail puffs according to directions on page 268, or use puffs purchased from a bakery. Cut off and set aside tops. Fill shells with vanilla ice cream; replace tops. Freeze on a tray in a single layer. When frozen, pack in plastic bags and store in freezer until ready to use.

To assemble, whip the cream; add sugar, vanilla, and chocolate syrup. Fold slightly thawed puffs and cherries into the cream. Layer into a glass trifle bowl and serve immediately.

Buttercream Frosting

6 cups powdered sugar

2 cups butter, room temperature

2 teaspoons vanilla extract

4 to 6 tablespoons heavy cream

In a medium bowl, mix powdered sugar and butter on low speed for 1 minute or until well mixed. Continue beating on high speed for 3 minutes. Add vanilla and cream and beat on medium speed for 1 minute. Add more cream in small amounts if needed to achieve a spreading consistency.

Variations: Here are some additional varieties to try for fun.

• **Raspberry/Strawberry:** Make Buttercream Frosting according to directions. When adding vanilla and cream, add 1 cup of raspberry or strawberry jam or preserves (without pieces of berries). Beat 2 minutes on medium speed or until well blended.

• **Lemon:** Make Buttercream Frosting according to directions. When adding the vanilla and cream, add 2 teaspoons lemon extract and ⅛ teaspoon (5 drops) yellow food coloring. Beat for 2 minutes on medium speed or until well blended.

• **Peanut Butter and Jelly:** Use the Buttercream Frosting recipe, but substitute ½ cup peanut butter for ½ cup butter. Follow recipe directions. Frost cupcakes using a generous amount of frosting, leaving a small indention in the top of the frosting. Spoon 1 teaspoon grape jelly (or your favorite jelly) into the indention.

Cream-Filled Cupcakes

Makes 24 to 30 cupcakes

Cupcakes

1 (18- to 18.5-ounce) package cake mix, any flavor
1 cup hot water
⅓ cup vegetable oil
4 eggs

Filling

⅓ cup all-purpose flour
⅓ cup plus ¾ cup sugar, divided
1 cup milk
½ cup margarine
½ cup white shortening
1 teaspoon vanilla
Dash salt

Preheat oven to 350 degrees F. Line muffin tins with cupcake papers and set aside.

For cupcakes: In a large bowl, beat together cake mix, water, oil, and eggs until well mixed. Fill cupcake papers ⅓ to ½ full. Bake 13 to 15 minutes. Cool.

For filling: While cupcakes cool, combine flour, ⅓ cup sugar, and milk in a medium saucepan over medium heat. Stir out all lumps. Bring to a boil and cook until thick. Remove from heat and allow mixture to cool. Add margarine, shortening, remaining ¾ cup sugar, vanilla, and salt. Beat with an electric mixer for about 5 minutes until fluffy. Fill a decorating bag that has a number 4 tip attached. Insert tip into center of the cupcakes and squeeze in a small amount of filling. Frost tops of cupcakes with remaining cream filling.

Chocolate Frosting

4 tablespoons cocoa
3 cups powdered sugar
¼ cup butter or margarine, softened

2–3 tablespoons milk
1 teaspoon vanilla
2 tablespoons chopped walnuts, optional for garnish

In a mixing bowl, whisk together cocoa and powdered sugar. Add softened butter, milk, and vanilla. Beat with an electric mixer until smooth.

White Buttercream Frosting

2 tablespoons water
4 tablespoons granulated sugar
2⅓ cups powdered sugar

1 pasteurized egg*
⅔ cup shortening or butter
1 teaspoon vanilla

Boil water and granulated sugar 2 minutes. Mix powdered sugar and egg. Blend mixtures together. Add shortening and vanilla. Beat on low speed for 30 seconds and then on medium-high speed for 3 to 5 minutes until light and fluffy.

Pasteurized eggs can be found in the supermarket dairy section by the regular eggs.

Lion House White Surprise Cupcakes

Makes 20 to 24 cupcakes

Cupcakes

4 eggs
½ cup vegetable oil
1½ cups water
1 (18.25-ounce) white or yellow cake mix
1 (3.4-ounce) vanilla instant pudding mix
1 cup white chocolate chips

Filling

1 cup milk
1 (3.4-ounce) package vanilla instant pudding mix
½ (8-ounce) container frozen whipped topping, thawed

Buttercream Frosting

See recipe on page 270

Preheat oven to 350 degrees F. Line muffin pans with cupcake papers and set aside.

For cupcakes: In a medium bowl, mix eggs, oil, and water mix with electric mixer on low speed for 30 seconds. Add cake and pudding mixes and mix for 30 seconds on low speed. Scrape the sides of the bowl with a spatula; continue mixing on medium speed for 2 minutes. Spoon cake batter into each cup, filling ½ to ⅔ full. Place 6 or 7 white chocolate chips on top of each cupcake. Bake 20 to 25 minutes. Allow to cool. Fill cupcakes with filling and then frost using Buttercream Frosting.

For filling: In a small bowl, whisk together milk and pudding mix until it is smooth and starts to thicken. Fold in whipped topping. Place half of the filling in a decorating bag with a large round tip or in a quart-size zipper-lock bag with a corner snipped away. With a clean straw or the end of a round wooden spoon, make a hole in the top center of each cupcake halfway through. Squeeze filling into each hole until it comes to the top of the cupcake. Refill decorating bag as needed.

Variations: Use any flavor instant pudding for different flavors. Raspberry or strawberry jam also make great fillings. Here are some cupcakes variations (filled or unfilled) to make with this recipe:

• **Black and White:** vanilla or chocolate filling and chocolate frosting

• **Lemon:** lemon filling and lemon frosting

• **PBJ:** grape jelly filling and peanut butter frosting

• **Raspberry Lemonade:** raspberry filling and lemon and raspberry frosting swirled together

• **Raspberry/Raspberry:** raspberry filling and raspberry frosting

Lion House Chocolate Cupcakes

Makes 20 to 24 cupcakes

Cupcakes

4 eggs
½ cup vegetable oil
1½ cups water
1 (18- to 18.5-ounce) package chocolate cake mix
1 (3.4-ounce) package chocolate instant pudding mix
1 cup semisweet or milk chocolate chips

Filling

1 cup milk
1 (3.4-ounce) package vanilla or chocolate instant pudding mix
½ (8-ounce) container frozen whipped topping, thawed

Buttercream Frosting

See recipe on page 270

Preheat oven to 350 degrees F. Line muffin pans with cupcake papers and set aside.

For cupcakes: In a medium bowl, mix eggs, oil, and water with an electric mixer on low speed for 30 seconds. Add cake and pudding mixes and mix for 30 seconds more on low speed. Scrape the sides of the bowl with a spatula; continue mixing on medium speed for 2 minutes. Spoon cake batter into each cup, filling ½ to ⅔ full. Place 6 or 7 chocolate chips on top of each cupcake. Bake 20 to 25 minutes. Allow to cool. Fill cupcakes and frost using Buttercream Frosting.

For filling: In a small bowl, whisk together milk and pudding mix until it is smooth and starts to thicken. Fold in whipped topping. Place half of the filling in a decorating bag with a large round tip or in a quart-size zipper-lock bag with a corner snipped away. With a clean straw or the end of a round wooden spoon, make a hole in the top center of each cupcake halfway through. Squeeze filling into each hole until it comes to the top of the cupcake. Refill decorating bag as needed.

Variations: Here are some fun variations to make with this recipe.

• **Chocolate/Chocolate:** chocolate filling and chocolate frosting

• **Chocolate/Raspberry or Strawberry:** chocolate filling and raspberry or strawberry frosting

• **German Chocolate:** chocolate filling with a ring of chocolate frosting around the edge of the cupcake and German chocolate frosting inside the ring

• **Chocolate/Peanut Butter:** chocolate filling and peanut butter frosting

Black Devil's Food Cake

⅓ cup shortening
1½ cups sugar
3 eggs, well beaten
⅔ cup cocoa
½ cup hot water

2 cups flour
½ teaspoon salt
1 teaspoon baking soda
1 cup thick sour cream
1 teaspoon vanilla

Preheat oven to 350 degrees F. Grease and flour 3 (8-inch) or 2 (9-inch) round cake pans. Cream shortening and sugar until light and fluffy and well incorporated; add eggs. Beat cocoa in hot water until smooth; add to creamed mixture. Sift dry ingredients together; add to sugar mixture alternately with sour cream. Add vanilla and beat well. Divide batter evenly between prepared pans and bake 20 to 30 minutes or until cake tests done. Remove cake from oven to wire racks. Let cool 10 minutes. Turn from pans and cool on wire rack. Frost with desired frosting.

Black Forest Torte

Makes 12 to 14 servings

1 (18- to 18.5-ounce) package chocolate cake mix
2 (21-ounce) cans cherry pie filling
1 (12-ounce) container frozen whipped topping, thawed

1 (16- to 18-ounce) package chocolate sandwich cookies, finely ground

Preheat oven to 350 degrees F. Grease and flour two 9-inch round cake pans. Set aside.

Prepare and bake cake mix according to package directions. Allow cake to cool completely. (For easier handling, freeze cake layers.) Split the cake layers in half horizontally. Recipe will use only 3 of the 4 layers. Freeze remaining layer for later use.

Place one layer on a serving plate. Spread ¾ can of cherry pie filling on top of cake. Place second layer of cake on top of the filling and then spread ¾ of the second can of filling on this layer. Place third cake layer on top of filling.

Generously frost the top and sides of cake with whipped topping. Place cookie crumbs all around the side of cake. Gently spoon remaining filling from both cans on top of the cake, bringing it to 1 to 1½ inches from the edge of the cake. Refrigerate 1 to 2 hours before serving (longer is better). It must be stored in the refrigerator.

Note: This cake may be made the day before it is to be served.

Quick German Chocolate Cake

1 package white or yellow cake mix*
1 (3-ounce) package instant chocolate pudding mix*
¼ cup flour

2 cups milk
3 egg whites, beaten stiff
1 recipe Coconut Pecan Frosting (see page 282)

Preheat oven to 375 degrees F. Grease and flour a 9x13x2-inch pan. Set aside. Combine cake mix, pudding mix, flour, and milk and beat according to cake package directions. Fold in egg whites. Spoon into prepared pan and bake 35 to 40 minutes, or until a wooden toothpick inserted in center comes out clean. Frost with Coconut Pecan Frosting.

*A cake mix that already contains pudding mix may be used. Prepare according to package directions.

Sinfully Delicious Cake

Makes 12 servings

1 (18- to 18.5-ounce) package German chocolate cake mix
1 (14-ounce) can sweetened condensed milk
½ (11-ounce) bottle caramel ice cream topping

1 (12-ounce) container frozen whipped topping, thawed
1 Skor candy bar, crushed

Preheat oven to 350 degrees F. Grease and flour a 9x13-inch cake pan. Prepare and bake cake mix according to directions on package.

While cake is still hot, poke holes over the surface of the cake with a straw or the end of a wooden spoon. Pour condensed milk evenly over holes, followed by caramel topping. Refrigerate cake until time to serve. Before serving, spread whipped topping on top and sprinkle with crushed candy bar.

Chocolate Cream Cake

Makes 14 to 16 servings

Cake

1 (18- to 18.5-ounce) package devil's food cake mix

Stabilized Whipped Cream

1 envelope (1 tablespoon) unflavored gelatin

¼ cup cold water

3 cups heavy cream

¾ cup powdered sugar

1½ teaspoons vanilla

Chocolate Frosting

4 tablespoons cocoa

3 cups powdered sugar

¼ cup butter or margarine, softened

2 to 3 tablespoons milk

1 teaspoon vanilla

2 tablespoons chopped walnuts, optional for garnish

For cake: Prepare and bake cake according to package directions for two 9-inch round layers. Cool and split cake layers horizontally. Only 3 of the 4 layers are used in this recipe. Freeze extra layer for later use.

For stabilized whipped cream: In a small saucepan, combine gelatin with water; let stand until gelatin softens, about 5 minutes. Turn heat to low and stir constantly until gelatin is just dissolved. Remove from heat and allow to cool slightly, but do not allow to thicken. In a large mixing bowl, whip cream, sugar, and vanilla until slightly thick. On low speed, gradually add gelatin and then beat on high until cream is thick and peaks hold their shape.

For frosting: In a mixing bowl, whisk together cocoa and powdered sugar. Add softened butter, milk, and vanilla. Beat with an electric mixer until smooth.

Place one layer of cake on a serving plate. Spoon half of the stabilized whipped cream on cake layer and spread evenly to within half an inch of edge of cake. Place second cake layer on top of cream. Spoon remaining cream on top of layer and again spread evenly to within half an inch of edge of cake. Place third layer on top of cream and gently press down on top layer to set layers together. Frost entire cake with Chocolate Frosting. If desired, garnish with chopped walnuts.

Note: Stabilized whipped cream will hold up for 4 to 5 days without separating. It may also be used in any recipe calling for whipped cream or whipped topping.

Chocolate Decadence

Makes 8 to 10 servings

Cake

6 ounces semisweet baking chocolate
7 ounces unsweetened baking chocolate
½ cup water
¾ cup plus ⅓ cup sugar, divided
1 cup butter, softened
6 eggs

Topping

2 cups heavy cream
½ cup powdered sugar
1 teaspoon vanilla
Chocolate shavings, optional

Preheat oven to 350 degrees F.

For cake: Spray one 9-inch cake pan with nonstick cooking spray. Finely chop both chocolates. Bring water and ¾ cup sugar to a boil. Remove from heat and stir in chocolate until completely melted. Stir butter into chocolate mixture.

Whip eggs with ⅓ cup sugar to form soft foamy peaks. Fold egg mixture into chocolate mixture. Pour into cake pan and bake 40 minutes. It is important to place another baking dish with an inch of water in it on the rack below the cake to create a moist baking environment. Chill at least 2 hours before unmolding.

For topping: In a mixing bowl, whip cream, sugar, and vanilla until soft peaks form and hold their shape.

To serve, spread the topping over the entire chocolate cake. Add dollops of topping around the edge as a garnish. Sprinkle with chocolate shavings, if desired.

German's Sweet Chocolate Cake

Makes 12 to 14 servings

Cake

- 1 (4-ounce) bar Baker's German's sweet chocolate
- ½ cup boiling water
- ¾ cup shortening, butter, or margarine
- 1¾ cups sugar
- 4 eggs
- 1 teaspoon vanilla
- 2¾ cups sifted cake flour
- 1 teaspoon baking soda
- 1 teaspoon salt
- 1 cup buttermilk

Coconut Pecan Frosting

- 3 egg yolks
- 1 cup sugar
- 1 cup evaporated milk
- ½ cup butter or margarine
- 1 teaspoon vanilla
- 1⅓ cups flaked coconut
- 1 cup chopped pecans

Chocolate Frosting (optional)

- 4 tablespoons cocoa
- 3 cups powdered sugar
- ¼ cup butter or margarine, softened
- 2 to 3 tablespoons milk
- 1 teaspoon vanilla
- 2 tablespoons chopped walnuts, optional for garnish

Preheat oven to 375 degrees F. Line bottoms of three 9-inch cake pans with parchment paper.

For cake: Place chocolate in a small bowl and pour ½ cup boiling water over top. Let chocolate melt in water and cool. In a separate bowl, cream butter until light; gradually add sugar, creaming until light and fluffy. Add eggs, one at a time, beating well after each addition. Blend in vanilla and melted chocolate. In a separate bowl, sift flour with baking soda and salt. Alternately add flour mixture and buttermilk to chocolate mixture, beating after each addition until smooth. Pour cake batter into pans. Bake 30 to 35 minutes, or until toothpick inserted in center of each layer comes out clean. Cool cake in pans 10 minutes. Remove from pans and finish cooling on racks. Peel off paper.

For Coconut Pecan Frosting: Combine egg yolks, sugar, evaporated milk, butter, and vanilla. Cook and stir over medium heat until thickened, 12 to 15 minutes. Add coconut and pecans. Beat until thick enough to spread. Spread frosting between layers and over top of cake. If desired, use Chocolate Frosting to frost sides of cake.

Cupcake variation: Preheat oven to 375 degrees F. Fill cups ½ to ¾ full. If the cupcakes are filled a little fuller, they will crown better. (Crowning is the rounded dome that forms when the cupcake is baking.) Bake 18 to 24 minutes. Test doneness by inserting a toothpick into the middle of a cupcake. It should come out clean with no crumbs attached. Cool and frost. *Makes 20 to 24 cupcakes*

Chocolate Sheet Cake

Makes 24 servings

Cake

- ½ cup butter or margarine, softened
- ½ cup shortening
- 4 tablespoons cocoa
- 1 cup water
- 2 cups flour
- 2 cups sugar
- ½ cup buttermilk
- 1 teaspoon baking soda
- 1 teaspoon cinnamon
- 1 teaspoon vanilla
- 2 eggs, beaten
- Dash salt

Frosting

- ½ cup butter or margarine
- 4 tablespoons cocoa
- 1 teaspoon vanilla
- 6 tablespoons milk
- 4 cups powdered sugar
- 1 cup chopped walnuts, optional
- 1 cup mini marshmallows, optional

Preheat oven to 350 degrees F. Grease and flour a 13x18-inch jelly roll pan.

For cake: In a large saucepan, combine butter, shortening, cocoa, and water and bring to a boil, stirring often. In a separate bowl, sift together flour and sugar. Pour chocolate mixture over flour and sugar; mix well. Add buttermilk, baking soda, cinnamon, vanilla, eggs, and salt; mix well. Pour into jelly roll pan and bake 20 to 25 minutes. Five minutes before cake is done, prepare frosting.

For frosting: Melt butter in a large saucepan over medium heat; add cocoa, vanilla, and milk and bring to boil. Remove from heat and add powdered sugar, nuts, and marshmallows. Mix well. Frost cake while both cake and frosting are warm.

Cupcake variation: Preheat oven to 350 degrees F. Line muffin tins with cupcake papers. Set aside. Prepare cake as directed. Fill cups ½ to ¾ full. If the cupcakes are filled a little fuller, they will crown better. (Crowning is the rounded dome that forms when the cupcake is baking.) Bake 20 to 24 minutes. Test doneness by inserting a toothpick into the middle of a cupcake. It should come out clean with no crumbs attached. Frost while cupcakes and frosting are warm. *Makes 28 to 30 cupcakes*

Fudge Ribbon Cake

Makes 14 servings

Cake

1 (18- to 18.5-ounce) package chocolate cake mix

4 ounces cream cheese, softened

1 tablespoon butter

1 egg

1½ teaspoons cornstarch

1 teaspoon vanilla

½ (14-ounce) can sweetened condensed milk

Chocolate Cream Frosting

¾ cup butter, softened

5 tablespoons shortening

3 tablespoons cocoa

4⅔ cups powdered sugar

1½ teaspoons vanilla

¼ cup plus 1½ teaspoons water

Preheat oven to 325 degrees F. Grease and flour two 9-inch round cake pans.

For cake: Prepare cake batter according to package directions and divide evenly between 2 pans. Set aside.

Blend cream cheese and butter in a small mixing bowl until smooth and creamy. Add egg, cornstarch, and vanilla and mix well. Add sweetened condensed milk and beat for 1 minute. With a large spoon, gently place the cream cheese mixture evenly over the top of the cake batter, dividing it equally between the two pans. (This layer will sink as the cake bakes.) Bake 45 to 55 minutes, or until the center bounces back when lightly touched with your finger. Cool 10 minutes and then turn cakes onto wire racks to remove the pans and cool completely.

For frosting: Beat butter, shortening, cocoa, and powdered sugar in a large mixing bowl with an electric mixer until very creamy. Add vanilla and mix until well blended. Add water and mix until very light.

Place one layer of cake on serving platter and frost with Chocolate Cream Frosting. Place second layer on top and frost top and sides of cake.

Cupcake variation: Preheat oven to 350 degrees F. Line muffin tins with cupcake papers. Fill cups ⅔ full with cake batter. Spoon 1 tablespoon cream cheese filling on top of the batter. Bake 25 to 30 minutes. Test doneness by inserting a toothpick into the middle of a cupcake. It should come out clean with no crumbs attached. Cool and frost. Makes 20 to 24 cupcakes.

Devil's Food Cake

Makes 12 to 14 servings

⅓ cup shortening
1½ cups sugar
3 eggs, well beaten
⅔ cup cocoa
½ cup hot water

2 cups flour
½ teaspoon salt
1 teaspoon baking soda
1 cup sour cream
1 teaspoon vanilla

Preheat oven to 350 degrees F. Grease and flour three 8-inch or two 9-inch round cake pans.

Cream shortening and sugar together; add eggs. In a small bowl, beat cocoa in hot water until smooth; add to creamed mixture. Sift flour, salt, and baking soda together; add to creamed mixture alternately with sour cream. Add vanilla and beat well.

Pour into pans. Bake 20 to 30 minutes or until a toothpick inserted into the center of the cake comes out clean. Remove cakes from oven and place on wire racks. Let cool 10 minutes. Turn cakes from pans and cool on wire racks. Frost with Chocolate Frosting (see page 271), White Buttercream Frosting (see page 271), or Buttercream Frosting (see page 270).

Cupcake variation: Preheat oven to 350 degrees F. Line muffin tins with cupcake papers. Set aside. Prepare cake as directed. Fill cups ½ to ¾ full. If the cupcakes are filled a little fuller, they will crown better. (Crowning is the rounded dome that forms when the cupcake is baking.) Bake 18 to 24 minutes. Test doneness by inserting a toothpick into the middle of a cupcake. It should come out clean with no crumbs attached. *Makes 20 to 24 cupcakes*

Chunky Chocolate Peanut Cake

Makes 12 servings

Cake

2 cups all-purpose flour

⅓ cup unsweetened cocoa powder, sifted

2 teaspoons baking powder

¼ teaspoon salt

2 cups firmly packed brown sugar

1 cup chunky peanut butter, room temperature

⅔ cup butter, softened

4 large eggs

2 teaspoons vanilla

¾ cup milk

Peanut Butter Frosting

1½ cups chunky peanut butter, room temperature

¾ cup honey, room temperature

⅔ cup powdered sugar

6 tablespoons cream cheese, softened

½ cup peanuts, chopped, for garnish

Preheat oven to 350 degrees F. Grease and flour two 9-inch round cake pans.

For cake: In a large mixing bowl, sift together flour, cocoa, baking powder, and salt. In a separate bowl, beat together brown sugar, peanut butter, and butter at medium speed until light and fluffy. Add eggs, one at a time, beating well after each egg. Stir in vanilla. At low speed, alternately beat flour mixture and milk into peanut butter mixture. Pour batter into prepared pans; smooth tops. Bake about 50 to 55 minutes, or until tops spring back when lightly pressed or toothpicks inserted in the centers come out clean. Transfer pans to cooling rack for 10 minutes. Turn cakes out onto racks to cool completely.

For frosting: Beat together peanut butter, honey, powdered sugar, and cream cheese at medium speed until blended and smooth. Reserve about one cup of the frosting.

Place one cake layer on a serving plate. Spread ¼ of frosting on layer. Place second layer on frosting and spread remaining frosting on top and sides of cake. Using a pastry bag fitted with a star tip, make a border around the top and bottom edge of cake with reserved 1 cup frosting. Sprinkle peanuts on top.

Cupcake variation: Preheat oven to 350 degrees F. Line muffin tins with cupcake papers. Set aside. Prepare cake as directed. Fill cups ¾ full. Bake 25 to 30 minutes. Test doneness by inserting a toothpick into the middle of a cupcake. It should come out clean with no crumbs attached. Frost with Peanut Butter Frosting. *Makes 18 to 24 cupcakes*

Bûche De Noël (Yule Log)

Makes 10 to 12 servings

Cake

3 eggs

1 cup plus 2 tablespoons granulated sugar, divided

⅓ cup water

1 teaspoon vanilla

¾ cup flour

¼ cup cocoa

1 teaspoon baking powder

¼ teaspoon salt

½ cup raspberry preserves

¾ cup powdered sugar

1 cup heavy cream

Green and red candied cherries, for garnish

Yule Log Frosting

⅓ cup cocoa

⅓ cup margarine, softened

2 cups powdered sugar

1½ teaspoons vanilla

1 to 2 tablespoons hot water

Preheat oven to 375 degrees F. Line a 13x18-inch jelly roll pan with waxed paper; grease.

For cake: Beat eggs in a large mixing bowl on high speed until thick and lemon colored, about 5 minutes. Gradually beat in 1 cup sugar. Beat in water and vanilla on low speed. In a separate bowl, sift together flour, cocoa, baking powder, and salt; add to egg mixture, beating just until batter is smooth. Pour batter into jelly roll pan. Bake 15 minutes. Cool 5 minutes and then turn out onto a dish towel sprinkled with powdered sugar. Remove waxed paper and roll up cake and towel together from short end; set aside to cool.

While cake is cooling, beat heavy cream with 2 tablespoons sugar until stiff. Unroll cake and spread raspberry preserves evenly over cake and then spread whipped cream over preserves. Roll up again (without towel) and place seam side down on a serving plate. Cover roll with Yule Log Frosting, making strokes with tines of fork to resemble bark. Decorate with green and red candied cherries. Refrigerate until ready to serve.

For frosting: Beat cocoa, margarine, powdered sugar, and vanilla in a medium mixing bowl. Add hot water a little at a time until frosting is smooth and of spreading consistency.

North Pole Toffee Cake

Makes 12 to 14 servings

1 (20-ounce) package chocolate cake mix

1 (12-ounce) carton frozen whipped topping

⅓ cup chocolate syrup (optional)

7 toffee bars (Heath® or Skor®), crushed*

Grease and flour two 9-inch round cake pans. Prepare and bake cake according to package directions. Cool on wire rack. Carefully cut each layer horizontally to make 2 layers. In a bowl mix whipped topping with chocolate syrup and 6 crushed toffee bars. Place 1 layer of cake on serving plate and spread with chocolate mixture. Repeat with remaining 3 layers. Frost sides and top of cake. Sprinkle remaining crushed bars on top of cake.

*1 cup peppermint candies or candy canes, finely crushed, may be substituted for candy bars. Omit chocolate syrup.

Bûche De Noël (Yule Log)

Toffee Torte

Makes 12 to 14 servings

Cake

1 (18- to 18.5-ounce) package devil's food cake mix

1 (16-ounce) container frozen whipped topping, thawed, or a double recipe of stabilized whipped cream

7 to 9 English toffee bars (Heath or Skor), crushed

⅓ cup chocolate syrup, optional

Stabilized Whipped Cream

1 envelope (1 tablespoon) unflavored gelatin

¼ cup cold water

3 cups heavy cream

¾ cup powdered sugar

1½ teaspoons vanilla

For cake: Grease and flour two 9-inch round cake pans. Prepare and bake the cake according to package directions. Cool on a wire rack. (If time permits, freeze cakes for easier handling.) Carefully cut each layer in half horizontally. Recipe uses only 3 of the 4 layers. Freeze fourth layer for later use or to make Cake Balls (see page 319).

For stabilized whipped cream: In a small saucepan, combine gelatin with water; let stand until gelatin softens, about 5 minutes. Turn heat to low and stir constantly until gelatin is just dissolved. Remove from heat and allow to cool slightly, but do not allow to thicken. In a large mixing bowl, whip cream, sugar, and vanilla until slightly thick. On low speed, gradually add gelatin and then beat on high until cream is thick and peaks hold their shape.

Place whipped topping or stabilized whipped cream in a bowl and fold in 6 of the crushed candy bars and chocolate syrup, if desired. Place 1 cake layer on a serving plate and spread with ½ cup whipped topping mixture. Repeat with the remaining 2 layers. Frost sides and top with the whipped topping mixture. Sprinkle the remaining crushed candy bars on top of the cake.

Cupcake variation: Preheat oven to 375 degrees F. Line muffin tins with cupcake papers. Set aside. Prepare cake as directed. Fill cups ½ to ¾ full. If the cupcakes are filled a little fuller, they will crown better. (Crowning is the rounded dome that forms when the cupcake is baking.) Bake 18 to 24 minutes. Test doneness by inserting a toothpick into the middle of a cupcake. It should come out clean with no crumbs attached. Cool and frost with whipped cream. Sprinkle with crushed candy bars (you may need 2 or 3 more candy bars). *Makes 20 to 24 cupcakes*

Mint Chocolate Ganache Cake

Makes 14 to 16 servings

Cake

2 (18- to 18.5-ounce) chocolate cake mixes, any flavor

Chocolate Ganache

1 cup heavy cream
2 cups semisweet chocolate chips

Whipped Mint Frosting

3 cups heavy cream, whipped until stiff
1 (8-ounce) container frozen whipped topping, thawed
1/8 teaspoon mint flavoring (or more according to taste)
1 to 2 drops green food coloring
1 (7-ounce) semisweet chocolate bar, chocolate molding chocolate, or chocolate bark, for chocolate curls
Mint leaves, for garnish

Preheat oven to 350 degrees F. Grease and flour four 9-inch round cake pans.

For cake: Prepare and bake both cake mixes according to directions on the box. Allow to cool completely or freeze to make it easier to frost and assemble.

For ganache: Place cream in a small saucepan and heat on medium heat until bubbles start to form around the edge of the pan. Remove from heat. Pour chocolate chips into cream and stir until smooth. Set aside.

For frosting: Gently fold together whipped cream, whipped topping, mint flavoring, and food coloring. Do not beat.

Trim the tops off 3 cake layers where they start to round from the side to the top. (Reserve the trimmed tops and the fourth layer for other recipes such as Cake Balls, page 319.) Place 1 layer on serving plate, cut side up. Place 1/3 of the ganache on that layer and spread it so it will slightly run down the sides. Place 1/3 of the frosting on top of the ganache and spread just to the edge of the cake. Place second cake layer on top of frosting and repeat with ganache and frosting. Repeat with third cake layer. Garnish with chocolate curls and mint leaves.

For chocolate curls: Warm chocolate bar 10 seconds in the microwave and then peel with a vegetable peeler.

Banana Cream Cake

Makes 10 to 12 servings

2 cups cake flour

2 teaspoons baking powder

¼ teaspoon baking soda

½ cup shortening

¾ teaspoon salt

¼ teaspoon ginger

2 teaspoons vanilla, divided

1 cup sugar

2 eggs

¼ cup sour milk or buttermilk

1 cup mashed ripe bananas (approximately 3 medium bananas)

1½ cups heavy cream

⅓ cup powdered sugar

2 bananas, (not overripe) sliced

Preheat oven to 350 degrees F. Grease and flour two 8-inch cake pans.

Combine flour, baking powder, and baking soda in a small bowl; stir with a spoon to mix well. Set aside. In a medium bowl, combine shortening, salt, ginger, and 1½ teaspoons vanilla. Mix well. Add sugar; cream until light and fluffy. Add eggs, one at a time, beating thoroughly after each addition. In a separate bowl, mix milk and mashed bananas together. Add flour mixture and banana mixture alternately to creamed mixture, beating well after each addition. Divide batter evenly between pans and bake 25 to 30 minutes.

Whip cream in a medium bowl; add powdered sugar and ½ teaspoon vanilla. Spread whipped cream and sliced bananas on top of first layer of cake and top with second layer of cake. Spread whipped cream on top of cake. Garnish with sliced bananas. Cream Cheese Frosting (see page 307) also works well with this recipe.

Cupcake variation: Preheat oven to 350 degrees F. Line muffin tins with cupcake papers. Set aside. Prepare cake as directed. Fill cups ½ to ¾ full. If the cupcakes are filled a little fuller, they will crown better. (Crowning is the rounded dome that forms when the cupcake is baking.) Bake 25 to 30 minutes. Test doneness by inserting a toothpick into the middle of a cupcake. It should come out clean with no crumbs attached. Cool and frost using either whipped cream or Buttercream Frosting (see page 270). *Makes 18 to 22 cupcakes*

Applesauce Cake

Makes 15 servings

Cake

1 teaspoon salt

1 teaspoon cinnamon

1 teaspoon nutmeg

1 teaspoon cloves

2 cups flour

½ cup butter

1 cup granulated sugar

1 cup firmly packed brown sugar

1 egg

2 teaspoons baking soda

2 cups unsweetened applesauce

1 cup raisins

1 cup chopped walnuts

Caramel Frosting

½ cup butter

1 cup firmly packed brown sugar

¼ cup milk

1 teaspoon vanilla

2 to 3 cups powdered sugar

1 cup chopped walnuts or pecans, optional

Preheat oven to 350 degrees F. Grease and flour a 9x13-inch cake pan.

For cake: In a small bowl, place salt, cinnamon, nutmeg, cloves, and flour. Stir with a spoon to mix. Set aside. In a separate bowl, cream butter and sugars; add egg and beat well. Place baking soda and applesauce in a medium bowl and stir to mix. This will look foamy and will rise in the bowl. Add dry ingredients and applesauce mixture alternately to the sugar mixture, starting and ending with the dry ingredients. Stir in raisins and nuts. Mix well. Place batter in cake pan and bake 45 minutes or until a toothpick inserted in the center comes out clean. Allow to cool.

For frosting: Melt butter in a small saucepan; add brown sugar. Boil over medium heat, stirring constantly, for 2 minutes. Add milk. Keep stirring until mixture boils. Remove from heat. Add vanilla and stir. Cool. Add powdered sugar 1 cup at a time, beating well after each addition. Stir in nuts and frost cake. This spreads well on the top of the cake, but it doesn't stick to the sides.

Cupcake variation: Preheat oven to 350 degrees F. Line muffin tins with cupcake papers. Set aside. Fill cups ½ to ¾ full. If the cupcakes are filled a little fuller, they will crown better. (Crowning is the rounded dome that forms when the cupcake is baking.) Bake 18 to 24 minutes. Test doneness by inserting a toothpick into the middle of a cupcake. Cool and frost. *Makes 20 to 24 cupcakes*

Cherry Cloud Cake

Makes 10 to 12 servings

1 store-bought angel food cake

2 cups milk

1 (3.75-ounce) vanilla instant pudding mix

2 (20-ounce) cans cherry pie filling

1 (8-ounce) container frozen whipped topping, thawed

Slice cake in half diagonally and then cut or tear each half into bite-sized pieces. Place one-half of the cake pieces in a 16-cup glass bowl, trifle dish, or 3½-quart casserole dish. Set aside the remaining cake pieces.

In a medium bowl, whisk together the milk and the pudding until it starts to thicken and then pour pudding mixture over cake pieces. Gently press the cake down into the pudding so that the cake is almost covered. Spoon one can of pie filling on top of the pudding. Place reserved cake pieces on top of the pie filling. Place whipped topping in a medium bowl and fold in second can of pie filling. Spoon half of this mixture on top of the cake pieces, gently pressing as you go so the mixture will go around and in between the cake pieces. Spoon remaining filling on top, smoothing evenly over the top.

Chill 2 hours or overnight before serving.

Cherry Pineapple Cake

Makes 12 servings

1 (21-ounce) can cherry pie filling

1 (20-ounce) can crushed pineapple

1 (18.25-ounce) package yellow or white cake mix

¾ cup butter

Whipped topping or ice cream, optional

Preheat oven to 350 degrees F. Grease a 9x13-inch cake pan.

Pour pie filling in the bottom of pan and spread as evenly as possible. Pour crushed pineapple, juice and all, evenly over pie filling. Sprinkle cake mix evenly over the fruit. Do not stir.

Slice butter thinly and place pieces on top of cake mix, or melt butter and drizzle over top of cake mix, covering as much as possible. Do not stir or mix. Bake 45 minutes. Serve with whipped topping or ice cream, if desired.

Pineapple Bundt Cake

Makes about 15 servings

Cake

1 (18.25-ounce) package yellow (pudding in the mix) cake mix

½ cup cream of coconut

½ cup pineapple juice

4 eggs

⅓ cup vegetable oil

¾ cup crushed pineapple, drained, divided

1 cup sliced fresh strawberries, optional

Stabilized Whipped Cream

1 envelope (1 tablespoon) unflavored gelatin

¼ cup cold water

3 cups heavy cream

¾ cup powdered sugar

1½ teaspoons vanilla

Preheat oven to 350 degrees F. Grease and flour a 12-cup Bundt pan.

For cake: In a large mixing bowl, combine cake mix, cream of coconut, pineapple juice, eggs, and oil. Blend well and then fold in ½ cup crushed pineapple. Place in prepared pan and bake 40 to 50 minutes. Cake is done when a toothpick inserted near center comes out clean. Remove from oven and cool on a wire rack.

If desired, fold pineapple and strawberries into ½ recipe stabilized whipped cream and serve on the side, or spoon whipped cream onto cake and garnish with fresh fruit.

For stabilized whipped cream: In a small saucepan, combine gelatin with water; let stand until gelatin softens, about 5 minutes. Turn heat to low and stir constantly until gelatin is just dissolved. Remove from heat and allow to cool slightly, but do not allow to thicken. In a large mixing bowl, whip cream, sugar, and vanilla until slightly thick. On low speed, gradually add gelatin and then beat on high until cream is thick and peaks hold their shape.

Cupcake variation: Preheat oven to 350 degrees F. Line muffin tins with cupcake papers. Set aside. Prepare cake as directed. Fill cups ½ to ¾ full. If the cupcakes are filled a little fuller, they will crown better. (Crowning is the rounded dome that forms when the cupcake is baking.) Bake 18 to 24 minutes. Test doneness by inserting a toothpick into the middle of a cupcake. It should come out clean with no crumbs attached. Cool and frost with fruit and cream mixture. *Makes 20 to 24 cupcakes*

Pineapple Upside-Down Cake

Makes 9 servings

Fruit mixture

¼ cup butter or margarine
⅔ cup packed brown sugar
9 slices canned pineapple
9 maraschino cherries

Cake

1¼ cups flour
1 cup sugar

1½ teaspoons baking powder
½ teaspoon salt
¾ cup milk
⅓ cup butter or margarine, softened
1 egg
1 teaspoon vanilla
1 cup heavy cream, whipped and sweetened

Preheat oven to 350 degrees F.

For fruit mixture: Melt butter in an 8x8-inch baking dish in the oven. Remove dish from oven and sprinkle brown sugar evenly over melted butter. Cut pineapple slices in half and arrange with cherries over sugar-butter mixture; set aside.

For cake: Place flour, sugar, baking powder, salt, milk, butter, egg, and vanilla in a large bowl and blend on low speed for 30 seconds. Then beat on high speed, scraping bowl occasionally, for 3 minutes. Pour batter over pineapple topping. Bake 40 to 45 minutes, until a toothpick inserted in center of cake comes out clean. Remove from oven and immediately invert on heat-proof plate. Serve topped with a dollop of whipped cream.

Note: For variety, instead of pineapple slices, use drained crushed pineapple, apricot halves, or sliced peaches

Caramel Pudding Cake

Makes 20 to 24 servings

4 cups water
2 cups brown sugar
½ cup butter or margarine, divided
1 cup granulated sugar
1 cup peeled and chopped apples
2 cups flour
1 teaspoon nutmeg
1 teaspoon cinnamon

2½ teaspoons baking powder
½ teaspoon salt
1½ teaspoons baking soda
1 cup milk
1 teaspoon vanilla
½ cup raisins
½ cup chopped walnuts
Whipped topping or ice cream, optional

Preheat oven to 375 degrees F. Grease a 9x13-inch cake pan. Mix and boil together water, brown sugar, and ¼ cup butter or margarine; set aside. Cream together remaining ¼ cup butter and granulated sugar; add chopped apples. Sift dry ingredients together and add alternately with milk to creamed mixture. Stir in vanilla, raisins, and walnuts. Spread batter into pan. Pour hot brown sugar and butter mixture over batter. Bake 45 minutes. Cut into squares and serve, warm or cold, with whipped topping or ice cream, if desired.

Chiffon Cake

Makes 14 servings

Cake

1¼ cups sugar
1 tablespoon baking powder
2¼ cups cake flour
1 teaspoon salt
½ cup vegetable oil
5 egg yolks
¾ cup water
2 teaspoons vanilla
1 cup (7 to 8 large) egg whites
½ teaspoon cream of tartar

Filling

2 (15.75-ounce) cans lemon pie filling

Frosting

1 (15.75-ounce) can lemon pie filling
1 (8-ounce) container frozen whipped topping, thawed

Preheat oven to 325 degrees F.

For cake: Sift first 4 dry ingredients together in a large bowl. Add oil, egg yolks, water, and vanilla and mix until smooth. Set aside. In a separate, clean bowl with clean beaters, whip egg whites with cream of tartar until stiff. Pour batter over whipped egg whites, folding together until blended. Bake 55 minutes in an ungreased 10-inch tube pan. To test doneness, lightly press finger on the cake. It will spring back when done. Invert tube pan and let hang until cool. Once cake is cool, slice horizontally into 3 layers.

For filling: Spread a thin layer (about ¾ can) of lemon pie filling on cut side of bottom layer and then place the next layer on top of the pie filling. Spread the top of that layer with ¾ can of pie filling. Replace cake top.

For frosting: In a small bowl, fold one can of pie filling into the whipped topping and frost inside the hole, outside the cake, and on top of the cake. Store cake in refrigerator. You will have leftover pie filling.

Whipped Cream Valentine Cake

Makes 10 to 12 servings

1 (10-inch) angel food cake, baked and cooled
1 (10-ounce) package frozen strawberries or raspberries, thawed
1 envelope (1 tablespoon) unflavored gelatin
2 cups heavy cream, whipped until stiff
4 tablespoons sugar
1 teaspoon vanilla

Cut angel food cake into 3 horizontal layers. Drain juice from thawed strawberries or raspberries into small bowl. Sprinkle gelatin over juice and allow to stand until softened. Set small bowl in larger bowl of hot water and stir until gelatin dissolves. Combine gelatin mixture with berries and cool slightly. (If mixture cools too much, gelatin will set.) Add sugar and vanilla to whipped cream. Fold berries into cream. (Fruit that may seem too juicy will soon set up.) Alternate cake layers with generous layers of cream mixture. Adjust top cake layer and spread remaining cream over entire top and sides of cake. Refrigerate until firm.

Lemon Coconut Torte

Makes 12 to 14 servings

1 (18.25-ounce) white or yellow cake mix
2 (15.75-ounce) cans lemon pie filling

1 (12-ounce) container frozen whipped topping, thawed
2 cups flaked coconut

Grease and flour two 9-inch round cake pans. Set aside. Prepare and bake cake according to package directions. Allow cakes to cool on wire racks.

Slice cakes in half horizontally. Place first layer of cake on a serving plate and spread ⅔ can of lemon pie filling on top of the cake. Place next layer of cake on top of filling. Spread a ¼-inch layer of whipped topping on that layer and place the next layer of cake on top. Spread ⅔ of the second can of lemon pie filling on cake and place the last layer of cake on top.

Frost top and sides of entire cake with remaining whipped topping. Cover sides of cake with coconut. Spread remaining pie filling on top of cake and sprinkle with a small amount of coconut. This cake should be refrigerated.

Apple Cake

Makes 12 servings

Cake

2 cups sugar
½ cup butter
2 eggs
4 cups grated apples (or 3 cups applesauce)
2 cups flour
2 teaspoons baking soda
1 teaspoon cinnamon
½ teaspoon nutmeg
¼ teaspoon salt
½ cup chopped walnuts
1½ cups heavy cream, whipped

Butter Sauce

1 cup butter
2 cups sugar
1 cup light cream
2 teaspoons vanilla
Dash of nutmeg

Preheat oven to 350 degrees F. Grease and flour a 9x13-inch cake pan.

For cake: Cream together sugar and butter in a large bowl. Add eggs and beat until fluffy. Mix in apples, flour, baking soda, cinnamon, nutmeg, salt, and walnuts and pour into pan. Bake 50 minutes.

For sauce: Combine all ingredients in a medium saucepan and cook over low heat until thickened, allowing to boil 1 to 2 minutes.

Pour Butter Sauce over cake and top each serving with whipped cream.

Lemon Coconut Torte

Orange Sponge Cake

Makes 10 to 12 servings

Cake

- 8 eggs, separated
- ¼ teaspoon salt
- 1 teaspoon cream of tartar
- 1⅔ cups sugar, divided
- Zest from 1 orange
- ⅓ cup orange juice
- 1 cup plus 2 tablespoons flour, sifted
- ½ cup almonds, blanched and toasted, coarsely chopped, optional
- Whipped cream, optional

Orange Butter Glaze*

- 1½ tablespoons milk
- 1 tablespoon butter
- 1¼ cups powdered sugar
- 1 tablespoon orange juice
- ½ teaspoon orange zest

Preheat oven to 350 degrees F.

For cake: Beat egg whites and salt until foamy; add cream of tartar and beat until soft peaks form. Gradually add 1 cup sugar, beating until stiff but not dry; set aside. In a separate bowl, beat egg yolks until thick and lemon colored. Add remaining ⅔ cup sugar, orange zest, and orange juice; beat well. Add flour; mix well. Gently fold egg whites into batter. Pour batter into ungreased 10-inch tube pan. Bake 1 hour. Remove from oven and invert for 1 hour. Glaze with Orange Butter Glaze or Lemon Butter Glaze.* Alternatively, spread whipped cream on cooled cake and top with almonds.

For glaze: Heat milk and butter together. Stir in powdered sugar and mix until smooth. Add orange juice and zest; beat until shiny. Add a drop or two more orange juice if needed to make desired spreading consistency. Makes about ½ cup, or enough to glaze the top of a 10-inch tube cake, an 8- or 9-inch square cake, or a 9x5-inch loaf.

*__Lemon Butter Glaze:__ Prepare as for Orange Butter Glaze, substituting lemon juice and zest for orange juice and zest.

Key Lime Bundt Cake

Makes 12 to 14 servings

Cake

- 1 (18.25-ounce) white or yellow cake mix
- 1 (3.4-ounce) package vanilla instant pudding mix
- 3½ tablespoons lime gelatin
- 5 eggs
- ½ cup vegetable oil
- 1 tablespoon lime zest
- 1 cup lime juice
- ½ cup powdered sugar, optional

Glaze

- 2½ cups powdered sugar
- 1 teaspoon lime zest
- 2 to 3 tablespoons lime juice
- ¼ cup butter, melted
- 1 to 3 tablespoons heavy cream

Preheat oven to 350 degrees F. Spray a 9-cup Bundt pan with cooking spray that contains flour, making sure the spray covers the grooves.

For cake: Place the cake mix, pudding mix, and gelatin in a medium bowl. Add eggs, oil, lime zest, and lime juice. Mix on low speed until dry ingredients are combined and then mix on medium speed until batter is thick and well incorporated, about 2 minutes. Pour batter into prepared pan, tapping the sides and bottom of the pan to ensure batter goes into the grooves.

Bake 45 minutes or until a toothpick inserted into the center of the cake comes out clean. Cool the cake in the pan for 10 minutes and then shake it a couple of times to help the sides release. Place a serving plate over the top of the cake pan and invert the pan to turn the cake onto the plate. Allow the cake to finish cooling. Dust with ½ cup powdered sugar or frost with glaze.

For glaze: Place all ingredients in a small bowl and mix with a spatula or electric mixer until smooth. It should be fairly thick. Add additional lime juice and cream to get correct consistency. Spoon glaze around the top of cake and allow it to drape (run) down the sides.

Cupcake variation: Preheat oven to 350 degrees F. Line muffin tins with cupcake papers. Set aside. Prepare cake as directed. Fill cups ½ to ¾ full. If the cupcakes are filled a little fuller, they will crown better. (Crowning is the rounded dome that forms when the cupcake is baking.) Bake 18 to 24 minutes. Test doneness by inserting a toothpick into the middle of a cupcake. It should come out clean with no crumbs attached. Cool and frost with thickened glaze. *Makes 18 to 22 cupcakes*

Strawberry-Filled Cake

Makes 12 servings

Cake

4 eggs

1 cup sugar

1 teaspoon vanilla

¾ cup flour

¼ cup cornstarch

1½ teaspoons baking powder

¼ teaspoon salt

Filling

2 cups heavy cream, whipped and sweetened

1 quart strawberries, sliced

½ cup sugar

Preheat oven to 350 degrees F. Grease and flour three 9-inch round pans.

For cake: Beat eggs until light and fluffy. Add sugar gradually, beating until thick. Add vanilla. Sift flour with cornstarch, baking powder, and salt and fold carefully into egg mixture. Pour into prepared pans and bake 25 to 30 minutes. Cool and remove from pan. This will make 3 thin cakes.

For filling: Whip the cream and sweeten to taste. Mix sliced strawberries with sugar. Place the first layer of the cake on a serving plate. Spread ⅓ of the whipped cream on top. Spread ⅓ of the strawberries on the cream. Repeat with second and third layers, with the strawberries as the final topping. Chill until serving; refrigerate any leftovers.

Strawberry Angel Torte

4 egg whites

¼ teaspoon salt

¼ teaspoon cream of tartar

1 cup sugar

1 cup heavy cream, whipped

1 quart fresh strawberries (washed, hulled, and halved) or 1 (10-ounce) package frozen strawberries (drained)

1 tablespoon powdered sugar

Preheat oven to 275 degrees F. Butter a 9-inch pie pan. Set aside. To make torte shell, place egg whites, salt, and cream of tartar in a small bowl. Beat at high speed until eggs are frothy and begin to stiffen. Add sugar gradually and beat to very stiff peaks (8 to 10 minutes). Spread meringue in prepared pie pan. Bake until dry, about 1 hour.

To make filling, spread one-half of whipped cream in the torte shell. Put shell in refrigerator and let it stand five hours or overnight. If using fresh strawberries, toss with powdered sugar and spoon into torte shell. Top with remaining whipped cream. If using frozen strawberries, fold into remaining whipped cream and pile into torte shell. Drizzle with juice drained from frozen berries. Serve.

Strawberry-Filled Cake

Carrot Cake

Makes 12 servings

Cake

- 2 cups all-purpose flour
- 1 teaspoon salt
- 1 teaspoon baking soda
- 2 teaspoons cinnamon
- ½ cup coconut
- ½ cup chopped walnuts
- ½ cup raisins
- 2 cups sugar
- 1 cup vegetable oil
- 4 eggs
- 3 cups peeled and grated carrots

Cream Cheese Frosting

- 2 (8-ounce) packages cream cheese, softened
- ½ cup butter, at room temperature
- 5 cups powdered sugar, divided
- 2 teaspoons vanilla

Preheat oven to 350 degrees F. Lightly grease and flour three 9-inch round or square cake pans or a 9x13-inch cake pan and set aside.

For cake: Whisk together flour, salt, baking soda, and cinnamon in a large bowl and set aside. Combine coconut, walnuts, and raisins in a food processor or blender and process until very fine (or chop with a knife until very, very fine). In a large mixing bowl, combine sugar and oil and mix well. Add eggs, one at a time, beating until creamy. Add dry ingredients and mix until well blended. Add ground nut mixture and grated carrots and beat until blended. Divide batter equally into pans and bake 40 to 45 minutes. Allow to cool 10 minutes before removing from pans and placing on cooling racks. When completely cool, frost with Cream Cheese Frosting.

For frosting: Beat cream cheese until smooth. Add butter and mix until blended. Add 3 cups powdered sugar and beat until blended. Add remaining powdered sugar and vanilla and beat until smooth and fluffy. Do not overmix or frosting will be runny.

Cupcake variation: Preheat oven to 350 degrees F. Line muffin tins with cupcake papers. Set aside. Prepare cake as directed. Fill cups ½ to ¾ full. If the cupcakes are filled a little fuller, they will crown better. (Crowning is the rounded dome that forms when the cupcake is baking.) Bake 30 to 35 minutes. Test doneness by inserting a toothpick into the middle of a cupcake. It should come out clean with no crumbs attached. Cool and frost. *Makes 20 to 24 cupcakes*

Poppy Seed Cake

Makes 14 servings

1 (18.25-ounce) package yellow cake mix
1 (3.4-ounce) vanilla instant pudding mix
4 eggs
1 cup sour cream
½ cup water

1 teaspoon rum flavoring
½ cup butter or margarine, melted
¼ cup poppy seeds
¼ cup powdered sugar, optional

Preheat oven to 350 degrees F. Grease and flour a Bundt pan and set aside.

In a large mixing bowl, combine cake and pudding mixes, eggs, sour cream, water, rum flavoring, melted butter, and poppy seeds. Blend well on low speed and then beat at medium speed for 5 minutes. Pour batter into prepared Bundt pan. Bake about 45 minutes, or until a toothpick inserted near center comes out clean. Remove from oven and cool in pan 15 minutes. Turn out onto cake rack and cool completely. Sift a light dusting of powdered sugar over cake, if desired.

Cupcake variation: Preheat oven to 375 degrees F. Line muffin tins with cupcake papers. Set aside. Prepare cake as directed. Fill cups ½ to ¾ full. If the cupcakes are filled a little fuller, they will crown better. (Crowning is the rounded dome that forms when the cupcake is baking.) Bake 18 to 24 minutes. Test doneness by inserting a toothpick into the middle of a cupcake. It should come out clean with no crumbs attached. Cool and dust with powdered sugar. *Makes 20 to 24 cupcakes*

Note: *This delicious dessert cake may also be sliced thin and served as a bread with fruit salad.*

Coconut Cake

Makes 16 servings

Cake

- 1 (18.25-ounce) package yellow cake mix
- 1 (3.4-ounce) package vanilla instant pudding mix
- 1⅓ cups water
- ¼ cup vegetable oil
- 4 eggs
- 2 cups flaked coconut
- 1 cup chopped walnuts or pecans

Cream Cheese Frosting

- 4 tablespoons butter, divided
- 2 cups flaked coconut, divided
- 1 (8-ounce) package cream cheese, softened
- 2 teaspoons milk
- 3½ cups sifted powdered sugar
- ½ teaspoon vanilla

Preheat oven to 350 degrees F. Grease and flour three 9-inch round cake pans and set aside.

For cake: Blend cake mix, pudding mix, water, oil, and eggs in a large bowl. Using an electric mixer, beat 4 minutes at medium speed. Stir in coconut and nuts. Pour into prepared pans and bake 30 to 35 minutes. Cool in pans for 15 minutes and then turn out onto wire racks. Cool completely.

For frosting: Melt 2 tablespoons butter in a large skillet over low heat. Add coconut, stirring constantly, until golden brown. Spread coconut out on absorbent paper to cool and drain off excess butter. Cream remaining butter with cream cheese. Add milk and gradually beat in sugar and vanilla. Stir in 1¾ cups of the buttered, toasted coconut.

Place bottom cake layer on serving plate and top with a generous mound of frosting. Spread frosting to within ½ inch of edge of cake. Place second layer on top and repeat, topping with third layer. Frost top of third layer and sides of cake with remaining frosting. Sprinkle remaining toasted coconut on top of cake. This cake is very rich, so small slices are recommended when serving.

Cupcake variation: Preheat oven to 350 degrees F. Line muffin tins with cupcake papers. Set aside. Prepare cake as directed. Fill cups ½ full. Bake 20 to 25 minutes. Test doneness by inserting a toothpick into the middle of a cupcake. It should come out clean with no crumbs attached. Allow to cool completely before frosting. Sprinkle tops of cupcakes with toasted coconut after frosting. *Makes 24 to 28 cupcakes*

Coconut Brunch Cake

Makes 10 to 12 servings

Cake

    4 eggs
    2 cups sugar
    1 cup vegetable oil
    3 cups flour
    ½ teaspoon baking soda
    ½ teaspoon baking powder
    ½ teaspoon salt

    1 cup buttermilk
    2 teaspoons coconut flavoring
    1 cup flaked coconut
    1 cup chopped walnuts

Glaze

    1 cup sugar
    ½ cup water
    3 tablespoons butter or margarine

Preheat oven to 350 degrees F. Generously grease and flour a 10-inch Bundt pan.

For cake: In a large mixing bowl, beat eggs, sugar, and oil. In a separate bowl, sift flour, baking soda, baking powder, and salt. Add dry ingredients to creamed mixture alternately with buttermilk. Add coconut flavoring, coconut, and walnuts. Pour batter into pan. Bake for 1 hour.

For glaze: In a saucepan, mix sugar, water, and butter or margarine. Bring to a boil and cook 5 minutes. When cake is done, pour hot syrup over top of cake. Allow to stand for 4 hours and then remove from pan.

Old-Fashioned Pound Cake

Makes 2 loaves, 10 to 12 slices

    1 cup butter
    2 cups sugar
    1 teaspoon vanilla
    8 eggs
    3¾ cups cake flour

    2 tablespoons lemon juice
    Lemon zest to taste
    Whipped cream (optional)
    Strawberries (optional)

Preheat oven to 350 degrees F. Grease and flour two 8x4x2½-inch loaf pans. Set aside.

In a large mixing bowl, cream butter and sugar until very fluffy. With mixer on low speed, add vanilla and eggs alternately with cake flour. Beat on low speed until light and fluffy. Add lemon juice and zest, beating again until light.

Pour into loaf pans and bake 45 to 60 minutes or until a toothpick inserted into center of cake comes out clean. Serve with whipped cream and strawberries, if desired.

Angel Food Cake

Makes 12 to 14 servings

1 cup plus 2 tablespoons cake flour
1½ cups sugar, divided
1¾ cups (10 to 12) egg whites, at room temperature
¼ teaspoon salt

1¼ teaspoons cream of tartar
1 teaspoon vanilla
¼ teaspoon almond extract

Preheat oven to 375 degrees F.

Sift together flour and ½ cup sugar. Set aside. In a large bowl, combine egg whites, salt, cream of tartar, and flavorings. Beat with a flat wire whip, sturdy egg beater, or at high speed of electric mixer until soft peaks form. Add remaining 1 cup sugar gradually, ¼ cup at a time, beating well after each addition. (If beating by hand, beat 25 strokes after each addition.) Sift in flour mixture, one-fourth at a time, folding in with 15 fold-over strokes each time, turning bowl frequently. Do not stir or beat. After last addition, use 10 to 20 extra folding strokes.

Pour batter into ungreased 9- or 10-inch tube pan or angel food cake pan. Bake 35 to 40 minutes for 9-inch cake or 30 to 35 minutes for 10-inch cake, or until cake springs back when pressed lightly. Cool cake in pan, upside down, 1 to 2 hours. After cake is cool, loosen from sides and center tube with knife and gently pull out cake. An angel food cake pan with a removable bottom is ideal for removing cake in perfect condition.

Brunch Cake Supreme

Makes 12 servings

Cake

1 cup butter
1¼ cups sugar
1 egg
1 teaspoon vanilla
2 cups cake flour
¼ teaspoon salt

¾ teaspoon baking powder
½ teaspoon baking soda
1 cup sour cream

Topping

1½ cups brown sugar
1 scant tablespoon cinnamon
1 cup chopped walnuts

Preheat oven to 350 degrees F. Spray Bundt pan with nonstick cooking spray.

For cake: In a large mixing bowl, cream butter and sugar. Add egg and vanilla. In a separate bowl, combine flour, salt, baking powder, and baking soda. Alternately add flour mixture and sour cream to creamed mixture.

For topping: In a medium bowl, combine brown sugar, cinnamon, and nuts.

Layer half the batter on the bottom of the Bundt pan, spreading evenly. Sprinkle with a light layer of topping mixture and then spread remaining batter evenly on top of mixture. Top with a light sprinkling of topping mixture. Bake 40 minutes. Serve with fresh fruit.

Danish Almond Gift Cake

Makes 14 to 16 servings

1⅓ cups margarine

2½ cups sugar

4 eggs

2½ cups plus 2 tablespoons flour

1 teaspoon baking powder

½ cup warm water

4 teaspoons almond extract

1 cup sliced almonds

½ cup pearl sugar*

Preheat oven to 375 degrees F. Grease two 9-inch or three 8-inch round cake pans and set aside.

In a large bowl, cream margarine and sugar until fluffy. Beat in eggs, one at a time, until batter is light and fluffy, about 7 to 10 minutes. In a separate bowl, sift together flour and baking powder; add to creamed mixture alternately with water and almond extract, mixing after each addition.

Pour batter into cake pans and sprinkle tops with sliced almonds and pearl sugar. Bake 30 to 35 minutes, or until a toothpick inserted in the center of cake comes out clean. Remove from oven and invert on wire rack to cool. Store in covered cake container or cover with foil or plastic wrap.

Cupcake variation: Preheat oven to 375 degrees F. Line muffin tins with cupcake papers. Set aside. Prepare cake as directed. Fill cups ½ to ¾ full. If the cupcakes are filled a little fuller, they will crown better. (Crowning is the rounded dome that forms when the cupcake is baking.) Sprinkle tops with almonds and pearl sugar before baking. Bake 18 to 24 minutes. Test doneness by inserting a toothpick into the middle of a cupcake. It should come out clean with no crumbs attached. *Makes 20 to 24 cupcakes*

*Pearl sugar is available in the gourmet section of grocery stores.

Red Velvet Cupcakes

Red Velvet Cake

Makes 12 servings

Cake

- ⅔ cup shortening
- 1½ cups sugar
- 2 eggs
- 2 ounces or ¼ cup red food coloring
- 4 tablespoons cocoa powder
- 1 teaspoon salt
- 1 teaspoon baking soda
- 2¼ cups all-purpose flour
- 1 cup buttermilk
- 2 teaspoons vinegar
- 1 teaspoon vanilla

Baker's Frosting

- 1½ cups milk
- 4½ tablespoons all-purpose flour
- 1½ cups butter (no substitutes)
- 1½ cups sugar
- 1 tablespoon vanilla

Preheat oven to 350 degrees F. Grease and lightly flour two 9-inch round cake pans.

For cake: In a large bowl, cream shortening, sugar, and eggs. Make a paste of food coloring and cocoa; add to creamed mixture and blend. In a medium bowl, mix salt, baking soda, and flour. In a separate bowl, mix buttermilk, vinegar, and vanilla together. Add the flour mixture and the buttermilk mixture alternately to the creamed mixture. Mix until blended.

Divide batter evenly between the 2 prepared pans and bake approximately 30 minutes. Overbaking will cause the cakes to be very dry. Cool layers for 10 minutes. Invert and remove from cake pans. Cool completely. Cut each layer in half horizontally so that you have 4 layers.

For frosting: Combine milk and flour in a small saucepan; mix well. Cook over medium heat, stirring constantly until thick. Cover and let cool. Cream butter, sugar, and vanilla until fluffy. Add the cooled flour mixture and beat until fluffy, approximately 5 minutes. When frosting is done, you should not be able to feel the sugar granules.

Place a cake layer on a serving platter and spread with ¾ cup Baker's Frosting. Repeat for all layers. Frost top of cake with frosting.

Cupcake variation: Preheat oven to 375 degrees F. Line muffin tins with cupcake papers. Set aside. Prepare cake as directed. Fill cups ½ to ¾ full. If the cupcakes are filled a little fuller, they will crown better. (Crowning is the rounded dome that forms when the cupcake is baking.) Bake 18 to 24 minutes. Test doneness by inserting a toothpick into the middle of a cupcake. It should come out clean with no crumbs attached. Cool and frost with Baker's Frosting. To garnish, finely crumble one cupcake on a plate. Sprinkle crumbs on frosting. *Makes 20 to 24 cupcakes*

Pumpkin Cake Roll

Makes 10 servings

Cake

3 eggs

1 cup granulated sugar

⅔ cup canned pumpkin

1 teaspoon lemon juice

¾ cup all-purpose flour

1 teaspoon baking powder

2 teaspoons cinnamon

1 teaspoon ginger

½ teaspoon nutmeg

½ teaspoon salt

½ cup chopped walnuts

1 cup powdered sugar

Filling

¼ cup margarine, softened

2 (3-ounce) packages cream cheese, softened

1 cup powdered sugar

½ teaspoon vanilla

Preheat oven to 350 degrees F. Line a 13x18-inch jelly roll pan with parchment paper, grease, and set aside.

For cake: In a large bowl, beat eggs with an electric mixer until lemon colored. Gradually add granulated sugar. Stir in pumpkin and lemon juice. In a separate bowl, sift together flour, baking powder, cinnamon, ginger, nutmeg, and salt; fold into pumpkin mixture. Pour batter into prepared pan, smooth out top, and sprinkle with chopped nuts. Bake 15 minutes.

Lay a clean kitchen towel on the counter. Sprinkle powdered sugar on towel. Turn the warm cake onto towel and remove parchment paper. Roll up cake and towel together lengthwise. Cool in refrigerator or freezer.

For filling: While cake cools, beat margarine and cream cheese together until smooth. Beat in powdered sugar. Add vanilla. Unroll cake, spread with filling, and then roll up again, using the towel to help lift and roll the cake. Cut cake roll in half. Wrap each roll in plastic wrap until served. Store in refrigerator, or freeze for later use. Cut rolls into 1-inch slices to serve.

Peppermint Torte

Makes 14 to 16 servings

Cake

1 (18- to 18.5-ounce) package devil's food cake mix

Filling

¼ cup finely crushed peppermint candies

½ (10.5-ounce) bag miniature marshmallows

1 cup chopped walnuts (optional)

2 (12-ounce) containers frozen whipped topping, thawed

½ (16- to 18-ounce) package chocolate sandwich cookies, crushed

15 to 20 starlight mints

Preheat oven to 350 degrees F. Grease and flour two 9-inch round cake pans.

For cake: Prepare and bake devil's food cake mix according to package directions. Cool 10 minutes and then turn out of pans and allow to cool completely on wire racks. When cakes are cool, slice each layer in half horizontally to make 4 thin layers. Place a piece of waxed paper between each layer and put sliced cake in the freezer while you make the filling.

For filling: Combine peppermint candies, marshmallows, nuts, and 1 container of whipped topping. Mix until smooth. Chill, covered, in refrigerator 2 to 3 hours.

Remove cake layers from the freezer and separate. Spread one-third of the peppermint filling on the first layer and then place another layer of cake on top of the filling. Repeat this process with the next 2 layers. Place last layer on top and frost sides and top with second container of whipped topping. Take a handful of cookie crumbs and gently pat onto the side of the cake. Repeat until sides of cake are covered with crumbs. Garnish with rosettes of whipped topping, starlight mints, and cookie crumbs.

Cake Balls

Makes 30 to 40 servings

1 (18 to 18.5-ounce) cake mix, any flavor

1½ cups frosting or cream cheese, any flavor that complements cake

1 package chocolate bark, regular or white

Cocoa (optional)

Shredded coconut (optional)

Finely chopped nuts (optional)

Sprinkles (optional)

Prepare and bake cake as directed on the box for a 9x13-inch cake. Line a jelly roll pan with waxed or parchment paper.

After cake has cooled completely, crumble into a large bowl. Mix thoroughly with the frosting or cream cheese. (It may be easier to use your hands to mix this, but they will get messy.) Roll dough into walnut-sized balls. Place on parchment-lined pan. Chill 2 to 3 hours or place in the freezer for 45 to 60 minutes.

Melt chocolate in the microwave according to package directions. (Chocolate will burn easily.) Dip each ball into the chocolate and allow to cool.

Variations: This recipe is a great way to use up trimmings from cakes or the extra layer from a 3-layer cake. Any flavor of cake and frosting can be used. Adjust the amount of frosting to the amount of cake.

Instead of dipping the balls in chocolate, they can be rolled in cocoa, coconut, finely chopped nuts (any kind), or sprinkles. Try your own variations.

To make a fun treat for children, place a lollipop stick in the cake ball before it is dipped in chocolate.

Wedding Cake

Makes 6 cups of cake batter

Cake

- 3 egg whites
- 1½ cups water
- ¼ teaspoon lemon flavoring
- ¼ teaspoon orange flavoring
- ½ teaspoon almond flavoring
- 1 teaspoon vanilla
- 1 (18.25-ounce) package white cake mix
- ¼ cup all-purpose flour
- ¼ cup shortening

White Buttercream Frosting

- ⅔ cup plus 1 tablespoon water
- 4 tablespoons meringue powder (available in craft stores in the cake decorating aisle)
- 12 cups powdered sugar, divided
- ¾ teaspoon salt
- 1 teaspoon clear vanilla
- 1 teaspoon almond flavoring
- ½ teaspoon lemon flavoring
- ½ teaspoon orange flavoring
- 1¼ cups shortening

Use the charts below to determine the amount of batter, baking temperature, baking time, and quantity of frosting required for desired cake size. When planning the servings, remember that wedding serving sizes are smaller than regular dessert portions.

For cake: In a large mixing bowl, combine egg whites, water, and flavorings. In a separate bowl, mix the cake mix and flour together and then add to liquid ingredients. Add shortening and mix on low speed until moist. Turn mixer to medium speed and beat 2 minutes. Cake batter should be thick; it should not be thin and runny.

For frosting: Combine water and meringue powder; beat at high speed until peaks form. Add 4 cups powdered sugar and beat on low speed until well incorporated. Add salt and flavorings; beat slightly. Alternately add shortening and remaining powdered sugar. Beat on low speed until smooth. *Makes 7½ cups frosting*

Frost the cake with a thin "crumb coat" to hold the crumbs in. Let sit ½ hour or more. Then frost the cake as usual.

Sponge cake variation: Replace water with milk for a little denser cake.

Wedding Cake Baking Chart

Size	Servings	Cups Batter*	Baking Temperature	Baking Time
6"	14	2	350° F.	25 minutes
8"	25	3	350° F.	25 to 30 minutes
10"	39	6	350° F.	35 to 40 minutes
12"	56	7	350° F.	35 to 40 minutes
14"	77	10	325° F.	50 to 55 minutes
16"	100	15	325° F.	55 to 60 minutes
18"	127	17	325° F.	60 to 65 minutes

Wedding Cake Frosting Chart

Size Cake	Cups Frosting
6"	3
8"	4
10"	5
12"	6
14"	7+
16"	8+
18"	10+

*One cake mix yields 4 to 6 cups of batter. Pans are usually filled ⅔ full.

Almond Cookies

Makes 1½ dozen cookies

1 cup butter, softened (no substitutions)
½ cup powdered sugar, plus more for dusting baked
    cookies
1 teaspoon vanilla
½ teaspoon almond extract

1¾ cups all-purpose flour
¾ cup finely chopped almonds
¼ teaspoon salt
1 (8-ounce) can or tube marzipan

Cream butter in a large bowl and then gradually beat in powdered sugar. Add vanilla, almond extract, flour, almonds, and salt. Blend well. Chill 1 hour in refrigerator.

Preheat oven to 300 degrees F. Line cookie sheets with parchment paper and set aside.

Roll out dough about ¼-inch thick. Cut out with scalloped cutter (about 2 inches in size) and place on prepared cookie sheets.

Sprinkle counter with powdered sugar and roll marzipan out to ¼-inch thick. Cut out 1-inch circles and press one in the center of each cookie. Bake 15 minutes, until set but not browned. Remove from oven and dust with powdered sugar. Cool. Store in an airtight container.

Applesauce Cookies

Makes 5 dozen cookies

1 cup butter
2½ cups packed brown sugar
4 eggs
2 teaspoons vanilla
1½ cups applesauce
5½ cups all-purpose flour
2 teaspoons baking soda
1½ teaspoons salt

1½ teaspoons ground cloves
2 cups raisins (optional)

Almond Cream Cheese Icing

¼ cup butter
1 (8-ounce) package cream cheese, softened
2½ cups powdered sugar
1 tablespoon milk
2 teaspoons almond extract

Preheat oven to 350 degrees F. Line cookie sheet with waxed paper.

Cream together butter and sugar in a large mixing bowl. Add eggs and vanilla and beat until light and fluffy. Mix in applesauce and then add flour, baking soda, salt, and cloves. Add raisins, if desired. Mix all ingredients together, making sure to scrape the sides of bowl. Drop by rounded tablespoonfuls onto prepared cookie sheet. Bake 8 to 10 minutes or until lightly browned at the edges. Frost with Almond Cream Cheese Icing while cookies are still warm.

For icing: Cream butter and cream cheese together in a medium mixing bowl. Add powdered sugar, milk, and almond extract; mix well.

Crescent Cookies

Makes 2 dozen

1 cup butter, room temperature
2 egg yolks
2 cups powdered sugar
2¼ cups flour
1 teaspoon cinnamon

½ teaspoon cloves
⅛ teaspoon salt
2 cups ground, blanched almonds
Powdered sugar

Preheat oven to 350 degrees F. Grease a cookie sheet and set aside.

Beat butter and egg yolks together in a large bowl. Add powdered sugar and beat until well mixed. Add flour, cinnamon, cloves, salt, and ground almonds. Mix well. Pinch off a piece of dough about the size of a walnut; roll it into a 2-inch rope and form it into a crescent shape. Place on prepared cookie sheet. Repeat with remaining dough. Bake for 20 minutes. While cookies are still warm, roll them in powdered sugar.

Spritz Cookies

Makes 2 dozen cookies

½ cup butter, softened
⅓ cup sugar
¼ teaspoon vanilla or almond extract

1 egg yolk
1¼ cups flour
Maraschino cherry halves, if desired

Preheat oven to 375 degrees F. In a large mixer bowl cream together butter and sugar. Add flavoring and egg yolk. Mix in flour gradually. Put dough into cookie press and force into desired shapes onto an ungreased baking sheet. Decorate each cookie with a maraschino cherry half, if desired. Bake 7 to 10 minutes. Remove cookies immediately from baking pan to wire racks.

Danish Shortbread

Makes 3 dozen cookies

2 cups butter, softened
1 cup sugar
Pinch salt

4 scant cups sifted flour
1 egg, beaten well
Chopped almonds

Preheat oven to 375 degrees F. Cream butter, sugar, and salt in a large bowl until light and fluffy, about 7 to 10 minutes. Gradually add flour, ½ cup at a time, beating after each addition. Roll out dough about ½-inch thick on floured board or pastry cloth. Cut dough lengthwise in 1-inch strips. Then cut strips on an angle into 2-inch lengths; place on ungreased cookie sheets. Press each cookie down slightly with back of fingers. Brush tops with beaten egg. Sprinkle with chopped almonds. Bake 20 minutes or until light brown. Cool on wire rack. Store in covered container.

Easy Macaroons

Makes 3½ dozen cookies

1 pint pineapple sherbet, softened

2 teaspoons almond extract

1 (18.25-ounce) package white cake mix

6 cups flaked coconut

Preheat oven to 350 degrees F. Grease cookie sheets.

Combine sherbet, almond extract, and dry cake mix in a large mixing bowl; mix well. Stir in coconut. Drop by tablespoons 2 inches apart onto greased cookie sheets. Bake 12 to 15 minutes or until edges are lightly browned. Allow to cool 5 minutes and then place on a wire rack to finish cooling.

Variations: The flavor of these cookies can be changed by changing the flavor of sherbet or by using 1 pint vanilla ice cream for plain macaroons.

Coconut Macaroons

Makes 2½ dozen cookies

3 tablespoons light corn syrup

¾ cup plus 2 tablespoons hot water

6 cups desiccated coconut (available at Asian markets)

2 cups granulated sugar

1 teaspoon salt

1½ cups pastry flour

1 egg

1 teaspoon vanilla

Preheat oven to 350 degrees F. Grease 2 cookie sheets and set aside.

Add corn syrup to water in a small bowl and set aside. In a medium bowl, mix coconut, sugar, salt, and flour. Add water mixture, egg, and vanilla. Mix on low speed until evenly blended. Allow to rest 30 minutes. Spoon by table-spoonfuls onto greased cookie sheets. Bake 18 to 20 minutes.

Easy Macaroons

Peanut Butter Cookies
and Snickerdoodles

Peanut Butter Cookies

Makes 5 dozen 3-inch cookies

5¼ cups flour
2 teaspoons baking soda
1 teaspoon salt
1 cup butter, room temperature
¾ cup shortening

1¾ cups granulated sugar
1¾ cups packed brown sugar
4 eggs
1 teaspoon vanilla
¾ cup chunky peanut butter

Preheat oven to 350 degrees F. Line cookie sheet with waxed paper; set aside.

Combine flour, baking soda, and salt in medium bowl; set aside. Cream butter, shortening, sugars, eggs, and vanilla in large mixing bowl. Stir in peanut butter. Add flour mixture and stir until well blended. Drop dough by tablespoonfuls onto cookie sheet. Using fork dipped in flour, flatten each cookie slightly in a crisscross pattern. Bake 8 to 10 minutes or until slightly golden around the edges. Do not overbake.

Snickerdoodles

Makes 5 dozen 3-inch cookies

3 cups granulated sugar, divided
1¼ teaspoons ground cinnamon
1 cup butter, softened
4 eggs
1 teaspoon vanilla

2½ tablespoons water
6 cups all-purpose flour
2 teaspoons cream of tartar
1 teaspoon baking soda
½ teaspoon salt

Preheat oven to 350 degrees F. Line cookie sheets with parchment paper.

Mix ½ cup of the sugar with the cinnamon in a medium bowl and set aside.

Combine butter and remaining 2½ cups sugar in a large mixing bowl and cream until light and fluffy. Add eggs, vanilla, and water and beat until fluffy. Add flour, cream of tartar, baking soda, and salt, pulsing mixer at low speed until flour is nearly blended in. Continue mixing at medium speed until well mixed. Shape dough by rounded tablespoonfuls. Roll in cinnamon-sugar mixture and then place on prepared cookie sheets. Bake 9 to 10 minutes, or until golden brown.

Lemon Crackle Sugar Cookies

Makes 3½ dozen cookies

1¾ cups sugar, divided
¼ cup finely chopped walnuts
1 teaspoon nutmeg
1 tablespoon packed brown sugar
2½ cups flour
1 teaspoon baking soda
1 teaspoon cream of tartar

1 teaspoon salt
1 cup shortening
3 eggs, beaten
1 teaspoon vanilla
1 teaspoon lemon extract
2 teaspoons lemon zest (optional)

Preheat oven to 350 degrees F. Grease cookie sheets or line cookie sheets with parchment paper.

Place ¼ cup sugar, walnuts, nutmeg, and brown sugar in a shallow bowl and stir together; set aside. Stir flour, baking soda, cream of tartar, and salt together in a medium bowl and set aside. Cream shortening and 1½ cups sugar in a large bowl until fluffy; add eggs and beat well. Stir in vanilla, lemon extract, and lemon zest. Add flour mixture, stirring until well blended. Shape into 1-inch balls. Roll each ball in the first sugar mixture. Place on parchment-lined or greased cookie sheet. Bake 12 to 15 minutes.

Ginger Cookies

Makes 4 dozen cookies

¾ cup shortening
1 cup sugar
¼ cup molasses
1 egg
2 cups flour

2 teaspoons baking soda
¼ teaspoon salt
1½ teaspoons ginger
1 teaspoon cinnamon

Cream shortening and sugar in a large bowl. Add molasses and egg and beat well. Sift together flour, baking soda, salt, ginger, and cinnamon in a separate bowl. Add gradually to creamed mixture, mixing well. Chill dough for 30 minutes.

Preheat oven to 350 degrees F. Lightly grease cookie sheets.

Form dough into 1-inch balls. Place on prepared cookie sheets and bake 8 to 10 minutes. Don't overbake. Cool on wire rack. Store in covered container.

Sour Cream Cookies

Makes 5 dozen 2½-inch cookies

1 cup butter, softened
1⅓ cups sugar
2 eggs
2 teaspoons vanilla
1 cup sour cream
6 cups all-purpose flour
1½ teaspoons baking soda
1 teaspoon salt
1 (8-ounce) can crushed pineapple, drained, juice reserved

Pineapple Cream Cheese Frosting

1 (3-ounce) package cream cheese, softened
¼ cup margarine
3 cups powdered sugar
1 teaspoon vanilla
1 to 3 tablespoons pineapple juice, reserved from main recipe

Lemon Cream Cheese Frosting (variation)

1 (3-ounce) package cream cheese, softened
¼ cup margarine
3 cups powdered sugar
1 teaspoon vanilla
1 to 3 tablespoons lemon juice
1 teaspoon lemon zest

Preheat oven to 350 degrees F. Grease cookie sheets.

Blend butter, sugar, eggs, and vanilla in a large mixing bowl. Fold in sour cream; mix on low speed. Add flour, baking soda, and salt and mix until all ingredients are combined. Stir in pineapple until just mixed. Drop cookies by rounded tablespoonfuls onto greased cookie sheet and bake 12 minutes. Frost as desired.

For Pineapple Cream Cheese Frosting: Whip cream cheese and margarine in a large mixing bowl; add powdered sugar and vanilla. Add pineapple juice and mix until smooth. Add more pineapple juice if needed to reach desired spreading consistency.

Lemon Sour Cream Cookie Variation: Substitute 1½ teaspoons lemon extract and 1½ teaspoons lemon zest for pineapple. Frost with Lemon Cream Cheese Frosting.

For Lemon Cream Cheese Frosting: Whip cream cheese and margarine in a large mixing bowl; add powdered sugar and vanilla. Add lemon juice and lemon zest and mix until smooth. Add more lemon juice if needed to reach desired spreading consistency.

Chewy Oatmeal Raisin Cookies

Makes 2½ dozen cookies

1 cup packed brown sugar

1 cup granulated sugar

1 cup butter, softened

4 eggs

2 teaspoons vanilla

2¼ cups all-purpose flour

1 teaspoon baking soda

½ teaspoon salt

2½ cups quick-cooking rolled oats

1 cup raisins

Preheat oven to 350 degrees F. Grease cookie sheets or line cookie sheets with waxed paper.

Cream sugars and butter in a large mixing bowl. Add eggs and vanilla. Mix in flour, baking soda, salt, oats, and raisins. Drop by large rounded tablespoonfuls onto prepared cookie sheets. Bake 8 to 9 minutes.

Oatmeal Raisin Cookies

Makes approximately 12 dozen cookies

2 cups water

2 cups raisins

3 cups sugar

1½ cups shortening

4 eggs

2 teaspoons vanilla

5 cups flour

1 teaspoon baking powder

2 teaspoons soda

2 teaspoons salt

2 teaspoons cinnamon

2 teaspoons cloves

4 cups quick oats

Preheat oven to 350 degrees F. Bring 2 cups of water to a boil in a medium saucepan. Add raisins to boiling water; remove from heat and set aside.

In a large mixing bowl cream sugar and shortening until fluffy. Stir in eggs one at a time. Drain liquid from raisins, reserving 1 cup. Add reserved liquid to the sugar and shortening mixture. Add vanilla. Mix until well blended. In a separate bowl, mix together flour, baking powder, soda, salt, cinnamon, cloves, and oats. Add to the creamed mixture. (This may require hand mixing.)

Carefully stir in the raisins. Scoop walnut-sized scoops onto ungreased cookie sheets and bake for 12 minutes.

Chewy Oatmeal Cookies

White Chocolate Macadamia Cookies

Makes 5 dozen cookies

1 cup butter, softened
1 cup shortening
1½ cups granulated sugar
1½ cups packed brown sugar
1 teaspoon vanilla
4 eggs

4 to 4½ cups all-purpose flour
2 teaspoons salt
2 teaspoons baking soda
1 cup quick-cooking rolled oats
1 cup chopped macadamia nuts
1 (12-ounce) bag white chocolate chips

Preheat oven to 350 degrees F.

Cream together butter, shortening, and sugars in a large bowl until light and fluffy. Add vanilla. Add eggs, one at a time, mixing after each addition.

Whisk together flour, salt, baking soda, and oats in a separate bowl. Add flour mixture to creamed mixture and blend until incorporated. Gently fold in nuts and white chocolate chips.

Drop walnut-sized balls of dough onto ungreased cookie sheets and bake 12 to 15 minutes, or until edges are light golden brown.

Peanut Butter Buttons

Makes 3 dozen cookies

½ cup butter, softened
½ cup chunky peanut butter
½ cup granulated sugar
½ cup packed brown sugar
½ teaspoon baking soda
½ teaspoon baking powder

½ teaspoon vanilla
1 egg
1⅓ cups all-purpose flour
1 (12-ounce) bag miniature peanut butter cups (about 36 candies)
½ cup milk chocolate chips

Preheat oven to 350 degrees F.

Cream butter and peanut butter in the bowl of an electric mixer. Add sugars, baking soda, and baking powder. Beat until combined, making sure all ingredients are incorporated. Beat in vanilla and egg until light and fluffy. Beat in flour just until well combined. Unwrap miniature peanut butter cups. Shape each dough ball around a peanut butter cup until it is completely covered and no chocolate is visible. Place on ungreased cookie sheets and bake 8 minutes.

Cookies may look underdone, but do not overbake! Remove from oven and let cookies sit on hot cookie sheets for several more minutes. Transfer cookies to a wire rack to finish cooling.

After cookies are completely cooled, melt milk chocolate chips. Drizzle melted chocolate over cooled cookies with a fork or toothpick. Allow chocolate to set up. To help the chocolate set up faster, put the cookies in the freezer for a few minutes before drizzling with chocolate.

Chocolate Sandwich Cookies

Makes 2½ dozen cookies

6 tablespoons raisins
1 cup roughly cut walnuts
1 cup sugar
½ cup shortening
2 teaspoons corn syrup
6 tablespoons cocoa
1½ teaspoons salt
3 eggs
½ teaspoon vanilla
1¾ cups all-purpose flour

Mint Buttercream Icing

3 cups powdered sugar
½ cup butter, room temperature
6 to 8 tablespoons heavy cream or evaporated milk, divided
1 teaspoon vanilla
¼ teaspoon mint flavoring
1 to 2 drops green food coloring

Chocolate Ganache

½ cup heavy cream
2 teaspoons butter
1 cup semisweet chocolate chips
2 or 3 drops imitation rum flavoring (optional)

Preheat oven to 350 degrees F. Line a cookie sheet with waxed paper or grease well.

Mix raisins and nuts together and grind in a blender until very fine. Set aside. Cream sugar and shortening in a large mixing bowl until light and fluffy. Add corn syrup, cocoa, salt, eggs, and vanilla; mix well. Add nut and raisin mixture and flour. Mix well.

Drop by rounded teaspoonfuls onto prepared cookie sheet. Bake 8 to 10 minutes. Spread Mint Buttercream Icing on the flat side of one cookie and place the flat side of a second cookie on top of the icing. Drizzle Chocolate Ganache on the top of the second cookie.

For icing: Place powdered sugar in a mixing bowl. Add butter and 3 tablespoons cream. Blend on low speed until mixed. Slowly add the rest of the cream, 1 tablespoon at a time, until creamy and smooth, but not at all runny. Add vanilla, mint flavoring, and food coloring and mix again.

For ganache: Pour cream into a saucepan and boil for 1 minute, stirring constantly. Remove from heat and add butter, chocolate chips, and flavoring and stir until completely melted and smooth.

If mixture gets too thick to use, return it to medium heat on stove and reheat, stirring constantly.

Flavor Variations: Replace the mint flavoring with orange, lemon, or another favorite flavor that goes with chocolate. Most flavorings are not as strong as mint, so add ½ to 1 teaspoon. Use a complementary food coloring.

German Chocolate Variation: Lay the cookies flat and put 2 to 3 teaspoons of your favorite German chocolate frosting on top. Drizzle with ganache and allow to cool and set up.

Open-face Variation: Lay cookies flat on wax paper or parchment. Drizzle with ganache. Allow to cool and set up.

Vanilla Buttercream Variation: Omit the mint flavoring and the green coloring to the icing. Add 1 more teaspoon vanilla.

Wedding Cookies

Wedding Cookies

Makes 3 dozen cookies

½ cup granulated sugar
1 cup butter, softened
1 teaspoon vanilla

2 cups all-purpose flour
1 cup chopped walnuts or pecans
2 cups powdered sugar

Preheat oven to 350 degrees F. Line cookie sheets with parchment paper and set aside.

Cream together sugar, butter, and vanilla in a large mixing bowl. Add flour and mix well. Add nuts and mix. Roll into 1½-inch balls and place on prepared cookie sheets. Bake 10 to 12 minutes. (The tops of cookies should have slight cracks in them and the bottom edges should be just barely light golden brown.) Roll cookies in powdered sugar while very warm.

No-Bake Caramel Cookies

Makes 5 dozen cookies

2 cups granulated sugar
¾ cup butter
⅔ cup evaporated milk

1 (4-ounce) package instant butterscotch pudding mix
3½ cups quick-cooking rolled oats

In a large saucepan, combine sugar, butter, and evaporated milk. Bring to a rolling boil, stirring frequently. Remove from heat and add butterscotch pudding mix and oats; mix together thoroughly. Cool 15 minutes. Drop by spoonfuls onto waxed paper. Allow cookies 15 minutes to set.

Chocolate Kiss Cookies

Makes 5 dozen cookies

1 cup granulated sugar	2 eggs
1 cup packed brown sugar	¼ cup milk
1 cup shortening	3½ cups flour
1 cup chunky peanut butter	2 teaspoons baking soda
1 teaspoon salt	60 Hershey's Kisses
1 teaspoon vanilla	

Preheat oven to 350 degrees F. Line a cookie sheet with waxed paper. Set aside.

Combine sugars, shortening, peanut butter, salt, and vanilla in a large mixing bowl; mix well. Alternately add eggs and milk and mix until creamy. Fold in flour and baking soda.

Transfer the dough to a clean, flat surface and do the final mixing by hand. Roll into walnut-sized balls and place on prepared cookie sheet or drop by rounded teaspoonfuls. Flatten with a fork or the bottom of a glass dipped in sugar. Bake 8 to 10 minutes. Press a Hershey's Kiss into each cookie as soon as cookies are removed from oven.

Chocolate Crackle Cookies

Makes approximately 5 dozen cookies

¼ cup shortening, melted	2½ cups all-purpose flour
¼ cup cocoa	½ teaspoon salt
½ cup vegetable oil	1½ teaspoons baking powder
2 cups granulated sugar	½ cup chopped walnuts
4 eggs	½ cup chocolate chips (optional)
2 teaspoons vanilla	½ to 1 cup powdered sugar

Mix shortening, cocoa, oil, sugar, eggs, and vanilla in a large mixing bowl until well mixed. Add flour, salt, and baking powder. Mix well and then add walnuts and chocolate chips, if using. (Dough will be very sticky and almost runny.) Refrigerate dough for 2 to 3 hours or overnight.

Preheat oven to 350 degrees F. Line cookie sheet with parchment paper or grease well.

Place powdered sugar in a shallow bowl. Drop and gently roll dough by tablespoonfuls in powdered sugar, being careful not to overhandle dough. Place on prepared cookie sheets. Bake 9 to 10 minutes. Do not overbake.

Note: The cookie dough may be stored in the refrigerator for up to 5 days. Baked cookies will store for at least 2 weeks, if well covered and refrigerated. These cookies freeze beautifully.

Rich Chocolate Nut Cookies

1 cup butter, softened
1 cup sugar
1 cup brown sugar
2 eggs
3¼ cups oatmeal
2 cups flour
½ teaspoon salt

1 teaspoon baking powder
1 teaspoon soda
1 teaspoon vanilla
1½ cups walnuts, chopped
1 (12-ounce) bag semisweet chocolate chips
1 (4-ounce) Hershey® bar, grated

Preheat oven to 350 degrees F. Line cookie sheets with waxed paper or parchment paper.

In a large mixing bowl, combine butter and sugars. Add eggs and beat until light and fluffy. Blend the 3¼ cups oatmeal in a blender. This should measure 2½ cups after blending. In a separate bowl, mix together flour, salt, baking powder, soda, and vanilla. Add oatmeal. Stir in nuts, chocolate chips, and grated Hershey bar until all ingredients are well blended. Drop by rounded tablespoonfuls onto prepared cookie sheet and bake for 10 minutes, or until slightly brown at the edges.

Cocoa Puffed Chocolate Chip Cookies

Makes about 20 cookies

2 cups Cocoa Puffs® cereal
2½ cups all-purpose flour
1 teaspoon baking soda
½ teaspoon salt
¾ cup packed light brown sugar
¾ cup granulated sugar

½ cup butter, slightly softened
½ cup butter-flavored shortening, chilled
2 eggs
1½ teaspoons vanilla
1½ cups semisweet chocolate chips

Preheat oven to 300 degrees F.

In a blender, blend Cocoa Puffs to small crumbs. Transfer to a medium bowl and whisk in flour, baking soda, and salt and set aside. In a large mixing bowl, blend sugars together, then add butter and shortening and cream well. Add eggs and vanilla and mix at medium speed until just blended. Add the flour mixture and chocolate chips and blend at low speed until just mixed. Using a large ice cream scoop, place on cold, ungreased cookie sheets 2 inches apart. Bake for 18 to 19 minutes, or until just browned. Transfer cookies immediately to a wire rack to cool slightly. For best taste, serve warm from the oven.

Chocolate-Dipped Orange Cookies

Makes 30 cookies

2 cups flour

½ cup yellow cornmeal

1 teaspoon salt

½ teaspoon baking soda

1 cup butter, softened

1 cup sugar

2 egg yolks

1 tablespoon grated orange peel

1 teaspoon orange extract

¼ cup ground walnuts

6 ounces milk chocolate or semisweet chocolate chips

In a bowl, stir together flour, cornmeal, salt, and baking soda. Set aside. In a large bowl, cream together butter and sugar. Beat in egg yolks, orange peel, and orange extract until fluffy. Add flour mixture and walnuts. Mix well. Divide dough in half. Wrap in plastic and refrigerate for 30 minutes.

Preheat oven to 350 degrees F. Roll half of the dough out to ¼-inch thickness on a lightly floured surface. Cut dough with a floured 3½-inch round or star-shaped cookie cutter. If using round cutter, cut each circle in half. Place 1 inch apart on a lightly greased baking sheet. Repeat with remaining dough. Bake 10 to 12 minutes or until lightly browned. Cool on a wire rack.

Line a baking sheet with wax paper. In a small saucepan, melt chocolate over low heat, stirring constantly. (Or chocolate may be melted in microwave in a microwave-safe bowl.) Remove from heat. Dip one end of each cookie into chocolate; place on prepared sheet. Let stand until chocolate hardens, about 1 hour.

Chocolate Chip Cookies

Makes 5 to 6 dozen 3½-inch cookies

1¾ cups (3½ sticks) butter, softened

1¾ cups packed brown sugar

1¼ cups granulated sugar

4 eggs

5½ tablespoons water

1½ teaspoons vanilla

6 cups all-purpose flour

1½ teaspoons salt

1½ teaspoons baking soda

3 cups chocolate chips

Preheat oven to 350 degrees F. Line cookie sheets with parchment paper or lightly grease sheets and set aside.

Cream together butter and sugars in a large mixing bowl. Add eggs, water, and vanilla; mix until creamy. Add flour, salt, and baking soda; mix well. Gently fold in chocolate chips, mixing only until chips are evenly distributed. (Overmixing results in broken chips and discolored dough.) Drop by spoonfuls onto prepared cookie sheets. Bake 8 to 10 minutes, or until golden brown.

Chocolate-Dipped Orange Cookies

Turtle Cookies

Turtle Cookies

Makes about 1½ dozen cookies

½ cup margarine, softened
¾ cup sugar
2 eggs
6 tablespoons cocoa
1 teaspoon vanilla
1 cup flour

Turtle Icing

½ cup light corn syrup
1 tablespoon cocoa
2½ tablespoons margarine
¼ cup cold water
½ cup sugar
½ teaspoon vanilla
2 cups powdered sugar

Heat a standard waffle iron. Cream margarine and sugar in a large bowl until light and fluffy. Beat in eggs, cocoa, and vanilla. Add flour and beat until incorporated. Drop by teaspoonfuls onto a hot waffle iron; cook 1 minute. Cook 4 to 6 cookies at a time, depending on the size of the waffle iron. Remove from iron and frost with Turtle Icing.

For icing: Place all ingredients except vanilla and powdered sugar in a medium saucepan and bring to a boil. Boil for 3 minutes. Remove from heat and let stand a few minutes to cool. Add vanilla and powdered sugar and beat with an electric mixer until smooth.

Peanut Butter Turtle Variation: Turn these into a peanut butter treat by decreasing the amount of margarine to ¼ cup and adding ½ cup peanut butter.

Candy Bar Cookies

Makes about 3 dozen cookies

1 (18-ounce) package milk chocolate cake mix
½ cup vegetable oil
2 eggs

35 to 40 pieces of your favorite candy bar, such as Rolos, Junior Mints, Snickers, or Milky Way

Preheat oven to 350 degrees F. Lightly grease cookie sheets.

Mix together dry cake mix, oil, and eggs in a large bowl. Form spoonfuls of dough into balls. Press a piece of candy bar into each dough ball and then roll to cover candy bar. Bake on prepared cookie sheets for 10 minutes. Cool cookies on cookie sheet for 5 minutes and then move to cooling rack.

No-Fuss Pumpkin Chocolate Chip Cookies

Makes 2 dozen cookies

1 (18.25-ounce) white cake mix	1 (15.5-ounce) can pumpkin
2 teaspoons pumpkin pie spice	2 cups semisweet chocolate chips

Preheat oven to 350 degrees F. Grease cookie sheets or line cookie sheets with parchment paper.

Mix cake mix, spice, and pumpkin in a large bowl. Stir in chocolate chips. Drop by heaping teaspoonfuls on prepared cookie sheets. Bake 10 to 12 minutes. Cookies are done when a toothpick inserted in the middle comes out clean.

Pumpkin Chocolate Chip Cookies

Makes 5 dozen cookies

¾ cup granulated sugar	2 teaspoons baking soda
¾ cup packed brown sugar	2 teaspoons baking powder
3½ teaspoons pumpkin pie spice	¾ teaspoon salt
1½ cups pumpkin, canned	4½ cups pastry flour
¾ cup vegetable oil	1½ cups semisweet chocolate chips
7 eggs	1¼ cups chopped walnuts

Preheat oven to 350 degrees F. Line cookie sheets with waxed paper or grease well.

Mix together sugars, pumpkin pie spice, pumpkin, oil, and eggs in a large mixing bowl until well blended. Blend baking soda, baking powder, salt, and flour in a separate bowl; combine with pumpkin mix. Mix together until well blended and then add chocolate chips and walnuts. Drop by spoonfuls onto prepared cookie sheets. Bake 8 minutes. These cookies may be frozen and stored for later.

No-Fuss Pumpkin Chocolate Chip Cookies

Date Pinwheels

Makes 6 dozen cookies

2 cups chopped dates	2 cups packed brown sugar
1 cup granulated sugar	3 eggs
1 cup water	4 cups flour
1 cup chopped walnuts	½ teaspoon salt
1 cup margarine, softened	½ teaspoon baking soda

Mix dates, granulated sugar, and water together in a small saucepan and cook 10 minutes over medium heat. Stir in nuts and set aside to cool.

Cream margarine and brown sugar in a large mixing bowl. Beat in eggs. Sift together flour, salt, and baking soda in a separate bowl; stir into creamed mixture (dough will be stiff). Divide dough in half and chill 1 hour, or until dough can be rolled easily.

On lightly floured surface, roll dough out into two 10x15-inch rectangles. Spread each rectangle with half of the cooled date filling. Carefully roll up jelly-roll style, beginning at long side. Wrap each roll in waxed paper and refrigerate several hours.

Preheat oven to 375 degrees F. Grease cookie sheets.

Cut chilled rolls into ¼-inch slices. Place on prepared cookie sheets and bake 12 minutes. Remove from cookie sheet and cool on wire rack. Store in covered container.

Raspberry Sticks

Makes 3 dozen sticks

1 cup butter, softened
¾ cup sugar
1 egg
1 teaspoon vanilla

2½ cups flour
¼ teaspoon salt
1 to 2 tablespoons water (if needed)
1½ cups raspberry jam

Cream butter and sugar together in a large mixing bowl until light and fluffy. Add egg and vanilla; beat well. Sift flour and salt together; add to creamed mixture a third at a time, mixing well after each addition. If dough is too stiff, add 1 or 2 tablespoons water. Wrap dough in plastic wrap and chill in refrigerator for about 1 hour.

Preheat oven to 375 degrees F. Grease cookie sheet.

Cut the chilled dough into 4 pieces. Roll each piece into a rope the length of your cookie sheet. Put ropes onto the cookie sheet, side by side. With your finger, make an indentation all the way down the length of each rope. Bake 6 minutes. Remove from oven and fill the indentation with raspberry jam. Put back into the oven for another 6 to 8 minutes. Place cookie sheet on rack to cool cookies. Cut on the diagonal.

Raspberry Bars

Makes 12 bars

1¼ cups flour
1 teaspoon baking powder
Pinch salt
3 tablespoons packed brown sugar

½ cup butter or margarine
1 cup (4 ounces) grated cheddar cheese
1 cup raspberry jam
½ cup chopped walnuts or almonds

Preheat oven to 350 degrees F. In a medium bowl, combine flour, baking powder, salt, and brown sugar; cut in butter or margarine with a pastry blender or fork until mixture resembles coarse crumbs. Stir in cheese. Remove ¾ cup of the mixture. Press remaining mixture evenly in the bottom of an ungreased 8x8-inch pan. Spread jam evenly over crust. Sprinkle on nuts then remaining crumb mixture. Press down gently. Bake 25 minutes or until golden brown. Cool in pan and cut into bars. Store in refrigerator.

Cutout Sugar Cookies

Cutout Sugar Cookies

Makes 5 to 6 dozen cookies

2 cups granulated sugar
1 cup shortening
3 eggs
1 cup milk
1 teaspoon vanilla
1 teaspoon lemon extract
6½ cups all-purpose flour
1 teaspoon salt
1 teaspoon baking soda
3½ teaspoons baking powder

Lemony Buttercream Icing

¾ cup butter, softened
¾ cup shortening
4⅔ cups powdered sugar
1½ teaspoons lemon juice
1½ teaspoons vanilla
⅓ cup water

Preheat oven to 400 degrees F. Line cookie sheets with parchment paper and set aside.

Cream together sugar, shortening, and eggs in a large mixing bowl. Add milk, vanilla, and lemon extract and mix at low speed. Whisk together flour, salt, baking soda, and baking powder in a separate bowl. Add to creamed mixture until well blended. Roll out dough ⅛-inch thick; cut into desired shapes and place on prepared cookie sheets. Bake 6 minutes, being careful not to overbake. Cookies should be light golden brown around the edges. Cool on wire racks before frosting with Lemony Buttercream Icing.

For icing: Combine butter, shortening, and powdered sugar in a large mixing bowl; beat until very creamy. Add lemon juice and vanilla and mix until well blended. Add water and beat until very light, about 2 to 3 minutes.

Cookie Wreaths

Makes about 4 dozen wreaths

1 cup sugar
1 cup margarine, softened
1 egg
1½ teaspoons almond extract
3½ cups flour

1 teaspoon baking powder
¼ teaspoon salt
½ cup milk
Green food coloring
Cinnamon candies

Cream sugar and margarine in a large bowl. Add egg and almond extract, beating until fluffy. Sift together flour, baking powder, and salt in a separate bowl; add to creamed mixture alternately with milk. Divide dough in half; tint half green (about 5 drops of food coloring), leaving other half white. Chill dough for 1 hour.

Preheat oven to 375 degrees F.

Sprinkle sugar on work surface. For each wreath, shape 1 teaspoon white dough and 1 teaspoon green dough into two 4-inch ropes. Twist ropes together and shape into wreath. Place on ungreased cookie sheets; press 2 or 3 cinnamon candies on each wreath to look like holly berries. Bake 9 to 12 minutes, or until light golden around the edges. Cool on wire rack. Store in covered container.

Banana Bars

Makes 24 (2x2-inch) bars

2 cups sugar

1 cup butter, softened

4 eggs

4 ripe bananas, mashed

2 teaspoons lemon juice

3 cups all-purpose flour

1 teaspoon salt

1 teaspoon baking soda

½ cup buttermilk

1 cup chopped walnuts, optional

Peter Pan Frosting

1 cup cold butter

1 pasteurized egg*

5 cups powdered sugar

1 tablespoon plus 1 teaspoon half and half or evaporated milk

Preheat oven to 350 degrees F. Grease and flour a 12x17-inch jelly pan.

Cream sugar and butter in a large mixing bowl until smooth. Add eggs and bananas and beat until smooth. Add lemon juice and mix briefly. Mix flour, salt, and baking soda together in a separate bowl; add to creamed mixture alternately with buttermilk. Fold in nuts with the last addition of buttermilk. Do not overmix. Pour into prepared pan. Bake 30 minutes. Allow to cool and then frost with Peter Pan Frosting.

For frosting: Beat butter in a large mixing bowl until smooth. (This works best if butter is cold.) Add egg and powdered sugar and beat just until combined. Add half and half or evaporated milk; beat until smooth and creamy. Spread on bars.

Note: Frosting recipe makes more than needed, but half the recipe is not enough. It will keep for a long time if refrigerated. Also, Banana Bars taste even better the second day.

*Pasteurized eggs can be found in the supermarket dairy section by the regular eggs.

Butter Pecan Squares

Makes 16 bars

½ cup butter, softened

½ cup packed brown sugar

1 egg

1 teaspoon vanilla

¾ cup flour

2 cups milk chocolate chips, divided

¾ cup chopped pecans, divided

Preheat oven to 350 degrees F. Grease an 8x8-inch baking pan.

Cream butter, sugar, egg, and vanilla in a large bowl until light and fluffy. Blend in flour. Stir in 1 cup of the chocolate chips and ½ cup pecans. Pour into baking dish. Bake 25 to 30 minutes. Remove from oven and immediately sprinkle with remaining 1 cup chips. When chips melt, spread evenly over top with knife. Sprinkle with remaining pecans. Cool and then cut into squares.

Banana Bars

Cherry Almond Squares

Cherry Almond Squares

Makes 36 bars

1 cup sour cream
¼ cup water
3 eggs
1 (18-ounce) box sour cream cake mix
1 (20-ounce) can cherry pie filling
¼ cup sliced almonds

Glaze

1½ cups powdered sugar
2 tablespoons milk

Preheat oven to 350 degrees F. Grease and flour a 10x15-inch jelly roll pan.

Mix sour cream, water, and eggs in a large bowl. Stir in dry cake mix until moistened. Batter will be slightly lumpy. Spread into prepared pan. Drop pie filling by generous spoonfuls onto batter. Bake 25 to 30 minutes or until cake springs back when touched lightly. Cool. Drizzle glaze over top. Sprinkle with almonds. Cut into bars.

For glaze: Combine powdered sugar and milk in a small bowl, stirring until a smooth glaze forms.

Caramel Almond Dream Bars

Makes 24 bars

35 caramels, unwrapped
1 (14-ounce) can sweetened condensed milk, divided
1 cup butter, softened
1⅓ cups packed brown sugar
2 teaspoons vanilla
½ teaspoon almond extract

½ teaspoon baking soda
1 cup all-purpose flour
3 cups quick-cooking rolled oats
1 cup slivered almonds
Whole almonds, for garnish

Preheat oven to 350 degrees F. Grease a 9x9-inch pan.

Melt caramels and half of the sweetened condensed milk together in a medium saucepan over low heat. While caramels are melting, cream together butter, brown sugar, vanilla, and almond extract in a large bowl. Add baking soda, flour, and oats. Press half of the mixture into prepared pan. Pour melted caramels over the top and spread almost to edge. Stir almonds into last half of oat mixture and spread on top. Place 1 whole almond on top of mixture every 1 to 2 inches; drizzle rest of condensed milk over top of pan. Bake 30 minutes. Cool on a wire rack and then cut into squares.

Nutmeg-Pineapple Marshmallow Squares

Makes 9 servings

24 large marshmallows, cut in squares

1¾ cups milk

⅛ teaspoon salt

½ envelope (½ tablespoon) unflavored gelatin

¼ cup cold milk

1 cup heavy cream, whipped

½ teaspoon ground nutmeg

¼ teaspoon grated lemon rind

1 (8-ounce) cup crushed pineapple, drained

½ cup graham cracker crumbs

Place marshmallows, milk, and salt in top of double boiler. Heat over hot water until marshmallows are melted. In the meantime, soften gelatin in ¼ cup cold milk, then stir into melted marshmallow mixture. Cool until mixture begins to thicken. Fold in whipped cream, nutmeg, lemon rind, and pineapple.

Press 4 tablespoons graham cracker crumbs in bottom of greased 9x9-inch pan. Gently spoon in marshmallow mixture; top with remaining graham cracker crumbs. Chill overnight or several hours in refrigerator. Cut into squares and serve.

Five-Layer Bars

Makes 24 bars

½ cup butter or margarine

1 cup graham cracker crumbs

1 cup flaked coconut

1 cup chocolate chips, milk or semisweet

1 cup butterscotch chips

1 cup chopped walnuts

1 (14-ounce) can sweetened condensed milk

Preheat oven to 350 degrees F.

Melt butter in 9x13-inch pan. Sprinkle cracker crumbs, coconut, chocolate chips, butterscotch chips, and walnuts over butter, in layers. Drizzle sweetened condensed milk over top. Bake 30 minutes. Immediately after removing from oven, cut cookies away from sides of pan. Cut in squares while still warm.

Granola Bars

Makes about 32 bars

1 (14-ounce) package chocolate or plain caramels

2 tablespoons water

¾ cup crunchy peanut butter

3 cups plain granola

1 cup golden raisins

½ cup salted peanuts

Melt caramels in water over medium heat in heavy saucepan, stirring often. Stir in peanut butter. Add granola, raisins, and peanuts; mix well. Pour into a buttered 9x13-inch pan, and cool. Cut into 1x2-inch bars.

Mock English Toffee Bars

Makes 36 servings

35 saltine crackers
1 cup packed brown sugar
1 cup butter

2 cups chocolate chips
½ cup chopped walnuts or pecans

Preheat oven to 350 degrees F. Line a 10x15-inch jelly roll pan with foil or parchment paper; grease the foil.

Line the pan with saltines, placing them close together. Combine sugar and butter in a small saucepan and bring to a boil, stirring often. Boil for 2½ minutes, stirring constantly. Pour butter sauce over crackers. Place coated saltines in oven for 5 minutes. Remove from oven and sprinkle chocolate chips on top. When the chips are melted, spread chocolate evenly over saltines and sprinkle nuts on top. Cool and cut or break into small squares.

No-Bake Chocolate Bars

Makes 16 bars

½ cup granulated sugar
½ cup light corn syrup
1 cup chunky peanut butter

1 teaspoon vanilla
3 cups Corn Flakes® cereal, crushed
¾ cup chocolate chips

Warm sugar, corn syrup, peanut butter, and vanilla in a medium saucepan; do not cook. Once mixture is warm and combined, add Corn Flakes (measured before being crushed). Stir together and spread in a 9x9-inch pan. Melt chocolate chips and spread on top.

Toffee Bars

Makes 40 small triangle-shaped bars

1½ cups butter
1 cup plus 2 tablespoons sugar
¼ teaspoon salt
2 eggs
1 teaspoon vanilla

4 ⅔ cups all-purpose flour
2 to 3 tablespoons water, if needed
2 cups toffee bar chips or crushed Heath Bars®
15 (1.55-ounce) Hershey® bars

Preheat oven to 375 degrees F. In a large mixing bowl, cream butter, sugar, and salt together until light and fluffy. Add eggs and vanilla; beat well. Measure flour and add to the mixture one-third at a time, beating well after each addition. If the dough is too stiff, add 2 to 3 tablespoons water and mix well. Spread evenly in a 12x15-inch jelly roll pan. Prick with a fork at about 2-inch intervals, then bake for 12 to 15 minutes or until the bars are light golden brown. Remove from oven and sprinkle with 1 cup of the toffee chips, then set unwrapped Hershey bars on top of the chips. (The heat from the bars will melt the toffee chips and chocolate.) Slightly spread the chocolate as it melts, then cut the bars into 3-inch squares. Cut each bar diagonally into triangles. Allow to cool slightly, then sprinkle remaining toffee chips over the bars.

Oatmeal Fudge Bars

Oatmeal Fudge Bars

Makes 36 bars

1 cup butter or margarine, softened
2 cups packed brown sugar
2 eggs
2 teaspoons vanilla
2½ cups all-purpose flour
1 teaspoon baking soda
½ teaspoon salt

1½ cups quick-cooking rolled oats
1 (14-ounce) can sweetened condensed milk
1 (12-ounce) package semisweet chocolate chips
¼ cup margarine
2 teaspoons vanilla
1 cup chopped walnuts (optional)

Preheat oven to 350 degrees F. Grease a 9x13-inch baking pan and set aside.

Cream together butter and brown sugar in a large mixing bowl; add eggs and vanilla. Sift flour, baking soda, and salt into a small bowl, and then add to creamed mixture. Mix in oats.

Combine sweetened condensed milk, chocolate chips, and margarine in a heavy saucepan and heat until chocolate is just melted. Stir in vanilla and nuts.

Spread two-thirds of the dough into prepared baking pan. Spread with chocolate mixture. Drop remaining one-third of dough on top by spoonfuls. Bake 25 minutes. Cool and then cut into bars.

Heavenly Cookie Bars

Makes 24 squares

¾ cup butter, softened
¾ cup granulated sugar
¾ cup packed brown sugar
3 tablespoons water
1½ teaspoons vanilla
1 egg

1½ cups all-purpose flour
1½ teaspoons baking powder
1 teaspoon salt
1½ cups chocolate chips
1½ cups flaked coconut
1 cup chopped nuts (optional)

Preheat oven to 300 degrees F. Lightly grease a 9x13-inch pan and set aside.

Beat butter in a large bowl until smooth. Add sugars and cream well. Mix in water, vanilla, and egg. Stir in flour, baking powder, and salt and mix well. Add chocolate chips, coconut, and nuts, if using. Mix together and spread evenly in prepared pan. Bake 25 to 30 minutes. Allow to cool and then cut into squares.

Chocolate Coconut Bars

Makes 24 bars

2 cups crushed graham crackers
½ cup margarine, melted
4 tablespoons sugar

2 cups flaked coconut
1 (14-ounce) can sweetened condensed milk
1 (12-ounce) package semisweet chocolate chips

Preheat oven to 350 degrees F. Grease a 9x13-inch baking pan.

Mix graham crackers, margarine, and sugar together and press into prepared baking pan. Bake for 7 minutes. Sprinkle the coconut on top of the crust and then pour the condensed milk over the coconut. Bake for 15 minutes. Remove from the oven and sprinkle chocolate chips on top. When the chips are soft, spread evenly over the coconut. Allow the chocolate to set up and cut into 24 pieces. It can be refrigerated to help the chocolate set up.

Coconut Chews

Makes 24 bars

1 cup flour
2 tablespoons granulated sugar
Pinch salt
½ cup butter
1½ cups packed brown sugar

2 eggs
2 teaspoons vanilla
1 cup flaked coconut
1 cup chopped walnuts

Preheat oven to 350 degrees F. Grease a 9x9-inch baking pan.

Combine flour, granulated sugar, and salt in a medium bowl; cut in butter with a pastry blender or fork until mixture resembles coarse crumbs. Press mixture into prepared pan. Bake 15 minutes. While crust is baking, beat brown sugar and eggs together in a medium bowl until smooth. Mix in vanilla, coconut, and nuts. Carefully spread over baked crust, then return to oven and continue baking 25 minutes longer. Cut into squares while warm. Cool and then cover pan to store.

Chocolate Coconut Bars

Pecan Bars (facing page),
Cream Cheese Brownies (page 360),
and Lemon Bars (facing page)

Lemon Bars

Makes 12 bars

Crust

- ½ cup butter, softened
- ¼ cup powdered sugar, plus more for dusting top
- 1 cup all-purpose flour

Lemon Layer

- 2 eggs
- 1 cup granulated sugar
- 2 tablespoons all-purpose flour
- 2 tablespoons lemon juice
- Zest of half a lemon
- 2 tablespoons powdered sugar

Preheat oven to 325 degrees F. Grease an 8x8-inch baking pan.

For crust: Cream butter and powdered sugar in a large bowl. Mix in flour. Spread into pan and bake 15 to 20 minutes.

For lemon layer: Beat eggs slightly. Add sugar, flour, lemon juice, and zest. Mix well and pour over hot crust.

Bake an additional 18 to 22 minutes, or until the center is set. Remove from oven and sprinkle with sifted powdered sugar. Cool slightly before cutting into bars.

Pecan Bars

Makes about 15 to 24 bars

Topping

- 1½ cups butter
- 1½ cups packed brown sugar
- 1½ cups honey
- ½ cup heavy cream
- 4 cups pecan halves

Crust

- 1 cup butter, softened
- 1 cup granulated sugar
- 3 eggs
- Zest of 1 lemon
- 4 cups all-purpose flour
- ½ teaspoon baking powder

For topping: Combine butter, sugar, and honey in a saucepan over medium heat. Bring to a boil and cook until it has boiled 5 minutes, stirring constantly. Remove from heat. Cool slightly and stir in cream and pecans. Cool while preparing crust.

For crust: Preheat oven to 375 degrees F. Grease a 10x15-inch jelly-roll pan.

Cream together butter and sugar in a large mixing bowl. Add eggs and lemon zest and beat until smooth. Add flour and baking powder and mix well. Press the dough into the bottom of the pan, pricking evenly with a fork. Bake 12 to 15 minutes, or until dough looks half done. (Overbaking at this point will cause the crust to be too hard by the time the second baking is complete.) Reduce heat to 350 degrees F. Remove crust from oven and spread topping evenly over the partially baked crust. Return to oven and bake an additional 30 to 35 minutes, or until topping is set. Cool completely. Cut into bars.

Cookie Pizza

Makes about 12 cookie wedges

1½ cups flaked coconut, divided	½ cup butter
Yellow food coloring (optional)	¾ cup packed brown sugar
¾ cup all-purpose flour	1 egg
¼ teaspoon salt	1 teaspoon vanilla extract
½ teaspoon baking powder	1 cup semisweet chocolate chips
½ teaspoon baking soda	½ cup chopped walnuts or your favorite nuts
1 cup quick-cooking oats	½ cup M&M's (optional)

Preheat oven to 350 degrees F. Grease or spray a 12-inch pizza pan with nonstick cooking spray.

If desired, tint ½ cup coconut with yellow food coloring. Place flour, salt, baking powder, baking soda, and oats in a medium bowl; stir to mix well and set aside. Beat together butter, brown sugar, egg, and vanilla in a large bowl until light and fluffy. Add first mixture and mix until well blended. Stir in 1 cup coconut.

Spread dough evenly on prepared pizza pan. Sprinkle with chocolate chips, nuts, and tinted coconut. Bake 13 to 15 minutes or until golden brown. Sprinkle with M&M's. Cut into wedges and place pan on a rack to cool.

Cream Cheese Brownies (shown on page 358)

Makes 9 to 15 bars

1 (18-ounce) package deluxe brownie mix	1 egg
1 (8-ounce) package cream cheese, softened	2 tablespoons milk
⅓ cup granulated sugar	

Follow package directions for preheating oven and preparing cakelike brownies. Pour batter into a greased 9x9-inch pan. Beat cream cheese and sugar in a separate bowl until creamy. Add egg and milk and mix until smooth. Drop cream cheese batter into the brownie pan in spoonfuls and swirl with a knife. Bake 35 to 40 minutes. Cut into 3-inch squares or size desired.

Raspberry Cream Cheese Brownie Variation: Dollop approximately ½ cup raspberry jam by spoonfuls on top of cream cheese before swirling.

Black-and-White Biscotti

Makes 7 dozen cookies

3 cups flour

½ cup granulated sugar

½ cup packed brown sugar

3 teaspoons baking powder

½ teaspoon salt

4 ounces unsweetened chocolate, melted

1 teaspoon orange zest

⅓ cup olive oil

¼ cup orange juice

2 teaspoons vanilla

3 eggs

6 ounces white chocolate, chopped

Topping

4 ounces white chocolate, chopped

1 tablespoon shortening

Preheat oven to 350 degrees F. Lightly grease 2 cookie sheets; set aside.

Stir together flour, sugar, brown sugar, baking powder, and salt in a large bowl. Add melted chocolate, orange zest, oil, orange juice, vanilla, and eggs. Blend well to make a stiff dough. Knead chopped white chocolate into dough. Divide dough into 4 equal parts; shape each part into a log about 14 inches long. Place 2 logs on each baking sheet; flatten with fingers to a width of about 2½ inches each. Bake 18 to 20 minutes or until firm to the touch.

Remove cookie sheets from oven. Reduce oven temperature to 300 degrees F. Cool logs on cookie sheets for 10 minutes. Cut warm logs diagonally into ½-inch-wide slices. Place slices, cut side up, on same baking sheets. Bake 7 to 9 minutes or until top surface is dry. Turn cookies over and bake an additional 7 to 9 minutes. Remove cookies from sheets and cool completely on wire racks. Drizzle with topping.

For topping: Melt white chocolate with shortening in a small saucepan over low heat, stirring until smooth.

Biscotti can be stored in an airtight container for up to 4 weeks.

Picnic Brownies

Picnic Brownies

Makes 16 brownies

4 ounces baking chocolate

1 cup butter

2 cups sugar

2 teaspoons vanilla

1 teaspoon salt

4 eggs

1¾ cups flour

⅔ cup walnuts, pecans, or almonds, chopped

1 cup chocolate chips

Preheat oven to 350 degrees F. Grease two 9-inch round pans. In top of double boiler or microwave-safe bowl, melt chocolate and butter. In medium bowl, mix sugar, vanilla, and salt; add to melted chocolate mixture and blend well. Add eggs, one at a time, beating well after each addition. Add flour and mix well. Divide batter equally into prepared pans. Spread evenly and sprinkle top of each with chopped nuts and chocolate chips. Bake 25 minutes. (Do not overbake.) Allow to cool completely before cutting. Run a thin knife between pan and brownies and turn upside down. You may need to shake hard to release brownies from pan. With knife that is longer than brownies are wide, cut brownies by pressing knife straight down through brownies; cut into 8 pie-shaped pieces.

Note: These brownies are named Picnic Brownies because they stack and travel very well.

Chewy Caramel Brownies

Makes 24 brownies

1 (18-ounce) package German chocolate cake mix

⅔ cup evaporated milk, divided

1 cup butter, melted

35 caramels, unwrapped

1 cup chocolate chips, milk or semisweet

1 cup chopped walnuts, optional

Preheat oven to 350 degrees F. Grease a 9x13-inch cake pan and set aside.

In a large bowl, blend dry cake mix, ⅓ cup of the evaporated milk, and the melted butter until all ingredients are incorporated. Spread two-thirds of this mixture into the prepared pan and bake 7 minutes. Remove from oven to cool.

Heat caramels and remaining evaporated milk in a medium saucepan over medium heat until caramels are melted. Pour caramel mixture over the cooled brownies. Sprinkle chocolate chips and nuts (if using) over caramel. Drop small spoonfuls of the remaining brownie batter over top of chocolate chips. Return to the oven and bake an additional 16 to 18 minutes. Cool for 15 minutes and then cut into servings.

Scottish Shortbread

Makes about 3 dozen cookies

>2 cups butter, softened
>1 cup sugar
>4 cups flour

Cream butter and add sugar; beat until light and fluffy. Add flour and mix well. Chill several hours.

Preheat oven to 325 degrees F.

Roll out dough about ¼-inch thick on floured board. Cut into 2x2-inch squares and place on ungreased cookie sheet. Prick each cookie several times with fork. Bake approximately 30 minutes, or until cookies are delicately brown. Cool slightly before removing from cookie sheet.

Layered Cream Cheese Brownies

Makes 42 (2x2½-inch) brownies

>1 (8-ounce) package cream cheese, softened
>⅓ cup sugar
>1 egg
>1 to 2 tablespoons milk
>1 cup water
>1 cup margarine
>5 tablespoons cocoa
>2 ounces unsweetened baking chocolate

>4 eggs
>2 cups sugar
>½ cup buttermilk
>1 teaspoon baking soda
>1 teaspoon vanilla
>3 cups flour
>1 recipe Cream Cheese Icing (see below)

Preheat oven to 350 degrees F. Grease a 12x17-inch cookie sheet. In a medium bowl beat cream cheese, ⅓ cup sugar, 1 egg, and milk until fluffy; set aside.

In a small saucepan, heat water, margarine, cocoa, and chocolate over medium heat until melted; set aside. In a large mixing bowl, beat eggs and sugar until light and well combined. Mix in melted chocolate mixture, then add buttermilk, baking soda, vanilla, and flour; mix well. Pour half of batter onto the greased cookie sheet. Spoon cream cheese mixture evenly over top of batter. Pour remaining chocolate batter over cream cheese. Bake 30 minutes. Remove from oven and cool on wire rack. Spread with Cream Cheese Icing.

Cream Cheese Icing

>1 (3-ounce) package cream cheese, softened
>¼ cup margarine, softened
>3 cups powdered sugar

>3 tablespoons cocoa
>1 teaspoon vanilla
>1 to 2 tablespoons milk

Make icing by whipping cream cheese and margarine in a medium bowl until fluffy; beat in powdered sugar, cocoa, and vanilla with a little milk until icing reaches spreading consistency. Spread over cooled brownies.

Chocolate Brownie Pudding

2 cups all-purpose flour	2 teaspoons vanilla
2 teaspoons baking powder	¼ cup butter, melted
1½ cups sugar	1½ cups walnuts, chopped
¼ cup cocoa	1½ cups brown sugar
1 teaspoon salt	½ cup cocoa
1 cup milk	3½ cups hot water

Preheat oven to 350 degrees F. Grease a 9x13x2-inch pan and set aside. Measure flour, baking powder, sugar, ¼ cup cocoa, and salt into a bowl and mix together. Add milk, vanilla, and melted butter and mix until incorporated. (This can be mixed by hand or with mixer.) Stir in the walnuts. Pour into prepared pan and set aside.

In a large bowl mix together brown sugar and ½ cup cocoa. Pour hot water over sugar and cocoa mixture and mix together. When well blended, slowly pour over the flour mixture in baking pan. (The baking pan will be very full, so handle carefully when putting it in the oven.) Bake for 35 to 40 minutes. Cut into 15 squares.

Marbled Caramel Surprise Pudding

Makes 6 servings

2½ cups water	1 cup brown sugar
1 cup brown sugar	1 cup raisins
2 tablespoons butter	1 cup chopped walnuts
1 cup flour	½ cup milk
2 teaspoons baking powder	1 teaspoon vanilla
½ teaspoon salt	Half and half or ice cream
¼ cup vegetable shortening	

Preheat oven to 350 degrees F. In a medium saucepan, bring water, 1 cup brown sugar, and butter to a boil. Boil, stirring occasionally, for 5 minutes. Pour sauce into an 8-inch square baking dish. In a medium mixing bowl, stir together flour, baking powder, and salt. Cut in shortening with a pastry blender. Add 1 cup brown sugar, raisins, walnuts, milk, and vanilla; mix just enough to form a sticky batter. Spoon batter into hot sauce in baking dish by rounded tablespoonfuls. It will spread and sink into sauce as it cooks. Bake in preheated oven for 45 minutes. Serve warm with half and half or ice cream.

Tapioca Pudding

Makes 6 servings

3 cups milk, divided	3 tablespoons minute tapioca
⅓ cup plus 1 tablespoon sugar, divided	Pinch salt
1 egg	1 teaspoon vanilla

Heat 2½ cups milk and 1 tablespoon sugar in top pan of a double boiler until skim forms and milk is scalded. In a medium bowl beat egg slightly and add tapioca, ⅓ cup sugar, salt, and the reserved ½ cup milk and whisk together. Pour this mixture very slowly into the scalded milk, stirring constantly. Stir for 1 minute and again every 2 minutes for the next 4 minutes. (Mixture will form a ball of tapioca on the bottom if not stirred enough; this ball can be stirred out, but pudding will not be as smooth and creamy.) Allow to cook 2 to 4 more minutes. Tapioca will swell and begin to turn clear. Turn off heat and allow pudding to sit over the hot water about 20 minutes. Add vanilla. Stir, then remove top pan from water. Serve warm or place in serving dishes and chill.

Note: Pudding can be made in a saucepan on the stove instead of in a double boiler but it must be stirred constantly and removed from heat when the tapioca has swelled and turned clear. Cool 5 to 10 minutes before dishing.

Creamy Vanilla Pudding

Makes 4 servings of pudding, or fills one batch of cream puffs or eclairs, or makes one 8-inch pie

2 cups 2% milk	¼ teaspoon salt
¼ cup sugar	1 teaspoon vanilla
2 tablespoons cornstarch	

Heat milk in the top of a double boiler until very hot. Combine sugar, cornstarch, and salt in a small bowl and stir in ½ cup of the hot milk. Stir until sugar is dissolved. Add sugar mixture slowly to the hot milk in double boiler, stirring constantly. Cook and stir until mixture thickens and is smooth, about 3 minutes. Cover and cook 5 minutes longer. Remove from heat and stir in vanilla. Cover with plastic wrap and let stand until cool. Refrigerate for 3 hours before serving.

Bread Pudding

Makes 16 servings

10 slices bread (any variety) or Lion House Dinner Rolls,
sliced in thirds
½ cup butter, melted
¾ to 1 cup raisins
6 eggs
6 cups milk (whole milk recommended)

¾ cup granulated sugar
Pinch salt
¾ teaspoon vanilla
¾ teaspoon nutmeg, plus more for dusting top of pudding
1 recipe Lemon Butter Sauce (see below)

Preheat oven to 350 degrees F. Coat a 9x13-inch pan with nonstick cooking spray and set aside. Cut off crusts from bread. Place one layer of bread slices in pan and brush with melted butter. Sprinkle raisins on top. Place another layer of bread on top of raisins and brush with melted butter. In a large bowl, mix eggs, milk, sugar, salt, vanilla, and ¾ teaspoon nutmeg with wire whisk. Pour over bread. Sprinkle nutmeg over top of pudding and allow to set for 30 to 45 minutes. Bake 45 minutes, or until custard is formed and knife inserted near center comes out clean. Serve topped with Lemon Butter Sauce.

Variation: 2 cups fresh or frozen raspberries can be substituted for raisins and vanilla butter sauce for lemon.

Lemon Butter Sauce

Makes 4 cups

2 cups granulated sugar
¼ cup plus ½ teaspoon cornstarch
¼ teaspoon salt

2 cups water
1 cup butter, cut in small pieces
1½ teaspoons lemon extract

Place sugar, cornstarch, and salt in a 4-quart saucepan and stir until blended. Add water. Bring to a boil and cook 5 minutes, stirring constantly. Remove from heat; stir in butter and lemon extract until butter is melted and mixture is creamy.

Variation: Omit lemon extract and add 2 teaspoons vanilla extract.

Caramel Bread Pudding

Makes 6 to 8 servings

4 to 5 Lion House Frozen Rolls, baked and cooled
½ cup packed brown sugar
½ cup butter

1 cup cream or half and half
1 teaspoon vanilla
2 eggs, beaten

Preheat oven to 350 degrees F. Tear rolls into pieces and put in a baking dish coated with cooking spray (a medium casserole dish works well).

Melt the brown sugar and butter in a small saucepan over medium-low heat. Take the pan off the heat and whisk in cream, vanilla, and beaten eggs. Pour over the rolls and let rest for 10 minutes. Bake 20 minutes.

Rice Pudding

Makes 8 servings

2 cups whole milk, divided

1 (5-ounce) can evaporated milk

½ cup plus 2 tablespoons granulated sugar, divided

2 eggs, slightly beaten

¼ teaspoon salt

1 tablespoon cornstarch

2 cups cooked rice

½ cup raisins

⅛ teaspoon nutmeg

⅛ teaspoon ground cinnamon

1 teaspoon vanilla

Place 1½ cups of the milk, the evaporated milk, and 6 tablespoons of the sugar in top of a double boiler. Heat until milk is scalded. In mixing bowl, whisk eggs; add salt and remaining 4 tablespoons sugar and whisk again. Slowly pour egg mixture into scalded milk, stirring constantly with wire whisk. Cook 15 to 20 minutes, stirring occasionally. In a small bowl, mix reserved ½ cup milk and cornstarch; slowly pour into milk mixture, stirring constantly until pudding begins to thicken. (Stir constantly or lumps will form.) Stir thoroughly and cook 10 to 15 more minutes, or until cornstarch flavor is gone. Add cooked rice and cook 7 more minutes. Remove from heat and add raisins, nutmeg, cinnamon, and vanilla.

Note: If double boiler is not available, place a stainless steel bowl on top of small saucepan of boiling water, or cook pudding in a heavy saucepan, stirring constantly. (Cooking time will be less in a saucepan.)

Almond Rice Pudding

Makes 8 servings

2 cups milk

½ cup uncooked rice

1 envelope unflavored gelatin

¼ cup cold water

¼ cup blanched almonds, chopped

1 teaspoon vanilla

5 tablespoons sugar

Dash salt

2 cups heavy cream, whipped

Fruit sauce of your choice

Bring milk to a boil over medium-high heat in a heavy saucepan. Add rice and reduce heat. Simmer, covered, until rice is tender, about 20 to 25 minutes. Dissolve gelatin in cold water in a small bowl; stir into rice, along with the chopped almonds, vanilla, sugar, and salt. Cool slightly. Fold in whipped cream. Pour into bowl. Refrigerate. Serve with cold fruit sauce, such as cherry sauce or Danish Dessert made according to package directions.

Rice Pudding

Chocolate Cream
Makes 10 servings

4 egg yolks
8 ounces Baker's German's Sweet Chocolate, coarsely chopped
½ cup butter or margarine

4 egg whites
2 tablespoons sugar
Finely chopped orange peel (optional)
Whipped cream (optional)

In a small bowl beat egg yolks until lemony in color. Set aside. Place chocolate and butter or margarine in a small, heavy saucepan. Heat over low heat, stirring constantly, until melted. Gradually stir about half the chocolate mixture into the beaten egg yolks. Return all to saucepan and continue cooking and stirring over low heat for an additional 2 minutes or until very thick and glossy. Remove from heat and let cool to room temperature.

In a mixer bowl beat egg whites until soft peaks form. Gradually add sugar, continuing to beat until stiff peaks form. Fold a small amount of the egg whites into chocolate mixture to lighten it; then fold the chocolate into the remaining beaten egg whites. Spoon mixture into dessert glasses by quarter-cupfuls. Cover and place in refrigerator for several hours or overnight. Garnish with chopped orange peel or whipped cream, if desired.

Crème Brûlée
Makes 6 servings

4 cups heavy cream
⅔ cup (about 7) egg yolks
½ cup sugar

¾ teaspoon vanilla extract
6 tablespoons sugar, for caramelizing

Preheat oven to 300 degrees F. Place 6 (7- to 8-ounce) ramekins in a large roasting pan; set aside.

In a heavy pot heat cream until just scalded. In a separate bowl, whisk together egg yolks, ½ cup sugar, and vanilla. Very gradually pour 1 cup of the hot cream into the eggs, stirring constantly. Slowly stir in remaining hot cream. Let the mixture stand 5 to 10 minutes and then skim off the foam that has risen to the top. While custard sets, melt 1 cup of sugar in a heavy pot, stirring continuously until it takes on a light caramel color. Slowly pour the caramelized sugar into the cream mixture. Blend well by hand or with a hand mixer. Skim off the foam.

Pour the cooled custard carefully into ramekins, then pour hot water into the roasting pan around the ramekins until the water comes halfway up the ramekins. Bake 50 to 60 minutes. Brûlée is done when the center is set. Cool; sprinkle granulated sugar on each brûlée. Place under a broiler and watch carefully. Remove from heat when sugar bubbles. Serve warm or chilled.

Chocolate Mousse

Makes 16 servings

4 tablespoons unsalted butter
12 ounces dark chocolate, broken up
6 eggs, separated

2 cups heavy cream
½ cup powdered sugar

Melt the butter and chocolate in the top of a double boiler set over simmering water. Stir until smooth. Pour into a large bowl and cool slightly.

Beat the egg yolks until blended and light yellow in color. Incorporate yolks into melted chocolate mixture. In a medium bowl, whip the cream until soft peaks form. Add powdered sugar and beat until stiff but not dry. Fold into the chocolate mixture. In a medium bowl beat the egg whites until stiff but not dry. Fold into the chocolate and cream mixture. Chill for service.

White Mousse

Makes 14 to 16 servings

1 (16-ounce) package Oreo® cookies
½ cup butter, melted
1½ cups white chocolate chips
½ cup heavy cream

1 (16-ounce) carton frozen nondairy whipped topping, thawed
Chocolate curls, for garnishing
Fresh berries, for garnishing

Place cookies in the bowl of a food processor and process until they become fine crumbs. Place in a separate bowl. Pour melted butter over the crumbs and mix thoroughly. Press crumbs into an 8-inch springform pan. Freeze 1 hour.

In a small saucepan over low heat, melt white chocolate chips with cream until cream almost scalds. Remove from heat and allow to cool slightly. Stir well to form a white ganache. It may look lumpy at first, but keep stirring until it looks smooth and beautiful.

Place thawed whipped topping in the bowl of a large mixer and whip in the ganache.

Fill the crust with the white mousse, smoothing top from the center outward. Freeze until solid, usually overnight. Garnish with chocolate curls and fresh berries.

Flan

Makes 6 servings

1 (14-ounce) can sweetened condensed milk
1 (12-ounce) can evaporated milk
4 ounces cream cheese (optional)

3 eggs
1 tablespoon vanilla
1 cup sugar

Preheat oven to 300 degrees F. for In a blender, combine condensed milk, evaporated milk, cream cheese (if desired), eggs, and vanilla and blend until well mixed. Sprinkle sugar over the bottom of a heavy frying pan. Place over low heat and cook, stirring constantly, until sugar melts and starts to turn golden brown. (Watch carefully; sugar burns easily at this point.) Pour caramelized sugar into an 8-inch round cake pan, tilting pan to coat bottom completely. Carefully pour the mixture from the blender over the sugar. Place the pan in a larger dish or baking pan and fill the larger pan with water to a depth of 1 to 2 inches. Bake 35 to 50 minutes or until the sides are firm and top is lightly browned. Let cool and flip pan upside down on a plate to serve.

Frosty Vanilla Ice Cream

Makes 4 quarts

4 Junket Rennet tablets
¼ cup cold water
8 cups milk
2 cups heavy cream

2 cups sugar
⅛ teaspoon salt
4 teaspoons vanilla

In a small bowl dissolve junket tablets in cold water. In a large saucepan mix milk, cream, sugar, and salt, and heat to lukewarm. Add dissolved junket tablets and vanilla. Pour into freezer can. Put dasher in place and let stand 10 minutes to set. Freeze according to freezer directions.

Variations: Add 2 cups mashed fresh or frozen fruit (thawed), such as raspberries, strawberries, peaches, or boysenberries.

Harvest Peach Ice Cream

Makes 4 quarts

8 large ripe peaches
Juice of 2 lemons
3 cups sugar

2 cups heavy cream
1 (14-ounce) can sweetened condensed milk
4 cups milk

Peel and mash peaches. Combine mashed peaches, lemon juice, and sugar in a large bowl and refrigerate 2 hours. Whip cream; fold into peach mixture with sweetened condensed milk and regular milk. Pour mixture into a 4-quart ice cream freezer and freeze according to manufacturer's directions.

Creamy Pineapple Sherbet

Makes 12 servings

¼ cup sugar
1 envelope unflavored gelatin
½ cup water
1 (15-ounce) can crushed pineapple in juice, undrained

⅔ cup sugar
2 tablespoons honey
1 teaspoon vanilla
2 cups nonfat buttermilk

In a small saucepan, stir together ¼ cup sugar and gelatin; add water. Cook and stir over low heat until sugar and gelatin are dissolved. Remove from heat and cool the mixture slightly.

In a blender or food processor, combine pineapple with juice, ⅔ cup sugar, honey, vanilla, and gelatin mixture. Cover and blend until smooth. Stir in buttermilk.

Freeze the mixture in a 4-quart ice cream freezer according to the manufacturer's directions.

Frozen Fruit Dessert

Makes 35 servings

1 gallon pineapple sherbet, softened
3 (10-ounce) packages frozen raspberries, thawed

5 bananas, cubed

Fold ingredients together. Put into covered plastic containers and freeze. Dessert may be made ahead of time and stored in freezer.

Note: You can also use equal parts pineapple sherbet and vanilla ice cream, softened.

Snowballs

Vanilla ice cream

Toasted coconut or chopped pecans

Chocolate, caramel, or other favorite toppings

Maraschino cherries, stems on

Line a baking sheet with waxed paper or parchment paper; set aside. Scoop ice cream with large ice cream scoop into desired size balls. Make balls as rounded and smooth as possible. Drop ice cream balls into bowl of chopped pecans or toasted coconut and roll around until well coated. Place on prepared baking sheet. With your thumb, make an indentation on the top of each snowball. Place pan in freezer until time to serve. At serving time, place snowballs in individual serving bowls. Pour a small amount of chocolate, caramel, or other favorite topping on top of snowball and top with a stemmed maraschino cherry.

To toast coconut: Spread desired amount of coconut on a cookie sheet and put in the oven at 350 degrees F. for 3 to 5 minutes or until light golden brown. Coconut will continue to brown a little after you remove it from the oven.

Note: Snowballs can be made up to one week ahead if they are well covered after they are frozen solid.

Angel Fluff

Makes 8 servings

Cake

1 (9-ounce) loaf angel food cake

1 cup heavy cream

1 cup half and half

1 cup sugar

⅓ cup lemon juice

Pineapple Sauce

4 tablespoons cornstarch

1 cup sugar

2¼ cups pineapple juice

¼ cup lemon juice

For cake: Prepare or purchase a loaf of angel food cake. In a large, attractive, 2-quart serving bowl, break cake into bite-sized pieces. In a medium bowl, whip cream until stiff. In another bowl, whip half and half into a fluffy, thick liquid. Mix cream and half and half together. Beat sugar gradually into cream mixture and then slowly beat in lemon juice. Pour mixture over cake pieces. Chill at least 2 hours. Spoon onto dessert plates and serve with Pineapple Sauce.

For sauce: In a small saucepan, combine cornstarch and sugar; mix well. Add pineapple juice; cook on medium heat, stirring constantly, until clear and thickened, about 5 minutes. Add lemon juice and stir. Remove from heat. Chill.

Peppermint Angel Food Dessert

Makes 12 servings

1 angel food cake
¾ cup crushed red and white peppermint stick candy
½ cup milk
½ envelope (1½ teaspoons) unflavored gelatin

2 teaspoons water
2 cups heavy cream, whipped until stiff
½ cup chocolate syrup

Prepare or purchase an angel food cake. Slice into 3 horizontal layers when cool.

Combine candy with milk; heat and stir until dissolved. Soften gelatin in water and add to milk and candy mixture. Chill until mixture starts to set; fold into whipped cream. Spread whipped cream mixture over bottom layer of cake. Drizzle chocolate syrup over whipped cream mixture. Place another layer of cake on top and repeat layers of whipped cream mixture and chocolate syrup. Repeat with third layer. Cover outside of cake with whipped cream mixture. Chill and serve.

Chocolate-Peppermint Delight

Makes 9 servings

2 cups crushed vanilla wafers
¼ cup margarine, melted
½ cup butter
1½ cups powdered sugar
3 pasteurized eggs*

2 (2-ounce) squares unsweetened chocolate, melted
1 cup heavy cream
1 cup miniature marshmallows
½ cup crushed peppermint candies

Combine vanilla wafers with melted margarine and press into an 8x8-inch pan; set aside. In a large bowl, cream butter and powdered sugar until fluffy. Add eggs and continue to beat; slowly add chocolate, mixing until combined. Spread mixture on top of vanilla wafers; chill for 45 minutes. Whip cream until stiff; fold in marshmallows and spread over chocolate layer. Sprinkle crushed peppermint candy on top. Refrigerate several hours before serving.

Pasteurized eggs can be found in the supermarket dairy section by the regular eggs.

Luscious Layered Raspberry Delight

Makes 9 servings

14 whole graham crackers, divided
1 (3-ounce) package vanilla instant pudding
2 cups milk

1 cup frozen nondairy whipped topping, thawed
1 (21-ounce) can raspberry pie filling

Line a 9-inch square pan with enough of the whole graham crackers to evenly cover the bottom of the pan. If necessary, break the crackers to make them fit. Prepare pudding mix as directed on package, using 2 cups milk. Let stand 5 minutes, then blend in whipped topping. Spread half the pudding mixture over the crackers. Add another layer of crackers; top with the remaining pudding mixture and remaining crackers. Spread pie filling over top layer of crackers. Chill for 3 hours.

Pink Angel Dessert

Makes 15 servings

½ large angel food or chiffon cake, torn in medium pieces.
1 (3-ounce) package strawberry gelatin
1¼ cups boiling water
1 (8-ounce) package frozen, sliced, sweetened strawberries

1 tablespoon sugar
1 dash salt
1 cup whipped cream, whipped with 1 tablespoon sugar

In a 9x13-inch pan place half of the cake pieces. Dissolve gelatin in 1¼ cups boiling water. Stir in strawberries, sugar, and salt. Cool until gelatin becomes thick and syrupy. Fold in whipped cream. Pour half of this mixture over the cake pieces in the pan. Place the remainder of the cake in the pan and pour the rest of the strawberry mixture over it. Refrigerate for 1 hour or until it is set.

Cranberry Crunch

Makes 6 to 8 servings

2 cups (about ½ pound) sliced tart apples
2 to 3 cups raw cranberries
½ cup water
2 tablespoons butter or margarine, melted
½ teaspoon salt
1½ tablespoons cinnamon

1 tablespoon lemon juice
½ cup butter or margarine
1 cup sugar
3 tablespoons flour
1¼ cups crushed corn flakes or bran flakes*
Table cream (optional)

Preheat oven to 375 degrees F. Place apples and cranberries in a 2- or 3-quart baking dish. Combine water, melted butter, salt, cinnamon, and lemon juice. Pour over fruit. In mixing bowl, cream together ½ cup butter and 1 cup sugar; add flour and mix well. Add crushed cereal to creamed mixture. Press mixture over fruit. Bake, uncovered, 30 to 35 minutes. Serve with table cream, if desired.

Raisin Bran® is a good alternate.

Luscious Layered
Raspberry Delight

English Trifle

English Trifle

Makes 8 to 10 servings

2 to 3 cups cubed day old sponge cake or broken up vanilla wafers

2 cups sliced fresh fruit, such as strawberries, peaches, mangoes, kiwi, or a mixture of each

1 (3-ounce) package gelatin (raspberry, strawberry, or cherry)

1 (3-ounce) package instant vanilla pudding*

2 cups cold milk

2 cups heavy cream

Mint leaves, for garnishing

Additional sliced fruit, for garnishing

Line the bottom of a glass serving bowl or trifle dish with the pieces of sponge cake or vanilla wafers. Arrange the fruit atop the cake pieces. Make gelatin according to package directions, and while still warm, pour over cake and fruit. Refrigerate until set, about 2 hours. Beat vanilla pudding powder into cold milk; pour over set gelatin. Cover with plastic wrap and refrigerate. When ready to serve, whip cream and spread over top of pudding. Decorate with a few mint leaves and sliced fruit.

For a true English trifle, in place of the pudding use Bird's Custard powder, which is available at many food stores in the gourmet or imported foods section. Prepare according to directions on package.

Chocolate and Fresh Fruit Trifle

Makes 16 servings

1 angel food cake or 9-inch long cake

1 (3.5-ounce) package instant chocolate fudge pudding mix

2 cups skim milk

1 teaspoon vanilla

2 cups assorted sliced fresh fruit: bananas, nectarines, peaches, pineapple, strawberries, raspberries, or other choices

1 cup light whipped topping

1 tablespoon grated chocolate

1 tablespoon sliced almonds

Cut cake in ¾-inch cubes. Place half the cubes in the bottom of a large clear glass bowl. Prepare pudding as directed on package, using 2 cups of skim milk. Stir in vanilla. Spoon half of pudding on top of cake cubes; arrange half of fruit on top of pudding. Repeat layers, ending with fruit. Top with whipped topping. Cover and refrigerate until thoroughly chilled, at least 1 hour. Just before serving, top with grated chocolate and slivered almonds.

Banana Split Cake

Makes 15 servings

Crust

2 cups graham cracker crumbs

½ cup butter or margarine, melted

Filling

½ cup pasteurized eggs* (enough to equal 2 eggs)

2 cups powdered sugar

¾ cup butter or margarine, room temperature

Topping

4 large bananas

1 (20-ounce) can crushed pineapple, drained

1 (12-ounce) container frozen whipped topping, thawed

1 bottle fudge ice cream topping

¼ cup chopped walnuts or pecans

¼ cup quartered maraschino cherries

For crust: Mix together graham cracker crumbs and butter; press into the bottom of an ungreased 9x13-inch cake pan. Refrigerate 10 to 12 minutes.

For filling: In a large bowl, beat together eggs, powdered sugar, and butter until light and fluffy, approximately 10 to 12 minutes. Spread filling on top of crumb mixture.

For topping: Slice bananas on top of the filling; spread crushed pineapple on top of the bananas. Spread whipped topping on top of the pineapple. Warm fudge topping slightly and drizzle on top of the whipped topping. Garnish the top with nuts and cherries.

Refrigerate at least 4 hours. For best results, refrigerate overnight. This dessert is very rich.

Pasteurized eggs can be found in the supermarket dairy section by the regular eggs.

Pistachio Pudding Dessert

Makes 12 to 15 servings

2 cups dry biscuit mix

2 tablespoons brown sugar

¼ cup margarine

½ cup chopped nuts

1½ cups powdered sugar

2 (8-ounce) packages cream cheese, softened

1 cup heavy cream

4 cups milk

2 (3.5-ounce) packages instant pistachio pudding

Whipped cream and green cherries, for garnishing

Preheat oven to 375 degrees F. Combine biscuit mix and brown sugar in a medium bowl; cut in margarine with a pastry blender or fork until crumbly. Add chopped nuts and press into a 9x13-inch baking pan. Bake 10 minutes. Cool on a wire rack.

While crust cools, cream powdered sugar and cream cheese in a large bowl until light and fluffy. Whip cream in a separate bowl, then fold into cream cheese mixture; spread mixture over baked crust.

Pour milk into a medium bowl. Add pudding mixes and beat until well blended. Pour over cream cheese layer. Refrigerate until set, about 2 hours. Top each serving with whipped cream and a green cherry.

Dipped Strawberries

Makes 12 to 16 dipped strawberries

1 pound high-quality milk chocolate, coarsely chopped
12 to 16 large strawberries, rinsed and thoroughly dried

Place chocolate in the top of a double boiler over simmering water, being careful to not let the water boil. Stir occasionally until the chocolate is smooth and melted. Carefully dip rinsed and dried strawberries into melted chocolate, covering three-fourths of the berry and leaving the stem end clean. Place each strawberry onto a cookie sheet lined with parchment or waxed paper. Refrigerate until chocolate is set.

Dipped Pretzels

2 (12-ounce) packages semisweet chocolate chips
2 (12-ounce) packages white chocolate chips
1 (16-ounce) bag pretzel knots

Line 2 cookie sheets with parchment or waxed paper. Place semisweet chips in the top of a double boiler and place over simmering water. Stir occasionally until chips are melted. If you want 2-toned decorations, you will need to melt the white chips in a separate pan at the same time. (You can also melt the chips in a glass bowl in the microwave in 30-second increments.) Pick up the pretzel by the single round loop and dip the double loop in the chocolate almost to your fingertips. Lay the pretzel on waxed paper to dry. You may choose to leave parts of the pretzel exposed or dip the other half in white chocolate after the semisweet chocolate has dried. You can also use the chocolate to "bond" several pretzels together in a variety of creative designs.

Christmas Caramels

Makes about 75 pieces

1 cup butter
1 cup packed brown sugar
1 cup granulated sugar

1 cup light corn syrup
1 (14-ounce) can sweetened condensed milk
Dash salt

Butter a 7x11-inch pan.

Combine butter, sugars, corn syrup, sweetened condensed milk, and salt in a heavy saucepan. Bring to a boil over medium heat, stirring constantly. Adjust temperature to maintain a steady boil and cook, stirring often, to firm-ball stage, 245 degrees F. (mixture forms a firm ball when dropped into cold water and won't flatten when removed). This will take 15 to 20 minutes. Pour into prepared pan. Cool and then cut into squares. Wrap each piece in waxed paper.

Pavlova

Makes 20 servings

6 egg whites, room temperature
3 cups sugar
3 teaspoons vanilla
3 teaspoons vinegar or lemon juice
½ cup boiling water

1 cup whipping cream
½ teaspoon vanilla
1 jar apricot preserves
Fresh fruit slices, such as peaches, strawberries, pineapple, blueberries, kiwi

Preheat oven to 450 degrees F. Line a baking sheet with foil. Using an 8-inch round cake pan as a guide, draw a circle on the foil.

In a large electric mixer bowl, beat together egg whites, sugar, 3 teaspoons vanilla, vinegar or lemon juice, and boiling water. Beat on high speed for about 12 minutes, scraping bowl constantly, until stiff peaks form and mixture holds its shape but is not dry. Spread the mixture onto the circle on the baking tray. Shape into a pie-shell form with a spoon, making the bottom ½-inch thick and the sides 2½ to 3 inches high. Form the edges into peaks or make a rim around the edge. Place baking sheet in center of preheated oven and turn oven off. Let stand 4 to 5 hours. Do not open oven door.

To serve: Remove meringue shell from foil and place on a serving plate. Whip cream with the ½ teaspoon vanilla until soft peaks form; spread in shell. In a small saucepan, warm the preserves until liquid. Arrange sliced fresh fruit on top of whipped cream and brush with melted preserves. Cut and serve immediately.

Note: Pavlova can be made into individual portions as pictured below.

Butter Cream Mints

Makes 90 mints

1 cup water
½ cup butter
2 cups sugar

6 drops food-grade peppermint oil or 1 teaspoon peppermint extract
Food coloring

In heavy saucepan heat water and butter until butter is melted. Add sugar and stir with wooden spoon until sugar is dissolved. Bring to a boil. Cover pan for 3 minutes to allow the steam inside the pan to melt the sugar crystals down from sides of pan. Remove lid and wipe sides of pan with brush to remove any remaining sugar crystals. Continue cooking until syrup reaches hard-ball stage, 260 degrees (when dropped in cold water, mixture forms a hard ball that is difficult to mold when removed from water). Pour onto cold buttered marble slab or a buttered cookie sheet (it will take longer to cool using a cookie sheet) without scraping pan. Sprinkle mixture with 6 drops peppermint oil and 2 or 3 drops of desired food coloring, but do not stir in. When cool enough to handle, pull mixture like taffy until candy is firm but elastic and loses its gloss. Pull out to a ½-inch thick rope; cut into ½-inch pieces. Store in covered container. Candy will mellow in 12 to 24 hours.

Bavarian Mints

Makes 48 to 64 pieces

1 pound milk chocolate, coarsely chopped
1 ounce unsweetened chocolate
1 (14-ounce) can sweetened condensed milk

2 tablespoons butter
Few drops vanilla
3 to 8 drops food-grade peppermint oil

Butter an 8x8-inch pan.

Place chocolate, sweetened condensed milk, and butter in the top of a double boiler over simmering water, being careful to not let the water boil. Stir until the mixture is smooth and melted; remove from heat. Add vanilla and peppermint oil to taste. Pour into prepared pan. Cool 4 hours. Cut into squares.

Chocolate Almond Balls

Chocolate Almond Balls

Makes about 4 dozen

1 (8-ounce) chocolate bar with almonds
1 (8-ounce) container frozen whipped topping, thawed to room temperature

30 vanilla wafers (crushed), candy sprinkles, coconut, or chopped nuts

Place chocolate in the top of a double boiler over simmering water, being careful to not let the water boil. Stir occasionally until the chocolate is smooth and melted. Cool slightly (don't let it become cold). Stir in thawed whipped topping. Using heaping teaspoonfuls of chocolate mixture, shape into balls and roll in vanilla wafer crumbs, candy sprinkles, coconut, or chopped nuts. Keep in freezer for 2 hours before serving. Store in freezer.

Old-Fashioned Taffy

Makes about 72 pieces

2 cups sugar
2 tablespoons light corn syrup
2 tablespoons butter

½ cup vinegar
⅛ teaspoon cream of tartar
Pinch salt

Butter a cookie sheet. Cut waxed paper into 72 3x3-inch pieces.

Combine sugar, corn syrup, butter, vinegar, cream of tartar, and salt in heavy saucepan. Stir until sugar is dissolved. Cook over medium heat until mixture reaches hard-ball stage, 260 degrees F. (when dropped in cold water, mixture forms a hard ball that is difficult to mold when removed from water). Remove from heat and pour onto buttered cookie sheet. Cool until lukewarm and can be handled comfortably. Take a small piece of taffy at a time and stretch and fold repeatedly until taffy turns light and pliable. Form into twisted ropes and cut into pieces with clean scissors. Let cool completely. Wrap in waxed paper or plastic wrap.

Lion House Taffy

Makes 30 bite-sized pieces

2 cups sugar
1½ cups water
1 cup white corn syrup
1 teaspoon salt

2 teaspoons glycerine (available at drugstores)
2 tablespoons butter
1 teaspoon vanilla

Butter a cookie sheet.

Mix sugar, water, corn syrup, salt, and glycerine in a heavy saucepan. Bring to a boil and cook until temperature is 258 degrees F. Remove from heat and add butter and vanilla, stirring until butter is melted. Pour candy onto buttered cookie sheet. Cool until lukewarm and taffy can be handled comfortably. Wash and dry hands thoroughly. Take a small piece of taffy and stretch and fold repeatedly until the taffy turns white. Form taffy into desired shape. Place on a piece of waxed paper.

Caramel Turtles

Makes 2½ pounds

150 pecan halves
2 cups sugar
2 cups light corn syrup
2 cups light cream
½ teaspoon salt

¾ cup evaporated milk
6 tablespoons butter
1 pound dipping chocolate or plain chocolate candy bars (optional)

Line 3 cookie sheets with waxed or parchment paper. Arrange pecans in clusters of three pecans on the cookie sheets.

Combine sugar, corn syrup, cream, and salt in a heavy saucepan. Bring to a boil over medium heat, stirring constantly. Adjust temperature to maintain a steady boil and cook, stirring often, until mixture reaches soft-ball stage, 235 degrees F. (a soft ball should form when mixture is dropped into cold water). Slowly—so boiling doesn't stop—add evaporated milk and butter. Continue cooking and stirring until candy reaches firm-ball stage, 245 degrees F. (mixture forms a firm ball when dropped into cold water and won't flatten when removed); remove from heat.

Allow to cool 5 minutes, stirring every 1½ minutes. Drop a spoonful of caramel onto each pecan cluster. Cool. Drop 1 teaspoon of melted chocolate on top of the caramel or dip candies in melted chocolate, if desired.

Chocolate Truffles

Makes about 30 truffles

½ cup heavy cream
⅓ cup sugar
6 tablespoons butter

3 cups semisweet chocolate chips, divided
1 teaspoon vanilla
2 tablespoons shortening

Combine cream, sugar, and butter in a heavy saucepan and bring to a boil over medium-high heat. Remove from heat. Add 1 cup chocolate chips and stir until chips are melted. Add vanilla. Pour into bowl and let cool 30 minutes, stirring occasionally. Cover and chill in refrigerator several hours or overnight to allow mixture to ripen and harden.

Line a cookie sheet with waxed paper. Remove mixture from refrigerator and form into ½-inch balls, working quickly to prevent melting. Place on prepared cookie sheet. Chill again for several hours.

Make chocolate coating by melting 2 cups chocolate chips with shortening in the top of a double boiler. Remove from heat. Cool to 85 degrees F., stirring constantly.

Dip each truffle into chocolate with a fork. Gently tap fork on side of bowl to remove excess coating. Invert candies onto waxed paper. To store, layer truffles in an airtight container with waxed paper between layers.

Caramel Turtles

English Toffee

Makes 1½ pounds

1 cup chopped walnuts or pecans, divided
1 cup butter (no substitutions)
1 cup sugar
2 tablespoons water

3 tablespoons light corn syrup
1 teaspoon vanilla
1 (8-ounce) milk chocolate bar

Butter a 9x13-inch cake pan. Sprinkle ¾ cup chopped nuts in the bottom of the pan; set aside.

Combine butter, sugar, water, and corn syrup in a heavy saucepan. Bring mixture to a boil over medium-high heat, stirring constantly. Cook and stir until candy reaches hard-crack stage, 300 degrees F. (when dropped in cold water, mixture should form hard, brittle threads that break easily). Stir in vanilla. Pour candy over nuts in prepared pan and spread slightly. Break chocolate bar into squares and place on hot candy. Allow to melt 5 minutes and then spread chocolate over candy. Sprinkle with remaining ¼ cup nuts.

Cool until chocolate sets up (2 to 3 hours) and then cut into bite-sized pieces.

Holiday Divinity

Makes about 48 pieces

3 cups sugar
1 cup light corn syrup
½ cup water
2 egg whites, room temperature

1 teaspoon vanilla
Red food coloring
⅓ cup chopped maraschino cherries
½ cup chopped pecans

Line a cookie sheet with waxed or parchment paper or place waxed paper on work space.

Combine sugar, corn syrup, and water in a heavy saucepan and bring to a boil. Cover pan for 3 minutes to allow the steam inside the pan to melt the sugar crystals from sides of pan. Remove cover. Cook without stirring until syrup reaches hard-ball stage, 260 degrees F. (when dropped in cold water, mixture forms a hard ball that is difficult to mold when removed from water).

While syrup is cooking, place egg whites in a large bowl and beat until stiff peaks form. When syrup is done, pour over egg whites in a fine stream, beating vigorously. Do not scrape pan. Add vanilla and 2 or 3 drops of red food coloring to tint candy pink. Continue beating until candy is thick and creamy and holds its shape. Stir in cherries and pecans. Drop from a teaspoon onto waxed paper. Divinity does not keep well, so serve while fresh.

Rocky Road Fudge

Makes 25 pieces

1 (12-ounce) package semisweet chocolate chips

1 cup crunchy peanut butter

4 cups miniature marshmallows

1 cup chopped salted peanuts (optional)

Butter a 9x9-inch pan and set aside.

Place chocolate and peanut butter in the top of a double boiler over simmering water, being careful to not let the water boil. Stir occasionally until the mixture is smooth and melted. Alternatively, melt chocolate and peanut butter in a microwave-safe bowl on high power in 30-second increments, stirring after each. Fold in marshmallows and peanuts. Pour into pan and chill until set. Cut into squares.

Variations: Flavors can be changed by using different flavored chips and nuts. Nutella could be used in place of peanut butter.

Luscious Fudge

Makes 5 pounds

1 (12-ounce) milk chocolate bar, broken into pieces

1 (12-ounce) package semisweet chocolate chips

1 (7-ounce) jar marshmallow crème

1 (12-ounce) can evaporated milk

4½ cups sugar

⅛ teaspoon salt

2 teaspoons vanilla

2 cups chopped walnuts

Butter a 9x13-inch pan and set aside.

Combine milk chocolate bar pieces, chocolate chips, and marshmallow crème in large mixing bowl; set aside. In a heavy saucepan, combine evaporated milk, sugar, and salt. Bring to a boil over medium heat and boil for six minutes. Pour over chocolate mixture. Beat vigorously with wooden spoon until creamy. Add vanilla and chopped walnuts. Mix well. Pour into prepared pan. Let stand two hours and then cut into small squares.

Kettle Corn

Makes 6 quarts

½ cup corn oil (no substitutions)

1 cup popcorn kernels

⅔ cup sugar

1 teaspoon vanilla

1 to 1½ teaspoons kosher or sea salt (non-iodized)

You will need a 5 to 6 quart heavy bottom pan with a tight-fitting lid, a long-handled wooden spoon, thick oven gloves or heavy hot pads, and a 6-quart bowl. Measure all ingredients into separate bowls and have near the stove.

Place the oil and 3 kernels of popcorn in the pan. Put on high heat and wait until the kernels pop. This tells you the pan and oil are at the right temperature. Do not turn the heat down. Add the rest of the popcorn kernels and stir with the wooden spoon until a few more kernels start popping. Pour the sugar into the middle of the pan and quickly pour the vanilla onto the sugar and start stirring immediately. Stir until the popcorn starts popping again and then place the lid securely on the pan. Using the hot pads, shake the pan vigorously for 5 to 10 seconds every 15 seconds until the popping has almost stopped (about 3 minutes). Moving quickly, take the pan from the stove, remove the lid, and pour the popped corn into the bowl. Immediately sprinkle with salt while stirring. The salt will stick to the hot sugar coating.

Once you start cooking this, you cannot leave the area or the popcorn will burn. Mushroom or magic mushroom popcorn is used for commercial kettle corn. It pops a lot larger than regular popcorn. Check online for availability, as it is not available in most stores.

Popcorn Nut Crunch

Makes 12 servings

12 cups popped corn

1⅓ cups pecan halves

⅔ cup whole almonds (blanched or raw)

½ cup light corn syrup

1⅓ cups sugar

1 cup butter

½ teaspoon cream of tartar

1 tablespoon vanilla

1 teaspoon baking soda

4 cups miniature marshmallows, frozen

Butter 2 cookie sheets.

Mix popcorn, pecans, and almonds in a large bowl or pan; set aside. Combine corn syrup, sugar, butter, and cream of tartar in a heavy saucepan. Cook and stir over medium-high heat until mixture comes to a boil. Reduce heat to medium and maintain a steady boil for 10 minutes, until mixture reaches hard-ball stage, 260 degrees F. (when dropped in cold water, mixture forms a hard ball that is difficult to mold when removed from water); remove from heat. Stir in vanilla and baking soda. Pour over popcorn and nuts, stirring to coat evenly. Add frozen marshmallows and continue stirring until mixture is evenly coated with syrup. Spread on buttered cookie sheets to cool. Break into chunks and store in an airtight container.